INTO THE
ARENA

'The bullfighter-philosopher' John-Paul Flintoff, *The Times*.

'Whether or not the artistic quality of the bullfight outweighs the moral question of the animals' suffering is something that each person must decide for themselves – as they must decide whether the taste of a steak justifies the death of a cow. But if we ignore the possibility that one does outweigh the other, we fall foul of the charge of self-deceit and incoherence in our dealings with animals.' Alexander Fiske-Harrison, *Prospect*

'It is one of the best pieces ever written on the subject. An almost literally terrific piece of work.' Frederick Raphael.

ALEXANDER FISKE-HARRISON was born in 1976 and is an English writer and actor. He studied biology and then philosophy at the universities of Oxford and London and trained in acting at the Stella Adler Conservatory in New York. He writes for *The Times*, *Financial Times*, *Times Literary Supplement* and *Prospect* magazine. He wrote, and acted in, *The Pendulum* which debuted in London's West End in 2008.

INTO THE
ARENA

The world of the Spanish bullfight

ALEXANDER FISKE-HARRISON

P

PROFILE BOOKS

First published in Great Britain in 2011 by
PROFILE BOOKS LTD
3A Exmouth House
Pine Street
London EC1R 0JH
www.profilebooks.com

10 9 8 7 6 5 4 3 2 1

Typeset in Stone Serif by MacGuru Ltd
info@macguru.org.uk
Printed and bound in Great Britain by
Clays, Bungay, Suffolk

A CIP catalogue record for this book is available from the
British Library.

ISBN 978 1 84668 335 0
eISBN 978 1 84765 429 8

The paper this book is printed on is certified by the © 1996
Forest Stewardship Council A.C. (FSC). It is ancient-forest
friendly. The printer holds FSC chain of custody SGS-
COC-2061.

Contents

Ser un torero es como hablar con Dios
[To be a bullfighter is like talking to God]

Eduardo Dávila Miura (matador)

En el mundo de los toros, el único que tiene vergüenza es el toro
[In the world of bullfighting, the only one with a sense of shame is the bull]

Curro Sánchez (flamenco singer)

La larga cambiada a portagayola

The kneeling matador greets the charging bull with the cape at the Gates of Fear.

David Fandila Marín – El Fandi – *walked across the sand with 14,000 pairs of eyes watching him, weighing him. This was his first visit to the most judgemental bullring in Spain, La Plaza de Toros de la Real Maestranza de Sevilla, the oldest of the great rings. Madrid is the head of the bullfighting world, where money is aggregated and policy decided, but its heart is in Seville. This is where it was born, among the pastures where the bulls are created. Not only have the* aficionados *here seen more fights than their urban cousins in the north, but many have stepped into a ring themselves, even if only on a ranch with a 250lb cow. For this reason they don't easily accept the elegant safety of 'caping to the furthest horn' to keep the animal distant, or the showy trickery of leaning in after the horn points have passed so the bull's body brushes the man's without risk. The 250-year-old stones of this ring always demand truth, even if the price is a human life. As it was for the thirty-three-year-old Valencian Manolo Montiliú, who died on that same sand eight summers before. The footage is there on the internet for all to see, his body lifted clear of the ground by the 1,320lb might of the bull Cabatisto, the animal's left horn a foot deep in his chest. As the attending surgeon described it with chilling poetry, 'his heart was opened like a book'.*

Fandi was only nineteen and still a novillero, *a 'novice mata-dor', but he seemed supremely confident and oblivious to the June Andalusian sun hammering down on him as he crossed the line of shade on to the sunny side of the ring. Despite the 10lb of tightly-cut scarlet silk and gold braid on his body and the 15lb of compressed magenta and yellow cotton in his hands, he moved lightly on his feet until he was directly in front of the door through which the bull would enter. To the delight of the crowd, he dropped to his knees before these 'Gates of Fear' and began to spread the cape out over his thighs. He was to open with* la larga cambiada a portagayola, *'the long exchange at the cage-door'.*

His only thoughts were now about the animal: what were this one's strengths and weaknesses? How was its stamina and speed? Was it left-horned or right? Would it attack into his territory or merely defend its own? Most importantly, how would it respond to this bravura opening manoeuvre? Yes, it might impress even this jaded audience, but on the other hand, Franco Cardeño, a more experienced bullfighter who had tried this same manoeuvre in the same spot three years before, had ended his career serving in a bar named Portagayola for that very reason only 400 yards away, with half his face crushed. And he was lucky to walk – or rather, be carried – away with only that. Fandi carefully smoothed out the creases in the compressed fabric of the cape. When the cloth flew, it had to fly true or he would die there on his knees.

The gate was opened before him by Manolo Artero, a stout middle-aged man, who shouted to the rustling crowd the words he had shouted for thirty years: 'Silence! A man risks his life here today.' As Fandi's sun-blinded eyes stared into the darkness he heard the distant protest of heavy steel bolts sliding into their housings, followed by muffled shouting and the hollow sound of unshod hooves skittering on concrete. Then came the dull crash of horns against steel. The sounds repeated closer as further doors were opened, followed by more crashes. Then, from within the darkness, came a rearing, jolting black head, eyes focused, nostrils flaring, ears forward, a foot and a half of horns tapering to fine points above it. And behind it came a half-ton of pulsing muscle propelling it at a steady twenty-five miles an hour. The heightened senses of the bull perceived him as an immediate threat in a totally unknown world of smell, sound and colour. It arched its neck to aim its long horns and accelerated hard.

Fandi pulled the cape up in a single long smooth movement so it swung out in front of the speeding animal's eyes, catching their attention, and then spun out to the side of his head. Distracted by this extension of the creature it wished to destroy, the bull deviated mid-charge and dived after the movement. As its horn struck the cloth mid-air, it discovered there was no substance there, no satisfying penetration to confirm its dominance. As for Fandi, all he saw was the long horns, the striving head, the massive neck and shoulders, and the long driving flanks sailing by him.

He smiled. Then he stood up.

■ ■ ■ ■ ■

This was the first encounter between a bull and a man I ever saw, on 14 May 2000. That spring was my first visit to Spain, and at the time I was a twenty-three-year-old postgraduate philosophy student at the London School of Economics. I was on holiday in Seville with my family. My parents, who had seen a few bullfights over the years, including the phenomenon that was El Cordobés in the 1970s, decided it would be an interesting afternoon for the family. They said it could be cruel and it could be beautiful and that you had to make up your own mind. The other person present, my older brother, had just spent the day arguing with me about foxhunting. He is an ex-Army officer and investment banker. I was a member of the World Wildlife Fund and Greenpeace and had studied as an undergraduate with the wildlife biologist Malcolm Coe at Oxford. You can imagine the difference in perspective. The irony of that being my only other memory of the visit is not lost on me.

However, what I saw in that ring was something different. This was not the pursuit of gentlemen, mounted on the best horseflesh of the Home Counties and riding behind trained canine proxies to deal death to a terrified fox. This was a young athlete from humble origins using skill, mobility and deception – the cape – to defeat an animal eight times his weight and three times his speed, and then execute it with a single sword-thrust delivered over the top of its horns. And doing all of this with 'art'. Equally, this was no humble meat cow kept penned for its eighteen months of life before being shipped to its 'humane' mechanised death, to end up plastic-wrapped in a supermarket. No, this was a five-year-old animal that had grown up running on open pasture, learning to use its horns on its herd-brothers, and would die fighting in a spectacular and brutal manner within twenty-five minutes of entering the ring.

This was something important.

However, the next two bulls, fought by the other two novices, not only did not want to fight, but were fought and killed without skill. They died badly, scrabbling in their own blood. I watched in horror and disgust. I have killed animals myself, both to eat and to dissect in the laboratory, but even I cannot deny that my stomach and my conscience were turned.

Then El Fandi entered for his second bull, and again put on such a display that the crowd – myself included – not only applauded but rose to their feet and waved white handkerchiefs until the president of the ring awarded him an ear of the dead bull as reward. We didn't stay for the other two fighters' second bulls: our eyes could not stand the bloodshed.

My last memory of that event was talking afterwards about the fight. My father and brother were impressed with Fandi's bravery and dexterity. My mother – a sculptor – was particularly struck by the line of body and elegance of movement. I, on the other hand, was struck by the terrible quandary it presented: this thing, whatever it was, seemed balanced on a perfect moral borderline. When it was done well, it seemed a good thing; when done badly it was an unmitigated sin. How could anything straddle an ethical boundary like that? In the words of the poet García Lorca: 'the bullfight is the last serious thing left in the world today'. I had never understood what he meant before that afternoon.

■ ■ ■ ■ ■

Years passed, and I would come back to Seville when I could and would watch a bullfight – perhaps three or four in total, each of six bulls – and each time my thoughts would follow the same route: the bullfight existed on the edge of an ethical precipice. In 2007 I went to Seville for its annual festival, the Feria de Abril, and watched three fights in a row. I wrote about them for *Prospect* magazine, and in a rather longwinded essay I solidified my thoughts about the bullfight into the beginnings of a coherent argument. My final paragraph was this: 'Whether or not the artistic quality of the bullfight outweighs the moral question of the animals' suffering is something that each person must decide for themselves – as they must decide whether the taste of a steak justifies the death of a cow. But if we ignore the possibility that one does outweigh the other, we fall foul of the charge of self-deceit and incoherence in our dealings with animals.'

After the worldwide interest that article caused – from Al Jazeera to the *Dayton Daily News* – I realised that I should go one step further and give a final answer to that question myself. So I telephoned a friend in Spain and he invited me to see a bullfight with him in Madrid. I was on a plane the next day – 3 October 2008.

■ ■ ■ ■ ■

A final word about El Fandi. It turns out he was indeed unusually good. The next day the national newspaper *ABC* said of that fight: 'El Fandi saved the honour of Seville.' Four days later he took his *alternativa*, the fight in which you become a full matador, in his home town of Granada. Within five years he was ranked number one in Spain: a position he held for three years. The man I flew to see in Madrid in 2008, Miguel Ángel Perera, surpassed him that year. I didn't know that then. Nor did I know that Perera would be there the first time I would face an animal in the ring myself. I didn't even know I would end up in the ring. There was a lot I didn't know back then.

El Arenal, Seville
December 2010

1

La verónica

The matador cites the bull with the large cape gripped in both hands, sweeping it to the side of his body, so that as the bull passes through the cape, it brushes his face, as Saint Veronica wiped the face of Christ on his way to Golgotha. (Reputedly invented by Joaquín Rodríguez Costillares, born 1729, Seville)

It started with a quick shave and a drink in the bar of the Madrid Palace Hotel by way of a nod to the ghost of Ernest Hemingway – it was his favourite hotel in the city. It also gave me the chance to study the matador who was going to fight that October day in 2008, Miguel Ángel Perera; matadors of his level always stay at the best place in town.

I watched him in the foyer as I bought cigarettes: he was decked out in his full *traje de luces*, the suit of lights, and looked vaguely ridiculous to me, an uncomfortable twenty-four-year-old, slightly too tall, internally flinching at the press cameras. Later on I would get to know the man slightly better, but then I perceived only an air of bravado layered over nervousness, all of which looked out of place in the gilded hotel lobby. Of course, setting is everything; when I saw him nearly die three hours later, tying off his own femoral artery and killing a half-ton bull with a sword, the courage seemed very real.

But that was still to come. I went back to my drink and waited for Tanis.

Tanis is a contemporary urban *aficionado* of the bullfight: liberal-left in his politics, but with a nationalist streak which is singular to the Spanish. He is an architect: well-read and intelligent, although always scruffily dressed, a lean figure with a thin beard and spectacles. Our friendship was new then – his best friend married one of mine – and made somehow both closer and more delicate since his wife's identical twin, Sofí, had captivated and then discarded me in four remarkable days in the winter of 2007.

He looks uncomfortable when he arrives, but not because of that. The room, glossed smart with corporate money, makes him feel out of place. Which is ironic, since framed above his head is some handwritten verse praising the bar written by his great-uncle, Federico García Lorca, the greatest poet of Spain's ill-fated voyage through the twentieth century. A voyage which savagely killed García Lorca and so many others.

We get on a moped – Sofí's, I remember – and Tanis drives full-throttle, caping passing cars with the flaps of my jacket, determined not to be late for the fight. Our adrenaline is flowing nicely when we arrive at the bullring, Las Ventas, which is filling to its 25,000-seat capacity. It is my first time here and everything is different from La Maestranza, the bullring I know in Seville. This is twice the size and makes the whitewashed stone of Andalusia look rustic in comparison to the complex brickwork and towers of the Neo-Moorish style.

La Maestranza was begun in 1759, when the gently Borbón Carlos III inherited a solid Imperial throne and a growing economy and population. It was the first structure built to house an audience of this size since the Roman gladiatorial arenas, and came more than a century before the great Victorian football stadia of Britain. Las Ventas, by contrast, came a century and a half later. It was opened as part of the Great Exposition of 1929 by Alfonso XIII, an immaculately dressed failure of a king, his empire gone, the economy collapsed, the people so hungry that even the royalist press had to admit that the peasants were eating grass to stay alive. Two years later he abdicated his impoverished throne and set the dominoes tumbling towards the Civil War.

Proceedings start with all the ritual one would expect of a deeply Catholic monarchy carrying out a ceremony that derives from Imperial Rome. First, the constables ride out in sixteenth-century costume to ask the president of the ring for permission to begin. Then the band starts up, the brass archaic and tinny yet with a certain Latin grandeur. Then comes *el paseíllo*, 'the parade', of Perera, the two substitute matadors who will take his place should he fall, and all their teams, including three sets of three *banderilleros*, who place the short spiked sticks after which they are named, and three pairs of mounted picadors with their lances, followed by reserve picadors, sword-handlers, the *monosabios*, or 'wise monkeys' who sweep the ring (there is a story behind this name), carpenters, and finally two teams of bell-covered mules to drag out the bull carcasses.

However, save for the first-time tourists – a minority at this time of year in Las Ventas – everyone's eyes are on Perera alone, the 'man of the moment' in the taurine world, who has been awarded the rare honour of fighting a full *corrida*, or running, of six bulls solo – only the seventh time this has happened in Madrid in over a decade. Perera may have been born in a poor rural village of 500 people, but he swaggers like a king.

He is now a top-ranking matador, equal to the former child prodigy El Juli, or to Francisco Rivera Ordóñez, president of the Ronda bullring and a fourth-generation matador whose great-grandfather inspired the matador in the Hemingway novel *The Sun Also Rises,* and about whose grandfather Hemingway wrote an entire non-fiction book called *The Dangerous Summer*. Fran Rivera's father was less lucky, and one of the most chillingly brave moments I have ever seen is the footage of him reassuring and calming the panicking surgeons as he bled to death from a horn wound in 1984 (fulfilling superstition, the man who killed that bull was killed himself a year and six days later in the ring).

The top of this hierarchy is the phenomenon that is José Tomás, whose apparent contempt for death, in combination with abundant skill and an astonishing sense of drama, has captured the mind of the younger generation, who had seemed to be growing away from the bullfight. Following yet another near-fatal goring in 2002 he retired, only to return to the giant Barcelona ring La Monumental in 2007 to its first sell-out in years – touts were selling tickets at $4,000 each.

Even the English-language newspapers were aware of the scale of his comeback. The London *Times* went with the headline 'King of the Ring Returns to Save His Sport', while the *New York Times* ran with 'Bullfighting Is Dead! Long Live the Bullfight'. However, this was only a dull echo of the thunder that occurred in Spain, led by the right-wing national, *ABC* (comparable to the *Daily Telegraph* in the UK or the *Washington Post* in the US), with the truly religious 'And the Myth Was Made Flesh'. In Spain, at least, it is immediately clear that this €2.5 billion per annum industry employing over 200,000 people for 1,000 fights a year – as compared to 300 a year in the 'Golden Age' of the '30s – needs no saving. The top matadors earn millions of euros a year; more than all but a handful of Spanish movie stars and football players. Which cannot be bad for Perera, a kid from Extremadura, the poorest region in Spain and the fifth poorest in the entire European Union.

There is a pause before the fight proper begins and, as Tanis shouts to vendors for beer, I read the programme to catch up on the other half of the fight: the bulls. I haven't been to a bullfight in eighteen months, and I've only been to six in total, so there's still a lot to learn. The bulls are from a selection of breeders, which, like the matador, I do not know. The first bull, Saltarín, a Valdefresno, comes in fast, but flighty and nervous, his legs apparently weak for the 1,140lb (518 kilograms, 81 stone) bulk of his body. Perera passes him a few times with the *capote*, the large pink and yellow work-cape, and he seems pretty disgusted with what he finds. As the mounted picadors come in for the final stage of the first act of the fight – it has three – the audience already has its doubts, especially the notorious group seated in Tendido 7, an area of the stands known for both the discernment of its denizens and their vociferous expression of it.

The bull charges into the horse, his horns finding no purchase in its padded and armoured flank, and at the same time the picador's lance drives into his *morillo*, the vast goring muscle-mass that rises over his shoulders. As the bull is caped, stumbling, away from the horse by Perera, it is abundantly clear that this bull is not the genuine article, not a *toro bravo*, a 'fierce bull'.

The audience demands the removal of the tepid animal from the ring by whistling. The president of the ring bites the proverbial bullet – a substitute at this level ups the cost of the fight by €15,000 or more – and the steers are let in. The moment the bull feels it is in a herd again it becomes placid once more and is led out to the tender mercies of the ring's vet. No bull once fought may fight again, and this one would hardly be wanted for his breeding potential.

The second bull is little better, although Perera lives up to his title, matador, 'killer', and ends his life quickly and cleanly. At this point I judge that Perera is showing skill, but little art, although the bulls aren't exactly helping.

Bull three is more interesting: he's wiser, more aggressive and appears to be conserving his energy. He gives two charges to the horse, taking two wounds from the lance, and during his extrication from this the matador trips, upping the drama momentarily. The small, spiked *banderillas* are placed without incident, and then we move to the 'third of death'.

At this point the wind in the ring is rising, and the bull seems to have chosen a *querencia*, a 'lair', which in bullfighting is where the bull feels safest and thus is able to think, making him unpredictable. My notes call it the '*querencia* of winds'. Given that the matador's sole protection at this point in the fight is his ability to create controlled flapping in the small red cape to distract the bull's movement-based vision from the solidity of his body, this is not a good place to fight.

Why Perera is allowing the bull to dictate the terrain is unclear, but he's clearly worried. At one point he even pushes the bull's horn away from him as it passes. Now sometimes a matador may stroke a bull's horn as it passes to indicate his courage and control over the situation, but Perera's actions are indicating to me fear or foolishness or both. He is telling the bull where solid matter is, as it is growing more frustrated with the insubstantial cape, and this bull is no novice. His five years on the ranch will have been spent fighting other bulls in the wide-ranging pastures. By Spanish law, he has never seen a man on the ground before – only mounted farm labourers – but the novelty will only last so long, which is why Spanish law also says this final third of the fight must end within a quarter of an hour. To make matters worse, in the next pass the bull bumps the matador with his shoulder. He is learning at an exponential rate now. What is more, the wind is so strong my notes say I can hardly write for the pages rustling.

Perera seems more than nervous now. We reach fifteen minutes and he still hasn't asked the president for permission to kill. The president signals the band and an *aviso*, a 'warning note', is played to tell the matador he's in extra time. If the bull isn't dead in three minutes, he is going to have his bull taken away and someone else will do the job, an utter humiliation for any matador, unthinkable for this one on this day. The crowd are being patient, which is rare for Madrid, often said to be the most discerning of all audiences. However, the law is the law. Perera takes the killing sword from his handler and lines the bull up with the cape, making it spread its shoulder blades and lower its head. He profiles his body, aiming down the blade of the sword, resembling some human-scorpion hybrid poised to sting.

Here are my notes in full: 'His kill-strike is perfect, but the bull hits him on its upstroke. He is thrown in the air and lands nearby. The bull plunges his horns towards the body, but is too accurate, they go either side. The matador does not move. The bull is distracted. He dies from the sword he carries in him. The matador limps off. The bull's body is whistled by the crowd for his not-straight charges. No *faena*, just skill.' (The *faena*, or 'work' – in the sense of work of art – describes the final section of the fight, when the matador is expected to dance with the bull and his cape.)

Perera is brave indeed. Not to move as 1,155lb of bull drives its horns into the dirt either side of your ribs takes notable self-control – the absence of motion also is the only thing that has kept him alive.

Perera then limps off to the infirmary, which leads to a twenty-minute pause where the crowd becomes worried that their star matador is going to short-change them and send in a substitute. So when Perera returns, still limping, the crowd cheers his courage and seems to settle forwards, for as Tanis says, 'Now, my friend, the bulls have pissed him off and we'll see what he's made of.'

Bull four is heavy – 1,245lb – and clever to boot, but nothing is stopping Perera now. He capes him into the ring, sets him up for the picador's lance, impatiently waits for the *banderilleros* to finish, and then he strides – lopsided – into the ring with the *muleta*, the small red cape used at the end of the fight. He begins caping the bull and by making each move closer, more dangerous, and more difficult for the bull than the last, steadily increases the emotion of this *faena*, this display. He is showing mastery now, although Tanis grumbles, 'His hand is not low enough on *naturales*.' Everyone's a critic, as they say in the theatre, but I'm still green enough to fall for the spectacle, and so when the bull is killed cleanly and quickly, I rise to my feet with the crowd and wave my handkerchief along with them, the stadium a sea of fluttering white. The president pauses like a modern-day Caesar, then lays out the piece of silk on his balcony-rail to indicate that the matador is to be awarded an ear. Perera does a lap of honour with the gory trophy, tossing it into the crowd, and as he passes each stand they throw flowers and gifts of cigars or money to him – which his team pocket – and items of clothing for his blessing, which he deftly tosses back. At the end, a wag from Tendido 7 throws him a crutch for his limp, which reduces the rather haughty audience to laughter and unifies it in its support for this young man.

Bull five comes out well, heavy in build but light on his feet. However, the picador lances him so hard you can see blood pumping into the air from the shoulder – at the very least a minor arterial breach. The crowd whistle this over-zealous action and Perera looks genuinely annoyed with his employee, not just the mock-annoyance a matador shows when his picador ruins a strong bull, the matador's voice saying one thing, his hand-signals quite another. However, Perera is on a roll now, and by offering the bull a closer target to charge he inspires another great fight, enhanced by the proximity of death for the matador. The kill is perfect: brave, fast, accurate, high risk.

It seems as though the boy can do no wrong. Then the sixth bull comes out – not the last, due to the earlier substitution. He is slow, seemingly dull. My notes open tersely, indicating that the freshness of the spectacle has now gone, along with the sensation in my legs from the stone amphitheatre seats. They say only, 'well pic-ed, went in for kill straight'. At that point the notes stop, because it was then that things went terribly, horribly wrong.

There is something searing in the sight of a human body moving against its own volition and impelled by a massive force, especially when that force also has a will of its own. The phrase 'rag-doll' is often used in these contexts, although that is not really how it appears to me when Bellotito's horn enters

Perera's thigh a few inches below the junction with his torso. Whether it is stuck into his femur, which can stand two tons per square inch of pressure, or has twisted itself into a firm enough bundle of his tendon and muscle to lift him, I don't know. What I do know is that he is thrust up from the ground with a remarkable rigidity given the speed of his upward trajectory, and he keeps going up and up until gravity does its job and brings him down ten feet away.

We can tell the wound is bad because he moves with the pain, into the pain, in vivid contrast to his earlier immobility when the bull had floored him and gone in for the kill. This time the bull doesn't get a chance to find him with its horns because the companions act quickly and distract it. Perera gets to his feet and it is then that we see, as does his *cuadrilla*, his 'team', the severity of the *cornada*, the 'horn-wound', as the blood begins to pump out on to the sand. His men surround him, each grabbing a limb, and run with him towards the infirmary, his bobbing head shouting at them to stop. They halt, unsure of what to do, and his manager comes over to confer.

They are putting him gently back on his feet and they move away so he can test his strength. We see the black ribbon tourniquet they have tied around the wound to reduce – but not stop – the flow of blood down his leg. The limp in his right leg now dwarfs the one in his left, but the 25,000-strong crowd of the Las Ventas bullring roar their approval at his courage. It isn't the limp that worries my friend and me, though, it is his pallor: a sickly, ghostly white, glossed in sweat and highlighted by the growing artificial light as the clock on the tower approaches half past seven. It doesn't matter whether the blood loss is worse than they think or he's going into shock; either way losing consciousness is now a possibility, and a fatal one with a bull which has already learnt that the man is a more satisfying target than the red cloth.

Perera stands his ground before the bull, although he is now considerably less functional than it is. It was only lightly lanced, and half the short barbs of the *banderillas* have bounced off its thick hide or missed entirely. It is a toss-up who is bleeding more – weight for weight – but Perera wants to fight on. There is a line of poetry by Tanis's great-uncle which goes, *La muerta me está mirando*: Death is watching me. Death *is* watching. Not me, though, but Perera and Bellotito.

I remember the nervous young man in the hotel lobby as Perera wavers on his feet, pale and bloodied. He completes a series of passes with the bull without grace but bravely nonetheless until he judges it is the time to kill, time for watching Death choose between its two objects of interest. Perera swaps his aluminium caping sword for a real one, the one with the killing weight of steel and the curved tip to better direct its trajectory when it is within the bull. Then he moves the scarlet *muleta* in his left hand on the ground, the bull tracking its movements with its head until its forehooves are together, its great shoulder blades splayed out, its broad, sharp and blood-slicked horns low. Perera raises the sword in his right hand to eye level, sighting down the blade like an eighteenth-century duellist with his pistol. Then he blurs, left arm sweeping across his body to his right, the bull following, leaping forward, the sword going between the shoulders as once again he goes between the horns that nearly killed him; then he moves left, the bull right, and we see – we see the man is alive, standing, the bull dead, standing also, the sword in to the hilt. The crowd are on their feet, our fear now dwarfed by our shared victory, also shared with the matador, but not with the bull who slowly capsizes, his hooves in the air. I turn to Tanis and say, '*Cojones*.' He has balls. '*Si, mi amigo,*' is the reply, '*pero no dos, cuatro.*' But not two, four.

The irony is that Perera almost ends up with only one, according to the surgeons who work on him in a series of interventions over two weeks. His only response to the press: 'I did what was necessary to finish the race.' And finish he does – the president awarding him both ears of the bull.

We pour out of the ring that night, not with the joyous existential thrill of having been in the presence of beauty and death which is usual after a great bullfight, but with the slightly disturbed feeling of too much blood and too little skill, like drinking an excess of fortified wine. (The hangover, the moral hangover, which I seem to be alone in having among those who have seen more than a few fights, comes the next day.) We join up with some Mexican and Spanish friends of Tanis's who have been sitting elsewhere in the amphitheatre and spill into a famous little taurine bar. As we drink and talk about the fight they replay the goring of Perera on the television. It is as I remember it, his body rigid as it joins with the bull via his horn, an odd sculpture of man and animal. However, they are more interested in me, a Brit who understands the bullfight. We are swept from bar to bar. The *aficionados* here are jaded, I notice. They have their views, but they are too urbane to argue them out. A hint here, a tip there, but nothing aggressively stated as I had seen in Seville: this is an intelligent and cultured young crowd.

Soon I find myself in a fashionable bar in the centre of Madrid talking to Sofí, who has come from seeing a band, her teeth white, her skin tanned, her eyes dark and flirtatious as she introduces me to her current boyfriend and I talk about my current girlfriend. We talk about theatre, and I notice a man at the bar taking cocaine from the crook between thumb and fore-finger and I can smell the sweet hashish coming in the window from someone in the street. All talk of bullfighting has gone; I am back in civilisation and I don't like it. This isn't why I came here. Las Ventas may be the toughest audience in Spain, but that is because these are Pan-European aesthetes who happen to include bullfighting in their list of arts. I am in the wrong place. I just saw Death stare at two creatures, wink at one and then leave. I need to follow him. South. That is where the bull-fight truly is. Andalusia. Seville.

2

La chicuelina

The matador cites the bull with the cape held out in front, and then twists his body and the cape in opposing directions, and encasing himself in cloth, drawing the bull close as it passes. (Invented by Manuel Jiménez Moreno, 'Chicuelo', born 1902, Seville)

The motto of the city is 'Seville, she has not deserted me', after the words spoken by Alfonso X in his war of untimely succession with his own son in the thirteenth century. This is emblazoned on everything in the city, from lampposts to garbage trucks, as 'No 8 Do' (the '8' is a looping length of yarn known as a *madeja,* making a heraldic pun, 'No *madeja* do', or '*No me ha dejado*'). I found the city one night in '98, returning overland from three months in the Moroccan Sahara. I stepped off a bus with sand still in my boots from the land of the veil, abstinence and Berber drums, to find a bar with a flamenco guitarist and filled with girls dancing *sevillanas* in summer dresses. I have not deserted Seville since.

The city is bound in orbit around its fourteenth-century cathedral, the largest on earth at that time, now looking like a great and aged beast slumped under the burning sun by day, or like some beautiful sunken and upturned ship at night, its floodlights making the distant hawks seem like moths as they circle its great tower, La Giralda, once the minaret of the mosque that stood here. Inside are the remains of the Genoese explorer Christopher Columbus, Cristóbal Colón to his Spanish paymasters. It is his discovery which made Spain and in particular Seville. The wealth of their entire American empire bled up the river Guadalquivir from the port of Cádiz until it clotted: too many galleons, too much silt. Then the city choked for three and a half centuries.

Seville is where the modern bullfight moved out of its informal and savage origins into the highly ordered three-act drama with its fatal conclusion which it now is; it is the site of the first ever school for matadors, founded by the inventor of the modern fight, Pedro Romero, in the mid-eighteenth century. It is also where flamenco was born, that near-sister of the fight, its origins distinct, but its fascination with death the same.

As García Lorca says of one of the greatest female singers of *el cante jondo*, 'the deep song':

On the dark stage
Parrala carries on
a conversation
with Death.
Calls her
she doesn't come,
calls her again.
The people
swallow their sobs.

When Death did finally come for her, in 1915, it was in Seville, around the corner from my then apartment in La Macarena. Ironically, that apartment was directly opposite the first ever Spanish anti-bullfighting organisation, La Sociedad Protectora de Animales y Plantas of 1872. It scratched my conscience when I saw that. Perhaps that was why I didn't like to write at home, preferring the dark and cramped wooden interior of Casa Matias, an old and decrepit bar round the corner from the bullring, where I would sit on my own under the stuffed head of a giant bull and eat crude tapas delivered by my friend Antonio – also known as Curro – the bartender, and the first person to ever call me Alejandro.

It is from there that I set off in November 2008 to meet my first bull, driven by the photographer Nicolás Haro. He was to become a friend, a fellow worker, a confidant, and another set of very powerful, and very different, eyes. However, back then he was a stranger working on a photo-documentary project about *los toros indultados*, bulls that have been pardoned from the ring. His feelings about the bullfight are mixed, torn even. At his heart, Nicolás dislikes the bullfight, despite growing up surrounded by it and having a grandfather who bred fighting bulls before he sold the family herd – an odd idea to the outsider, but this is Seville after all.

So we set off down the *ruta del toro*, the main road that connects Seville and Cádiz through fighting-bull country, a beautiful and epic landscape with rolling plains and ice-topped hills in the distance, while all around herds of bulls roam between meadows and woodland, a wilderness underwritten exclusively by the bullfight's audience – there's no room for corporate logos on the suit of lights.

We talk about the fight as we drive, trying to weigh up each other's intentions and character. I am asked for the first of what now seems like an infinity of times why someone British wants to write about the bullfight. I tell him how I am also torn, how it walks a moral line, how bulls that fight have at least four years out here learning how to use their horns, whereas British beef cattle are slaughtered at eighteen months, with a considerable proportion still coming from factory farms. A very different life, but then a very different death. Fifteen minutes in the ring or a moment in the abattoir. To put them side by side in the analogy I preferred back then: five years on free-release and then the arena, or eighteen months in prison and then the electric chair. Nicolás can see the logic, he says, but his eyes see the cruelty just as clearly.

The *finca*, or 'ranch', that we are headed to is owned by the Núñez del Cuvillo family, renowned breeders of bulls so good that they are currently treating not just one, but two pardoned from the ring, one by José Tomás himself. I wonder how Nicolás has managed to get access into this most private part of a private world, but I don't want to ask him directly. I soon discover that at every level of society the world of southern Spain is the world of the bulls.

We arrive at the end of the long drive at the sprawl of a luxurious white stone farmhouse built in the Andalusian style around a central courtyard. As we get out of the car two modern-day knights ride up casually on unusually muscular horses, reins in their left hands and long lances in their right. They slouch low into the shape of the horse, gaucho-style, looking both born in the saddle and careless about the conventions of riding. They talk through their cigarettes, their flat caps pulled low, and point out a small bullring.

Nicolás and I wander over and climb up on to a viewing platform, from where we spot one of the pardoned bulls in a stone-walled pen adjacent to the ring. He is looking uncomfortable in the enclosure, but there is no violence in him as he rubs shoulders with his two companions, two much bigger *cabestros*, steers of a different breed with their long, wide, blunt horns. A few minutes later the vet arrives, and we see far more closely the damage a bullfight can do.

The cattle are herded into a narrow stone corridor in single file, the bull book-ended between the steers at his head and tail to calm him, and the vet begins unpacking the antibiotic-soaked gauze wadding from within the picador's lance-wound in his shoulder (the *banderillas* wounds having quickly healed). The bull begins thrashing around at the interference, his blood flowing freely down the shoulder as the vet has his middle finger up to the hilt within the animal, cleaning the wound before pouring in diluted iodine and giving various injections.

He is healing well and his health and strength are undoubted – while helping the vet I make the mistake of trying to hold the bull's horn and almost have my wrists snapped for my trouble. I forget that a bull can lift the heavy horse of the picador, and his armoured rider, clean off the ground – a three-quarter-ton straight lift, with a lance in his shoulder. Some bulls appear barely to notice the lance through the haze of adrenaline and endorphins, pushing ever upwards into the horse so that were the crossbar missing from the haft they would drive it through their entire bodies. I am reminded of the words of another vet from the Madrid bullring: 'The only time I get really upset is when the bull is handled badly by man … Man has a responsibility to the bull to fight it expertly. And in a good *corrida* the bull feels no pain.' Perhaps, perhaps not, but there is no denying the damage.

Afterwards, Nicolás asks one of the farmhands if this is Idílico, the bull José Tomás fought, and they answer no, he is in the nearest field, although we can only see a herd of small calves in there. Then they show us the intricate tactics involved in moving an animal like this. The two farmhands ride off and collect two more steers from a neighbouring field – just as for humans three is a crowd, for bovids, three is a herd. They enter the pasture with the calves and begin a series of moves, endlessly cross-riding the field, calling, cajoling, driving calves away and steers in, until they have separated the bull from his former herd so that he attaches himself to the steers. Eventually, they manage to get this impromptu herd into a pen.

I have heard that the fighting bull has two psychological states, that in the herd he is a relatively placid animal, although capable of far more 'defensive' aggression than any other breed of bull, and that when solitary the beast within is released. The rather docile animal I see before me bears no relation to the bulls I have seen in the ring, let alone one so fearless and aggressive it wins reprieve from the matador's sword. Then, following another complex set of manoeuvres, they single out this nervous animal into a pen on his own.

■ ■ ■ ■ ■

I have never before seen such a startling change come over a living creature. This was not a change of temperament, but of character itself. His head came up, crowned with its fiercely pointed horns, and a vast surge of testosterone-enhanced adrenaline seemed to course through him. He literally began to dance, as a boxer dances, his 1,212lb bulk skittering on his hooves over the mud-slick stones. I climbed on to one of the six-foot walls of the pen and finally he caught sight of me.

The sensation of being the focus of such fury is a unique one. I stopped halfway along the wall, slowly turned, put my hands on the safety-rail and looked down at the explosive paranoia of horn and muscle less than five feet away from me. I moved the little finger of my left hand and his head flicked towards it. Then I moved the little finger on my right, and his head shot towards that. Bulls can jump – I've seen film of bulls clearing the almost six-foot barrier round the sand of the bull-ring – and I didn't particularly fancy ending up in hospital that day, so I kept my movement-level low, trying to gauge it so that I kept his attention but didn't exceed whatever psychological tipping point existed within that bovine brain. My overwhelming feeling at that moment was of smiling and thinking, perversely you may say, that this was an experience I would like to take further. However, it was enough for a first meeting with a bull. Now I had to meet my first matador.

■ ■ ■ ■ ■

I had been put in touch with Adolfo Suárez Illana by a family friend, and he had agreed not only to meet up, but to introduce me to the great matador Juan José Padilla. The plan was to meet at a farm in December and to watch them train together, but Spain was suffering a seemingly unending downpour and in the end we met in mid-January on the steps of the Cajasol Bank's Cultural Centre in Seville, where the two were due to take part in a filmed interview on stage as part of the bank's *'mano a mano'* cultural programme.

I had been told that Adolfo was an *aficionado práctico*, a 'fan who does', although it has a stronger meaning. This is not like football, where you can knock a ball around in the park: the bullfight does not allow for unskilled amateurism, not twice anyway. I was also told he was the eldest son of Adolfo Suárez González, not only the first democratic prime minister of Spain after Franco's death, but, with the King, a co-founder of democratic Spain responsible for its *'transición'* to a democratic state.

When I meet him, he is a lean, well-dressed figure in his mid-forties, speaking English immaculately without a trace of Spain or America in the accent (he spent time at Harvard). Everything about him projects confidence and I write in my notes that he has the air of a political matador. Which is not to say that anything Machiavellian lurks behind the ready smile. He merely possesses the self-awareness and multiple levels of thought that are required in his twin spheres of politics and the law where he practises. He somehow avoids the trap of coming across as what the Spanish call *un lobo que sabe*, 'a wolf who knows', and I wonder if the rough honesty and camaraderie of the bullfight is responsible for this.

His good friend Padilla is another animal entirely. Prominent sideburns, a sharp suit, a flash of gold on the wrist and a vastly larger-than-life manner, he gets away with it all through sheer charisma. There is something of the movie star about him, not in looks, but in the projection of character. And when you get up close you see the scar in the neck from the horn that pierced his oesophagus. What you don't see are the others that criss-cross his body in dense and irregular patterns, like coiled ropes.

On a stage in front of the cameras and 100 or so of Seville's *afición*, Padilla sits down in front of a mannequin bearing his suit of lights, complete with cape and hatbox. Adolfo is placed in front of a photograph of himself as a child alongside his father, in an eerie echo of images from the first *Godfather* film. The two are comfortable with each other and the stage, highlighting the nervousness of the journalist interviewing them. The first question is well placed.

INTERVIEWER: Which are more dangerous, political bulls or the real ones?

ADOLFO: Political bulls wound the prestige, real bulls the body.

INTERVIEWER: Which is worse?

ADOLFO: Take a look at Padilla's neck some time.

This sets the tone for the rest of the talk, a wry look at the life and friendship of two very different men.

INTERVIEWER: Would Padilla make a good politician?

ADOLFO: *Pause* … He's a great bullfighter … (*Laughter*).

What is most interesting as the Q&A continues is the esteem in which the two men from such different backgrounds and professions hold one another: Padilla was a baker's apprentice in Jerez de la Frontera before he became the matador he is today. The reason seems to me simple: they perceive each other as equals because each is better than the other at different things, but things that they both respect.

At the drinks afterwards Adolfo circles the room, but makes sure to introduce me to the right people along the way, not just those that can help me research my book, but those that should be met. These include the ageing, stocky figure of the man who opens the Gates of Fear in the Seville bullring. He proudly tells me with great dignity that it is his honour to shout every time he does so, 'Silence. A man is risking his life today.'

Padilla seems less at ease in the room – cultural centres are not his habitat, perhaps. We head out across the street to a typical Seville restaurant and a couple sitting in the gallery lay out a white handkerchief over the railing when they spot him, as though they are the president of the ring offering him an ear of the bull for his brilliance. The tone changes immediately and here Padilla comes into his own, holding court from a corner of the bar, Adolfo on one side of him, me on the other trying to blend into the background to observe, but being constantly underlined by Padilla's banter. I notice the smile never fades from his face, and he finds my now high-school-level Spanish amusing. When I taste the *jamón* that comes I judge it good and Iberian – *bueno ibérico, pero no cinco jota* – but not the five 'J' standard of the highest quality. He thinks this is hilarious from an Englishman, and '*cinco jota*' becomes my nickname for the night.

The entire bar seems to me aimed at this corner, everyone looking up towards the twin points of gravity that are Padilla and Adolfo. Someone finds out I am a writer and drags me a few yards away to meet a couple of young Portuguese *novilleros*, novice bullfighters, aged seventeen and twenty. However, although they are aware I am writing a book and they need the publicity, they can barely focus on me, their eyes sliding past me back into the corner of the room. I question the older one, Gonzalo Montoya, after he looks through me for the fifth time.

'*Señor*, I am sorry! Publicity is very important, but that, *that is Padilla!*'

A couple of hours and many glasses of red wine later we walk out of the restaurant (I still don't know who paid or whom to thank), and one of Padilla's friends, a *banderillero*, collects us in a car and drives us to another restaurant. We join a table with the president of a premier league football club and various breeders and bullfighters. At the other end sits a beautiful woman who sings unprompted with a sweet, sweet voice filled with sadness and power as we drink *cubas libres* made with more rum than Coca-Cola. At some point they ask Padilla to sing, but rather than flamenco he embarks on an entirely phonetic – he speaks no English – rendition of 'New York, New York'.

As the evening draws to a close, I notice a man in his thirties at the other end of the table, his face aristocratically handsome but grim, almost bitter. The group have been at this table for a while, and all eyelids are heavy, but his look is hooded. There is something of Death about him. I ask who he is.

'Eduardo Dávila Miura, the retired matador.'

A man who not only kills bulls, but is a descendant of the family that breeds bulls that kill matadors – most famously Manolete. We shake hands as we leave; he smiles coldly, but says nothing as he slides out of the room. A very different sort of killer – or that was my impression at the time. One year later we would meet again under different circumstances when he took me under his sole instruction for my own lethal debut in the ring.

The last thing Adolfo says as we share an umbrella in the rain is: 'You haven't seen anything until you have seen Padilla fight, or, even better, watched him train.'

3

La gaonera

The matador holds the cape spread behind his body like angel's wings, and calls the bull to charge him from in front, passing it through the cloth on one side. (Invented by Rodolfo Gaona Jiménez, born 1888, Mexico)

After much toing and froing of text messages in broken Spanish, Padilla eventually commits to a day of training with young cows at a ranch in February, and promises 'many animals, much Rioja, much *jamón* and many cigars'. It sounds like a light day of fun, but that would be to ignore that this is the matador's matador, a man usually regarded as the bravest of all in his craft.

The morning starts early, with me meeting Nicolás again at his apartment in the old Jewish quarter of Seville. He wants to come and see Padilla in action, and has agreed to share his photos with me for the book. We head off down a different road south, this time to Sanlúcar de Barrameda and Padilla's house, named Portagayola after one of his favourite moves in the ring – and one that has paid for the house many times over.

Padilla's house is a rather grand affair, with his mono-grammed minibus behind the electric gates for his *cuadrilla*, his 'team' of three *banderilleros*, two picadors and a sword-page, whose entire livelihood depends on the matador's skill. The housekeeper ushers us through the garden into the living room, where the heads of various bulls adorn the walls, and one Cape buffalo, alongside trophies and paintings of Padilla. The rooms seem heavily furnished, but comfortable, decorated but not cer-emonious. The taste is not mine, there is something strangely Los Angeles about the walls also being covered in photos and paintings of the Maestro, but it is in keeping with his character.

The man himself bounds into the room with an energy I had not noticed on our previous meeting; it seems as if he is holding on to himself in preparation for something. Yes, he wants to make a good impression, but there is more to this internal force than that, much more.

He takes us into the dining room, with each placement along the table overshadowed by a Miura bull's head. The bulls that kill matadors have been killed in numbers by Padilla at the *feria* in Pamplona, and now they lean over the chairs, peering glassy-eyed into the middle distance.

We are shown around the gardens where, between the swim-ming pool and a children's play area littered with plastic slides and see-saws, there is a miniature bullring. Next to it are two simulated bull's heads with horns mounted on wheels, known as the *carretón*, or 'cart'. The pavilion overlooking this *arenita* is a place of solace and happiness for the Maestro, its walls adorned with photos of Padilla and great matadors, breeders and friends, living and dead. Its bar is well stocked and there is also a large flatscreen TV. The sign on the door proclaims, *Aquí ... sin problemas*, 'Here ... there are no problems.'

We are soon back on the road, heading towards our final destination at incredible speed with Padilla at the wheel, vari-ous crucifixes and charms hanging from his key chain and the wing-mirror, his hands constantly touching them for luck or merely for something to do with his excess energy. Los Albu-rejos, the *finca*, or 'ranch', where we are headed, belonged to one of the greatest of the *ganaderos* (breeders) – Álvaro Domecq Díez. The family are descended from French stock who moved to Spain and into the sherry business and vast wealth in the eighteenth century. The old Don was a remarkable man, a devout Catholic who joined the newly formed Opus Dei and served as a fighter pilot in the Civil War on the side of the King, whatever Franco later did with that victory.

In his personal life, he combined a love of horses and bulls, reinstating the almost defunct form of bullfighting from horse-back, the *rejoneo*. It doubtless helped that his father had taken over the ranches of the Duke of Veragua, whose bulls Heming-way once called 'the bravest, strongest, fastest and finest look-ing of all the bulls of the Peninsula', although the bloodlines have been completely changed.

Despite these riches and piety, there has always been a whis-per that the family is cursed. Of the nineteen children the old Don had, fourteen died at birth. Of the five surviving, an infant girl died during a blood tranfusion, a son at four months from dysentery and another son at six in a riding accident. In 1991 four of his granddaughters and their nanny died in a collision with a lorry on the road outside the house we are in. The trials of Job spring to mind. The press made much of the absence of tears from the family at the graveside and Nicolás repeats the story. I reply that when my own brother had his memorial service and I stood with my brother and parents greeting the people filing in, we didn't cry either. But my God did we love him.

We arrive at the *finca* to be greeted by the sole surviving son, the sixty-nine-year-old Álvaro Domecq Romero, on one of his beloved horses. He himself learnt to fight bulls from horseback, and spent time with the Spanish Riding School of Vienna to perfect his technique before founding the Royal Spanish Eques-trian Academy. He sits deep in the saddle in the morning sun, looking comfortable on the horse, if not at meeting someone who he suspects might be an English journalist. Padilla banters through the window to him, as does Nicolás, who knows him through other connections. The *finca* itself lives up to Padilla's description, 'the Cathedral of Bullfighting'. Set on the hillside in the shadow of a thirteenth-century Moorish castle, the white stone buildings of Los Alburejos sprawl out into the distance. Alongside the outdoor ring I was expecting, there is also an indoor one which is if anything larger. There is something almost decadent about having a full-size, indoor arena: man and beast braving death while the spectators refuse to brave the elements.

And then comes the arrival of the bulls. Or rather, the *vaquillas*, the young mothers of future bulls. For the bullfight is premised on the fact that the bull has never seen a man on the ground before, and he is herded entirely by mounted farm-hands. So, in order to test whether or not the lines are breeding true, it is the females who are brought into the corrals along-side the much larger steers (of another breed) who keep them calm. Despite this, as I approach the sunken corral, I notice that the *vaquillas* seem much more nervous than the steers. I won-der why this is. Perhaps the steers are more used to humans, although since I am appearing from far above, how can they identify me as such?

After much cajoling, shouting and prodding, they single out the first *vaquilla* to be tested. Yet again I witness the psychologi-cal shift that occurs, although it is much less marked than in my encounter with the pardoned bull Idílico. There is a tran-sition from fear to aggression. The *vaquilla* begins to charge shadows on the walls of the holding pen, stopping just short of actual collision with a nimbleness no bull has. Everything that moves is constantly assessed for its threat status.

The ethology student in me wonders if this is a revolution-ary transition inside the mind of the animal, or merely an evo-lutionary one. Is this massive, overwhelming fear that I am witnessing, or have the switches and channels in the bovine brain actually flipped from defensive to offensive? And is there really a difference between these two things? I can't decide, and walk away as the day proper is about to begin.

■ ■ ■ ■ ■

I find myself next to Padilla in the main *burladero*, or recess, of the outdoor bullring in my shirtsleeves, Padilla wearing a *traje corto*, an unembroidered and sombre-coloured variant of the bullfighter's 'suit of lights'. The first day of spring sun is in our eyes and a flicker of trepidation is in my chest. It has been suggested that perhaps I enter the ring today, but only lightly. However, I don't feel there is any way I could say no, as thirty pairs of eyes are wondering who the young man is standing next to the Maestro.

Behind the other three *burladeros* are various young matadors, *novilleros* or novice matadors, and a *banderillero* from Padilla's *cuadrilla*, along with a picador on an armoured horse from Don Álvaro's staff. Around the ring are seated various friends of the Don, including someone from one of the major bullrings who wishes to see the future stock from this, one of the greatest of the *ganaderías*, the 'breed houses'.

The gates then open and in flies the first *vaquilla* with a lightness of hoof and variability of direction which is quite a surprise to someone who has only seen the charges of fully grown, male *toros bravos*. Padilla walks out into the ring and for the first time today I see that he is calm, seemingly at home. He presents the animal with the large pink and yellow *capote de brega*, the work cape, and it begins its lightning fast and unpredictable charges, which even the Maestro seems to find difficult. His rather calm interest comes from the fact that although these animals are dangerous, they are not usually lethally so. One would have to be very unlucky to die in a testing ring with a *vaquilla*, although it does happen, most famously to the great matador Antonio Bienvenida in 1975. There is always risk in the ring.

After a few passes with the cape, Álvaro gestures for the *vaquilla*'s courage against the horse to be tested. Padilla dexterously lines up the *vaquilla* until the horse dominates its field of vision, before slipping out of it himself, sharing a joke with the picador on his way. There is something impressive in the way an experienced *torero*, the general term for 'bullfighter', is both aware, and supremely confident in that awareness, of where the animal's attention is at any given moment in time. Equally interesting is how little room for subsidiary ideas there are in the animal's head.

I am reminded of the time at my family's house in Essex when a Harris hawk plummeted to earth with a pheasant in its claws. It began to feast on the still-living game bird as I watched with equal parts disgust and admiration through the study window. Moments later a strange-looking man with a TV aerial in his hand came wandering across the lawns. He was the falconer to whom the bird – with radio-collar attached – belonged. As we chatted over a mug of tea, he took a semi-devoured wood pigeon carcass out of his leather bag and put it next to the hawk. He physically nudged the bird until it was atop the new corpse, which it pecked at with the same staccato efficiency. He then removed the pheasant for his own cooking pot and explained that the bird didn't even perceive the difference. For the raptor, there is merely the Platonic idea of 'prey', indivisible and pure. For the bull, likewise, there is the perceived threat at that moment and nothing else. One can easily see the evolutionary pressure on wolves to hunt in packs if their prey – for example, that precursor of domestic cattle and fighting bull, the aurochs – can only focus on one of them at a time.

Returning to the dancing *vaquilla*, it hurls itself at the horse – which at over 1,500lbs, plus stout rider, padding, armour, etc., is left unmoved – and is received on the picador's lance, although this one has had its sting curtailed, the lance point shortened from four inches before the crossbar to three-quarters of an inch. Again and again the *vaquilla* throws herself into the point, Álvaro's low voice growling across the echoing sands, '*otra vez*', 'one more time'. In the *vaquilla*, fear becomes aggression and aggression seems to cancel out, or remove the significance of, pain.

Then, following very roughly the structure of the bullfight – but with no *banderillas*, the colourful, barb-pointed sticks – we move straight on to the *muleta*, the smaller red cape used in the final act for the close work with the bull.

The animal, faster than any bull, would seem to be impossible for a bullfighter to create any elegance in caping. However, Padilla does exactly that. He uses delicate movements at the base of the cape to bring her head down, horns grazing the arena floor, drawing neat half circles in the sand, while his body strikes and maintains the long lines, so reminiscent of flamenco: the line and the curve, calm conflicts of geometry.

Despite the skill, Padilla still takes a battering from the cow, both horns into his waist, not hard enough to penetrate but hard enough to knock him down, causing a bleeding gash in his hand. I watch closely and ponder the reason why he doesn't even look at the wound. Has the adrenaline removed the sensation or is it so low on the list of priorities; or is it pride, the kissing-cousin of vanity? These are the sorts of questions I can't ask; not yet. As he dusts himself off, several of the younger *toreros* wrestle the *vaquilla* to the ground and I am surprised to see the farm manager cut the tips of its horns off with bolt-cutters. When it gets up, blood pumps out of the horns with little pulses of the heart, like water from a drinking fountain on an alternating current. I do not ask why they do this, I merely watch. Padilla capes her twice more; she seems absolutely undiminished, despite the new sensitivity this causes and the often-heard opinion that this reduces the animal's spatial awareness, like clipping a cat's whiskers. As Padilla leaves the ring, she is busy flying at the *novilleros*, who are having a hard time of it. He shakes my hand, his blood and the cow's mixed on his palm, and informs me that he thinks I would be wise not to step into the ring today.

My feelings at the time are mixed. Watching the skill of even the youngest of the novices, I realise that I have never lifted a *capote* or a *muleta*, I don't even know how to hold it.

Also, the meniscal tear in the cartilage in my right knee, and the double cyst and calcified tendons in my right shoulder (the former from cross-country running, the later from falling from a horse), make me wonder whether my natural reflexes will take me out of danger fast enough should I mess up. Perhaps a little practice ... however, I cannot help but feel in this company that somehow I should protest, should just leap in like the *espontáneos*, the spontaneous ones, usually boys, who illegally jump into the ring during a fight to show off and sometimes make their name. There is a bitter comfort in being reassured into a position you want, but I suspect it may be a touch – just a touch – cowardly. He sees this, and reassures me: next time. So next time it will be.

Soon after the *novilleros* have tested their skills, Álvaro's nephew, Antonio Domecq, comes in on one of the most beautiful horses I have ever seen – tall-bodied, long lines, but with a strident musculature, as though the muscled Hellenistic warhorses of the Parthenon frieze were crossed with English thoroughbreds. They dance around the ring in a slow gallop, the horse watching the *vaquilla* to make sure its horns never touch its flanks, the man leaning out of the saddle – impossibly far out – to stroke the cow's horns. His horsemanship, and this is one area I can claim a little knowledge, is exquisite.

I remember a description I read years ago in the book *The Royal Horse of Europe*, while I was perfecting my own riding on a *hacienda* in Argentina. According to the author, Sylvia Loch, the *rejoneador* and his mount are 'a symbol of complex dependence, one upon the other. The centaur–man and horse joined together in a way in which no other equestrian sport can demonstrate. Something deeply primeval within us is touched when we see such perfect empathy between a man and his horse.'

However, what we also see is the antipathy between the centaur and the ungainly bull who cannot catch him. There is here the slightly malicious hint of the favoured child, one domestic animal working with his master to taunt another. It is a difficult thing, sometimes, to keep an honest eye. I wonder about this spectacle. I have never seen a full fight from horseback. I wonder if, in lacking the pathos of unassisted man against beast, it collapses into an exercise of craft rather than art – fireworks not theatre – and thus is mere gladiatorialism.

A little while, and three cows, later, the event comes to an end and the crowd dwindles away, as do the *novilleros* and Padilla's team. Padilla is taken away to choose the bulls he will fight in Pamplona at some point in the year. I am annoyed to have missed this, since I would have enjoyed the introduction to the animals I am sworn to run with on a July morning (at risk to life and limb) alongside the man who will kill them – or die trying – that night. The sheer oddity – and gravity – of those phrases echoes through me now exactly as the thoughts did at the time. This is a very strange world I am moving into: sometimes beautiful, sometimes comical, always deadly – *lethally* – serious.

As those who are left wander down through high-walled courtyards, I cannot shake the feeling that I am in some way imposing on the Domecq family, that they had not counted on my presence at this *tentadero*, this testing, and that as a writer, an Englishman and a Protestant-born atheist, I may not be their idea of a perfect guest. However, when we come to a set of stables near the door to the house, I see the inquisitive head of a tall grey pure-blood Andalusian horse poking over his stall door. I go and talk to him as the others stand chatting about the *tentadero* and Álvaro comes over and opens the stall door so I can go in with the animal. I walk in and the giant leans affectionately against me. I notice he possesses an unusual combination of dignity and curiosity, and try to pass this on to Álvaro in broken Spanish; for the first time that day, he smiles, although whether it is at me or the horse, of which he is clearly fond, is unclear. He gestures at me to follow and to leave the stable door open, something I find strange, but he merely says the horse likes to feel involved. Again I note the favouritism among species.

Inside the main house, I am introduced to his wife Maribel and his sister Fabiola. When one of the uniformed servants asks what I want to drink, I say beer, which leads to a raised eyebrow, and I am steered towards the sherry – it is the Domecq house, after all. We sit on sofas under bulls' heads among statues of bulls. We talk and smoke for a while, Álvaro singing the praises of the matador José Tomás, before we head into the great hall for lunch.

There I am seated between Maribel and her nephew Antonio, the *rejoneador* I had seen practising with his horse and the *vaquilla* earlier, because they both speak English. There is a frigid politeness to them which I try to break through. I talk to Antonio about the polo players whom I met in Argentina, including the great Adolfo Cambiaso, 'the wizard', but he seems to regard their skills as parlour games.

At first, there is a formality to the lunch, despite the excellent food and wine. However, as I talk to Maribel about her childhood schooling not far from where I grew up in London, she does warm a little and laughs out loud. Across the table I catch the eye of Fabiola, Antonio's mother, and I can't help but think of her four daughters, aged eleven to twenty-one, and their twenty-nine-year-old nanny all dying on the road just outside the gates after a *tentadero* much like today's. There seems an unnatural amount of tragedy in the world I have come into.

By this point Padilla, either ignorant or careless of the looming air of death and good manners, has begun to hold court, regaling the table with stories, anecdotes, jokes and opinions so voluble and changeable that, lost in the labyrinth of his Spanish, I turn to Maribel and remark how amazing he is, to which she replies with an air of warning and sadness combined, 'Yes, but he fights Miuras.'

The bulls of death. I ask why.

'Because the other matadors, like Enrique Ponce, get to choose first. And they don't choose Miuras.'

And so I begin to see a picture: this matador in his mid-thirties, his contemporaries retired into other careers or of sufficient celebrity to afford to fight easy bulls, supporting his family and his *cuadrilla* by fighting with his intelligent and economical style – alongside some trademark flourishes – the most dangerous bulls on the circuit, seventeen serious injuries to his name and even the great houses of bull-breeding speaking of him in hushed tones.

Then I look across and he cracks another joke, talking simultaneously to Álvaro and Adolfo Suárez Illana on his mobile phone, while throwing down another glass of wine. And I remember the six Miura heads above the six place settings at his dinner table. This is not a man you feel sorry for: *es demasiado fuerte para la tragedia*, 'he is too strong for tragedy'.

As we leave the table for Domecq brandy and Padilla's Cohiba cigars, we pass a sideboard of photos: Álvaro's father with Manolete not long before the Miura Islero killed him; the ill-fated gypsy and the aristocrat rumoured to suffer a curse, both firm friends. Álvaro senior was in the stands when his friend died. He didn't fight on his horses again after that.

We get into Padilla's car and I sit and close my eyes, thinking about the fascinating day that has passed, thinking it is over. How little I know.

■ ■ ■ ■ ■

I wake up in the car half an hour later. We are in the streets of Jerez de la Frontera, the town of sherry itself. Padilla is shouting out of the open window at passers-by who recognise him. He has been steadily bantering with Nicolás as I have been dozing and now he is playing to his audience. Suddenly he shouts at

Nicolás to stop outside a nightclub called Lalola – it is 4.30 p.m.

'Here. It's my nightclub, let's check up on them.'

We follow, partly out of interest, partly for the novelty, but largely because of the irrepressible good humour of our host.

Inside, Padilla introduces us to the manager and the bar staff and I am given a large rum and Coke: and when I say large, I watch as a quarter of a bottle of Ron Barcélo empties into the huge glass before Padilla nods to his employee to stop.

What happens next is something of a blur, not helped by the utter illegibility of my notes and the fact that very few of Nicolás's photos are in focus. There is a plan to return to Padilla's house to collect our car and then return to Seville. However, that plan is scrapped under the barrage of Padilla's jokes, stories, and demonstrations of the perfect *muleta* pass on the dance floor of the empty nightclub.

More drinks come. I get through most of the rum bottle. Demands are made by all of us for food to Padilla, who eventually concedes. It is dark outside when we leave, but instead of going to Seville, we end up at a hotel where Padilla's friend and fellow matador Finito de Córdoba is staying before a fight. As Nicolás and I grab some food at the bar, Padilla goes to find Finito but for some reason he isn't in the room he's meant to be in. I find out months later from Finito himself that he had hidden under the bed rather than get caught up in the whirlwind of his friend's night out.

Now we need more company, Padilla decides, and we find ourselves in a dance studio with Antonio El Pipa, a master of flamenco who has danced on the stages of Broadway in New York and Sadler's Wells in London. He is a childhood friend of Padilla, and after another serving of rum – during which I don part of his costume and demonstrate my own flamenco as Padilla and this new maestro look on laughing – we get back in the car and return to Padilla's house, where we settle in to the longest argument about fighting and dance I have ever had in any language, not least my third. Nicolás's photos show Padilla, Antonio and me, at this point sworn brothers, arms around one another, huddled in the corner of a large room, gesticulating wildly with slack lips and glazed eyes. Nicolás manages to get me out alive at 5 a.m. We drive to Seville. Padilla sleeps in his bar, awaking three hours later to fight in another *tentadero*.

Before I leave, Padilla asks me to sign a cape he keeps in the bar, which has been inscribed by the greatest matadors of the past twenty years. I am insanely honoured and try to think of something memorable in Spanish. I settle for a drunken hybrid, my words in English, García Lorca's in Spanish. It goes something like this:

> To my Spanish brother, a maestro of elegance and
> generosity. When he enters the ring,

> '*La gente van suspirando*
> *con las guitarras abiertas.*'
> ('The people are sighing
> With open guitars.')

Padilla is happy, not fully understanding. Antonio El Pipa – who speaks English and knows his poetry – is almost in tears at the words of the long dead maestro.

4

La revolera

The matador cites with cape in front of him, transferring the cape into one hand as the bull passes. He swirls the cloth around his waist, changing hands, fixing the bull in place where it turns to follow, *para rematar la serie de pases*, 'to finish the series of passes'.

After I recover from my hangover, I receive an email from Adolfo Suárez Illana inviting me to another *tentadero* on a friend's ranch. He is getting back in training, as he intends to kill a full-size bull in a public arena later in the year. So he wants to work his way up from the *vaquillas* of the *finca* of Fuente Ymbro.

The event becomes much larger than this, as Adolfo, a strong defender of the bullfight, decides a little publicity would be good. So Miguel Ángel Perera, the number one ranked matador in Spain whom I had flown over to see fight in Madrid, is coming along too, with journalists from *¡Hola!* magazine.

When I arrive at the ranch – a much more modest and modern version of Los Alburejos – the heavy rain and wind of early March have turned the Cádiz countryside into a replica of my East Anglian homeland. It has a bleakness about it, the modern buildings huddling in the untimely weather as small groups of men stand around in the doorways smoking. Things are not looking good.

A few minutes later Adolfo arrives in his sleek Mercedes and gets out happily greeting all present, and exploding out of the other door comes the ever-innervating Padilla. Rough handshakes and embraces are exchanged all round. Once again a weight is lifted from my mind when Adolfo tells me that he doesn't want me to enter the ring today. The wind makes it far too dangerous – controlled manipulation of a hanging cloth is the essence of bullfighting, after all – and we should wait until he can get me out on to his father-in-law's ranch, where he can teach me in controlled conditions on younger and smaller *vaquillas* than they will be using.

Then another car arrives bearing the bullfighting 'man of the moment', Miguel Ángel Perera. He is flanked on one side by his PR handler, whose last job was for Disney, and on the other by his manager, whose last job was as a matador, but who retrained as a lawyer when he retired in 2006.

Perera and Adolfo shake hands with something like the wary mutual respect of birds of prey landing on the same perch. There is about him the same air of discomfort that I saw in the lobby of the Madrid Palace Hotel five months previously. We are all introduced, and, although he seems oblivious to me, his PR takes me to one side, complimenting me on my blog which she has been following, including my description of his fight in Madrid.

'Really, I had no idea an Englishman could understand the bulls so well. How is this possible?'

She is pretty, in her mid-thirties, and the embodiment of PR charm, flashing a smile with her hand on my arm. I try to remember what I had written three months before and can only think that I was quite critical of Perera's bullfighting, if not his courage.

'I just described what I saw.'

'Ah, a natural!'

She moves on to the journalists from the magazine. However, the more important discussion going on is between the owner of the ranch and the bullfighters. The wind and rain have relented, but the ring is like a swimming pool. The breeder says he will clean it up while we have lunch, so we pile into various cars and drive to a nearby roadside restaurant. The restaurant is large and shabby, with a run-down bar area where some locals sit watching television. A few come up to the table to say hello because the table is quite a line up. One of Spain's best breeders, Riccardo Gallardo, next to him its number one ranking matador, Perera, next to him Adolfo, then me and the breeder's garrulous and charming wife, then the even more garrulous Juan José Padilla, the PR and the writer from ¡Hola!. On another table sit Perera's bullfighting team and both a photographer and cameraman from the magazine.

Through lunch several things are happening at once. María-Paz begins an excitable interrogation about why an Englishman would want to write about her beloved bulls. And she does love them: she even tells me about how one bull during the unseasonal rains that winter became stranded on an island in the water. Since there was simply no way to rescue him – the idea of attempting to load him on to a small boat is as laughable as heaving a great white shark on to it – the local government was contacted and the nearby dam was opened, dropping the water-table for the entire region. For one bull. I chat with her out of the side of my mouth, and the side of my mind, because all my focus is on Perera. He is seated between Adolfo and Riccardo and yet he seems politely oblivious to them both, focusing on his food in the way a well-mannered child sitting between two adults at a dinner-party would as the grown-ups talk over his head. Except they keep trying to draw him into the conversation. In fact, they treat him with a slightly paternal reverence, like viziers with the heir to the throne, especially Riccardo, who has known and helped Perera throughout his career. Perera continues to contemplate the chips in front of him as though they are a particularly fascinating problem, judging each individually, then spearing his chosen victim with a fork before eating it slowly. I cannot help but remember research done on bullfighters by the Madrid psychiatrist José Carrasco, finding much lower than average levels of monoamine oxidase, a similar neurochemical phenomenon being found in those members of the prison population who have been classified as clinical psychopaths. Whatever the truth, the twenty-five-year-old Perera is a fascinating study in tranquility, although I did not see him smile once at that table.

■ ■ ■ ■ ■

When we arrived back at the ranch, there was much changing of clothing and posing for photos by journalists and friends. This meeting of Adolfo and Perera had something of the diplomatic about it, a nod between old Spain and her progeny. From here on in, I will give my diary entry written that night:

'At about six o'clock, the first *vaquilla* hurled herself into the ring at great speed much as they had done at the Domecq ranch. However, now we had two *toreros*, Adolfo and Perera, taking it in turns. Perera, whose professional life this is, had a far greater elegance of posture and mobility of wrist, but I was interested to see that there was no flaw, in technique or courage, in Adolfo's work. Both men not only caped the cattle, but also the wind, their capes angled so the air did not force them beyond the centuries-old shapes they were determined to cut through the moving air.

'Some *vaquillas* were good – one in particular sticks in the memory as it struggled and strove under the horse, trying to find purchase to eviscerate, to disembowel – and some were bad, wanting only to be elsewhere.

'And then came the surprise, then came blood and thunder.

'The fully grown bull sped into the ring with its trademark ferocity straight from the field, putting paid to the idea that it is the hours in transit and the goading before entry which gives them their trademark rage. From behind the *burladero* I could feel the ground bounce, the earthquake of its moving presence. And from its head rose smoke. The dust of its five years roaming free in the *campo*, the dry countryside, came off its horns as though from the devil itself.

'As I tried to photograph it, great clumps of sand struck the camera lens as the bull cornered. No seat in the ring, no close-up footage on television will ever come close to showing you the tangible, manifest threat presented by these animals in the ring. I found myself finally realising that when Hemingway said there was not a land mammal alive beside man which could survive in the ring with a bull – no elephant, lion or bear – he was speaking the truth. Only through illusion, only by giving the cape motion as the body remains still, could the movement-based vision – and movement-based brain – of the bull be tricked sufficiently to survive in that place.

'Although Adolfo has fought fully grown bulls in the past, and was to fight them again, this *toro*, this gift from the breeders who have supported Perera's career since its birth – worth the price of a Rolex or two – was for the maestro of that day.

'With only one small lance-strike from a picador to tire it – no *banderillas* – and a tiny ring in which tiring it by distance was impossible, Perera caped and caped and caped until its head grew lower and lower from fatigue. And its breathing louder. That is the other thing I remember, the breath. Rolling and sonorous, massive and deep, it echoed in the ring in a manner I had never heard, as it never reaches the stands in a proper arena.

'As is the dramatic structure of the fight, it reached its logical conclusion, and Perera was handed the killing sword by his *mozo de espadas*, his "sword-handler". Perera lined up the bull, then lined up himself and the sword, and went in hard and fast, stepping away from the horns at the last moment, the blade seated in the body to the hilt.

'As the bull toppled to the ground, Adolfo called me out into the ring to witness the great presence of the animal as it passes and diminishes. I reached down and touched the hide of its flank, my hand soon slick with its blood as I felt the relaxing of the huge muscles. As I did so, I saw its second eyelids close – the white crosswise-moving membranes underneath the dark ones – and when they opened the pupils were blank, unfocused. I felt something, an echo of something. I shook hands with people afterwards. No one commented on the blood running from my fingers.

'Night was beginning to fall by now and I was tired from a long day, the *toreros* more so with their undulating adrenaline levels. Adolfo began to cape the last *vaquilla* of the day, a larger beast, more steady but still feisty. The wind had fallen. At one point he passed me in the *burladero* and said, "Perhaps this one is for you. But if you do, only cape it backwards." I assume there are two reasons for this: in this direction the human body naturally moves the cape more smoothly; but also it has more protection from serious injury: its organs are better protected by lower spanning ribs and rising hip bones, the muscles tougher, the femoral arteries and genitals out of reach. My pulse began to rise. I was afraid, and happy, and excited, and afraid.

'As darkness covered us, and a couple of small floodlights came on, Adolfo walked up to me with his small, red cape, the *muleta* – sword inside it to widen – and began to show me how to hold it. This was my time. My pulse began to spike. I had had too long to wonder what would happen to me when this moment came. I knew the odds were massively against serious injury; no, my worry had only been that I would fail at the moment of testing. However, the world sometimes intervenes to take us outside of our inner thoughts.

'As I took the *muleta* from Adolfo, the *vaquilla* suddenly charged him, sending him out into the ring unprotected, the other *toreros* running out with large capes to distract it, and then I ran in after him, shouting the first thing I could think of, "¡Toro! Toro!" The *vaquilla* stopped and decided that I would make a more interesting target. At this point, there was still thought, and I did indeed turn my back on the beast and cite it with the *muleta*. It charged and passed through the cape.

'My internal state changes: "I can do this," I think. I face the animal and, shuffling forward, offer it the cape again. It charges, going through the red fabric, its pointed horns too close to my legs for comfort. It turns, frustrated, tired, and stares at me again. I cite it again, and this time something is off – in me, in it – and it turns for my legs halfway through. I dance to one side as I continue to cape, missing the horns by a few inches.

'This shakes me, but I try to lure it again. This time it is harder, it is less inclined to charge, and when it does it ducks in again for my legs. Looking back, I realise that my complete lack of experience – my having never even held a *muleta* – means that my body was changing, trying to learn what to do as it had no training, no muscle memory to fall back on. Again I am saved more by reflexes than skill, my insistence on continuing more pride than courage.

'I do not know how many times this went on. Memory and vanity are deceptive friends. Five, six? After this Adolfo took control of the beast again. As I stepped behind the *burladero* and my heart and hormones returned to the norm, I felt two things: one strong, one weak. The weak one was pride, the strong one embarrassment. Looking back on the photos of that day I can see that the line of my body is terrible, my failure to remain stationary during the pass unforgivable.

'We return to the main hall for food, the day over. I am universally praised for giving it a try, but the come-down from the adrenaline and a feeling of failing to do what I should have makes me quiet and pensive.

'However, I won't end on a note of false modesty. I sent Adolfo a message to ask about the caping, about how many passes I made. His response was as follows. "My dear friend, nobody could believe it: not less than fifteen. You were brave for the first time. Even more, not a lesson whatsoever before." I must admit an inkling of pride at this.'

■ ■ ■ ■ ■

What the diary entry does not contain is the fact that after I got out of Adolfo's car I went straight to Flaherty's, Seville's Irish pub where the staff speak English, and ordered a large glass of Johnny Walker, sitting staring at it with the blood from the great, dead bull staining my hands pink and my nails black. It took days to wash out.

5

La fanfarria

The trumpets announces the entry of the two picadors, bearing lances, riding upon armoured horses.

As spring came I moved into an apartment in the house belonging to my photographer Nicolás's mother. It is a large stone building in the old Jewish quarter of Seville, known either as Barrio Santa Cruz, or by its original name of La Judería, and without doubt the prettiest part of the city.

After Seville was taken from the Moors by Ferdinand III in 1248, the Jews began to gather in numbers second only to those of Toledo in Spain. More educated than the nobility, and more economically useful, they existed under royal protection for a time. They were given properties in this quarter of the city and built a palisade around it, but a ghetto it was not. They manned the gates themselves, and Alfonso IX gave them the three mosques within to turn into synagogues. However, royal favour faltered, and the fact that laws came in preventing them from charging annual interest on loans in excess of 20 per cent may give some indication of the feelings they were inspiring in an impoverished populace. By the time King Juan I of Castile died in October 1390 and his fourteen-year-old son took the throne as Enrique III, things were escalating rapidly. In the following summer the gates of the Jewish quarter were breached and men, women and children were dragged into the streets and hacked to death (estimates run from hundreds to 5,000). Property was expropriated and survivors forcibly converted in mass baptisms. This fire swept across Spain all summer and never truly died. Periodically recurring, usually originating in Seville, the most notable outbreak was the infamous Inquisition of 1478, which hounded those *conversos* who were thought to have secretly reverted to Judaism and burned 2,000 at the stake on the basis of such evidence as the absence of smoke from a chimney on Saturday, the Jewish Sabbath, and a dislike of *jamón*. This culminated in the Alhambra Decree of 1492, in which Ferdinand and Isabella, having just conquered the last Moorish stronghold, Granada, offered the Jewry of a finally unified Spain a stark choice: conversion, exile or death. (Another devout Catholic and Nationalist, Edward Longshanks, had done the same in England 100 years earlier.)

The house in which I lived, on calle Levíes (a surname derived from the tribe of the Levites), was one such grand merchant's house. The centrepiece of the building is a large courtyard with a fountain, surrounded by marble pillars, while on the walls there are ceramic depictions of the bullfight, even though its owner personally loathes bullfighting as a barbaric throwback (her own father having been a breeder of fighting bulls).

The apartment, on the ground floor, had a cavernous feel, the sitting room's black-timbered ceiling some forty feet up in the darkness. Down a narrow corridor was the similarly proportioned bedroom, but this was swamped with light because almost the entire wall of the bedroom opened, via a medieval iron portcullis, on to a small, sunny, jasmine-filled patio. A better place for writing this book I cannot imagine. A few days after I moved in, Nicolás's brother, Kinchu, invited me to a party in his apartment across the courtyard. So I wandered across and experienced my first taste of a different sector of Seville's society at play.

In a room full of people I am always that odd combination

of bored and nervous. The boredom comes because no one says anything; people who would be perfectly interesting facing you over a pint of beer in a pub or a glass of red wine at the corner table of a restaurant are reduced to the facile platitudes of small talk. The nervousness comes from being watched, a basic evolutionary hangover from our counter-predation instincts made worse by being almost half a foot taller than the male average in Seville.

Kinchu's apartment, a modernised and crisply furnished variant of my own, was filled with six dozen *sevillanos* in their mid-forties, dressed in a mixture of old-school English smart casual and preppie American. They were packed into the sitting room, speaking fast and loud over the flamenco-tainted electronica of Spanish pop-music. I walked in, said a quick hello to Kinchu, then virtually ran, head down, out on to the torch-lit, cobbled patio with its makeshift bar to fix myself a stiffener before I had to start with the small-talk. Before the first chunk of ice hit the bottom of my glass, a pretty brunette had sidled up and started interrogating me in incomprehensibly sibilant Spanish, standing close enough that pouring a drink became a form of foreplay, her animated conversation causing the tips of her breasts to bounce up and down against my arm. As a result, half the rum missed the glass and poured over my hand and for all I could see in the half-light down her cleavage.

Having managed to get some rum first into the glass and then into my mouth, I looked up (or rather, less down) to find that she had been joined by a bitter-eyed man whom she introduced as her husband, before continuing to jiggle against me while telling me about the wonders of Seville, Spain, flamenco, bullfighting, sherry, *jamón ibérico* and King Juan Carlos I, all the while with eyes that were saying something untranslatable (and unrepeatable).

I have absolutely no idea what was going through her husband's head, but he decided to take an aggressively diagonal approach to the problem.

'You are not English,' he spat at me.

'I'm sorry?' I replied.

'You are not English. You have not the English look. You are not Anglo-Saxon.'

The first thought that went across my mind was to suggest he read Stephen Oppenheimer's work on how three-quarters of British blood is actually from Basque Neolithic farmers, but I didn't think that would go down well and nor was my Spanish up to it.

'No, I am a Celt.'

'Hmm,' he said doubtfully. 'And what do you know about bulls?'

'Shut up, *coño*,' said his wife. (*Coño* is a hard word to translate, as the reference is the same as an English four-letter word beginning with 'c', but its significance is vastly less.)

'I was just asking ...'

' ... I know what you were doing. At least he has the balls to get in front of a *vaquilla*. What do you have?'

He fell silent, but didn't move away. Which made it all the more uncomfortable when she put her hand on my arm, fluttered her eyelashes and said, 'Nicolás tells me he took some photos of you. Could I see them?'

'Yes, but I don't have them on me.'

'I know, but you do have them in your apartment, no? The one across the courtyard.'

Was she really making a pass at me in front of her furious husband? I was pretty sure she was – and was half-fascinated to confirm it, if not interested in taking it up – but I decided that now was the time to bow out gracefully. I patted my pockets in a searching manner, looked apologetic, and said, 'I think my phone's vibrating.'

I then 'found' it, pushed a button and said in English, 'Hello, Alexander speaking ...'

I walked away across the patio, gesturing apologetically.

Re-entering the sitting room, this pattern repeated itself more than once, with slight variations, until I actually made a run for my own apartment and sat in the little garden listening to the increasingly drunken conversations next door while having a silent cigarette. I must admit I was smiling. And sweating. But still smiling.

I returned after the breather, this time to be scooped up by the tall, lean, blonde figure of Rocío, a particularly charming – and unmarried – *sevillana* who took me by the arm to a sofa and began to draw me into an hilarious and risqué conversation about infidelity, wife-swapping and why my poor Spanish was removing half my fun.

'English reserve is a wall, but uncomprehending English reserve is a fortress too formidable even for Spanish women. It is like flirting with the *Titanic*.'

'Don't you mean an iceberg?'

'Oh no. We are the ones with concealed depths, you are the one sinking.'

At some point someone took a photo of the two of us entwined which, despite the innocence of the flirtation, I hoped no one was going to put up on a social networking website of which my girlfriend was a member. I decided it was time to break the tryst. However, as I was leaving, Kinchu grabbed me and introduced me to a cousin of his lurking by the door whom he thought I might like to meet, as he had also studied biology at university.

This was how I met Tristán Ybarra, who is often referred to by his female admirers as the Spanish George Clooney (the comparison is half-fair). He was watching the entire room from the corner, drink in his hand.

'You looked like you were having fun,' he said.

'That's one way of describing it,' I replied.

'Well, what you should have done was taken her to the bathroom and ...' Tristán is now too good a friend for me to repeat in print what he said next, but it was explicit, lengthy, shocking and hilarious. It turns out he had indeed studied biology, and spoke perfect English after working at the fruit and vegetable market in Spitalfields during his gap year.

Most importantly, he invited me to a *tentadero* at another of his cousin's ranch – to which I couldn't go – and a *tertulia* (discussion group or salon) to which I could.

Leaving him to salivate over the increasingly lively group of people as the clock rolled on to 4 a.m., I gratefully left.

■   ■   ■   ■   ■

A few days later, I donned a suit and tie and strolled down calle San José, in the warm Seville night air, completely ignorant of the links in the chain of events that were being forged by me.

The *tertulia* was to be held in the Hotel Las Casas de la Judería, a hotel which I remembered from a passing visit some years before as a few small, pretty houses knocked together to form a dark little warren of rooms.

How different it was now. Crossing streets by using the network of defensive tunnels the original Jewish inhabitants had constructed, yet managing to maintain the feel of a small hotel by allowing each of the houses to maintain its original integrity, it was now the size of a small village of historic buildings, each with its own courtyard ranging from the pillared and fountained to tiny, overgrown grottoes.

The main entrance is now part of the largest building of all, decorated in the grand medieval Spanish style. When I mentioned the *tertulia* at reception, I was ushered up a flight of stairs on to a gallery and from there into a room that owes as much to the Louis of France as it does to the Philips of Spain. Inside the room was gathered an older generation of Spain in both senses of the word.

Tristán greeted me, and I was placed on an armchair next to Gola, a thin woman in her early sixties of immaculate manners who spoke English with a slight and unplaceable accent. There was something of the Spanish Katharine Hepburn about her. As we spoke, a man whose style was similar to hers, although with a slightly more knowing tone and energetic manner, leant over and said, 'Young man, you make smoking that cigarette look so elegant. Could I ask you for one?'

Gola spoke as I lit his cigarette.

'Ignacio, this young man has come to write about the bullfight.'

'Oh, bullfighting. I know nothing about that. It is of no interest to me. Although I have many paintings of it at home.'

He turned away and continued to talk in rapid Spanish to an older man in a cravat and blazer on his right who made me think of John Gielgud. Gola and I continued to talk for a couple of hours more before I went to stretch my legs.

And that was my introduction to the Duke of Segorbe and his wife, in whose hotel the *tertulia* was held.

I have no idea if it was the abundance of seats, the lack of sexual tension, or the slightly older average age, but I felt infinitely more comfortable at that *tertulia* than at the previous party. People were talking, discussing, looking each other in the eye and trying to draw out a nuanced opinion or deliver one.

Tristán then introduced me to his wife María, a lover of the bullfight, and his sister Cristina, a strikingly elegant painter.

'Oh, the bullfight is fine,' Cristina said, 'although I am more interested in your acting. I love theatre. Of course, we have bulls as well.'

'You have bulls?'

'Oh yes, my husband Enrique breeds them. The Saltillos. They are quite well known, although they are not like other bulls.'

María leant over and spoke in a conspiratorial whisper. 'Not like other bulls? They are buffaloes! No matador will fight

1. The matador Juan José Padilla and me at my first tentadero at Los Alburejos.

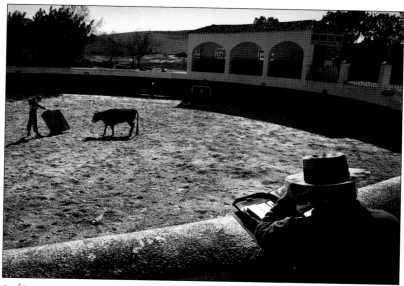

2. Álvaro Domecq watches Padilla test his calf, a 'Torrestrella', for ferocity and courage.

3. Padilla hones his smooth style and upright posture with the reduced danger of a calf.

4. Relaxing afterwards Padilla takes me to the studio of his childhood friend, the great flamenco dancer, Antonio 'El Pipa'.

5. Two Maestros: Padilla and his friend, the matador Finito de Córdoba let me try a calf of the Saltillo breed.

6. Finito steps into the rescue, without a cape. For some reason I am laughing, as is Padilla running up on the right.

7. Chatting to Cayetano Rivera Ordóñez before his fight at the ring in Sanlúcar de Barrameda, 2009.

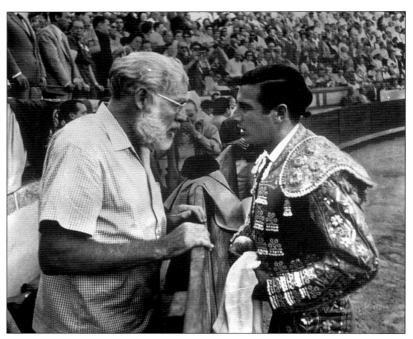

8. Ernest Hemingway with Cayetano's grandfather, Antonio Ordóñez, in Madrid, 1960. The author was writing about the rivalry betwen Antonio and his brother-in-law, Luis Miguel Dominguin, for *Life* magazine. It was later published as *The Dangerous Summer*.

9. The great matadors of 1959 in a charity 'festivale' in Valencia to raise money for the bullfighter, El Cobijano, who lost had his leg to a goring. From left to right: Domingo Ortega, Antonio Ordóñez (Cayetano's grandfather), Julio Aparicio, Luis Miguel Dominguín, Pepe Cáceres and Jaime Ostos, who dedicated the photo to the photographer, Angela Gracey.

10. Manuel Laureano Rodríguez Sánchez, 'Manolete', the greatest of Spain's post-war matadors. In 1947, aged thirty, he was killed by the Miura bull Islero in Linares, sending the entire nation into mourning.

11. The breeder of the Saltillos, Enrique Moreno de la Cova, and I lay out the ring. On the left is the matador Rafaelillo, to my right, his banderillero Abraham Neiro, and far right my Maestro Eduardo Dávila Miura.

12. I complete a series with a right-handed chest-pass. Directly above me in the audience are my parents amongst my many friends from Seville.

13. Conséjote, a 3-year old Saltillo bull, a novillo, being passed in a naturale. There are faults here. I am just happy to be alive.

14. Cayetano performing a perfect natural with a bull of Santiago Domecq in Sanlucar de Barrameda: note the long arm and the finger-tip control of the muleta causing the bull to throw itself headlong after the folds in the cloth.

them. They are not brave enough nowadays. But once upon a time, these were the best bulls. The best!'

I remembered a line from the autobiography of the greatest matador in history, Juan Belmonte: *What has happened to the breeds of Parladé, Saltillos and the others?* (All modern fighting bulls descend from these two breeds, along with Murube and Santa Coloma.) Now I was about to find out. Cristina gestured towards a relaxed man dressed in English tweed talking with a constant smile and authoritative hand gestures in the corner. He came over.

'This is my husband, Enrique Moreno de la Cova. This is Alexander. He is here to write about the bulls and I told him he must come and see our Saltillos.'

He shook my hand firmly. 'You must! The trouble is, no matadors want to fight them.'

'Ah, I think I have a friend who might be brave enough.'

'Who?'

'Juan José Padilla.'

There was a silence.

'You know Padilla.'

'Yes, he is like a brother to me. I will speak to him tonight.'

'Padilla, yes, Padilla who fights the Miuras, he is perfect,' said María (who I later discovered refers to Tristán as her 'Miura').

'Padilla, yes, he is just right for that,' said Cristina.

'And I must try them too!' I said.

They looked at each other doubtfully. Then Enrique smiled. 'It is done,' he said.

■ ■ ■ ■ ■

And that is how I became a bullfight impresario – in the most informal sense – for the day.

6

El puyazo

The picador shouts. The bull charges the horse in reply. As it does so, he aims the lance so that the point hits the bull between the shoulders. The bull strives up into the lance, the crossbar on its shaft preventing this apparent suicide.

I am eleven years old. My father walks into the Swiss hotel room where I am sulking because I have had to walk home alone. His eyes are red, and the bad mood and the annoyance with my parents for failing to collect me from ski-school evaporate. He calls me into the corridor and as we walk along, my eyes are on the carpet because I know something is horribly wrong.

He says in a cracked voice, 'Jules, lovely Jules, has been a very silly boy.'

And I know immediately my brother is dead.

■ ■ ■ ■ ■

I sit in front of a coffee table in my parents' room; my brother Byron is there as well. Everyone has been crying, but they have stopped before I arrive. They are watching me, and the only thought in my head is that I should be crying now but I can't. I don't even want to. All I can think about is how annoying my eighteen-year-old brother can be, always telling me what to do and making sure I'm not reading in bed when I should be sleeping. I dwell on this but my focus shifts. I remember the other things. I remember playing Frisbee with him, and computer games. I remember him teaching me the concept of infinity and how to build a radio. I remember him playing Vivaldi and New Order and talking about Milton and Tolkien. I remember his advice on what to wear to the school disco. I remember the story of him saving my life when I almost drowned as a toddler, diving in to pull me up from the bottom of the pool.

And then I understand that all of that is gone and that I will never see him again. I finally learn what the word 'never' really means. And then the pain comes in a pulsing mass of blackness, punctuated with the one word, 'Why?' I say it over and over again, maybe a hundred times. A doctor gives my parents a sedative for me. I can't remember if I took it or not.

■ ■ ■ ■ ■

I see him once more. Or rather his body. I kiss him goodbye in a mortuary in Zermatt, the skin of his cheek cold and rubbery. We bury the coffin in the village churchyard on the hill near my parents' house where we grew up. I pass his grave every time I visit that house and pause for a while to read the inscription from Tennyson's *In Memoriam*:

> *Death has made*
> *His darkness beautiful with thee.*

■ ■ ■ ■ ■

On the twenty-first anniversary of my brother's death, I am sitting in Seville with my parents discussing an article about him in *The Times*. It has been written by his best friend, the columnist Giles Coren, and we are all struck by the charisma of a young man whose friends still talk about him now he has been dead longer than he was ever alive. It is not hard to see why. Giles describes the highlight of one school trip being when 'Jules, a famously skilled and fearless skier, would rocket across the group, backwards, on one ski, smoking a cigar and laughing'.

And as we reminisce, I get a text message on my mobile: 'My English brother, if you want tickets to my bullfight tonight, call me. A hug, Padilla.'

My parents are fascinated by what they have been told about Padilla, so we hire a car and set off into the peaks and ravines of the Sierra Norte national park. We revel in the green of the countryside and the cool freshness of the mountain air.

We arrive at a small, white-walled village planted halfway up a hill called Cazalla de la Sierra, and make our way to a boutique hotel laid, palimpsest-like, over a medieval hermitage. As I walk in, I recognise Miguel, Padilla's sword-handler, who says that he is preparing for the fight in his room and would we like to come.

I have read about the ritual dressing of the matador. The accounts describe rooms shaded against the Spanish sun, where people speak in hushed tones as the naked matador rises from the bed to be cantilevered into his suit of lights. In part, this disrobed display shows the lack of concealed armour on the matador's body, also his physical pride. His focus at the time is completely on his forthcoming war with Death, and after he is dressed, which can take up to half an hour, he kneels before a portable altar to request the intercession of his patron saints with whatever destiny the Almighty may have in store for him.

I don't think my parents are quite ready for that, so I put them on a sofa with a glass of wine and head off with Miguel. I follow him down into just such a shaded room, although the scene is different. Fighting in a festival, Padilla will be wearing only the *traje corto* that he wore for the *tentadero*, so dressing takes less time and the entire atmosphere is less formal, although no less striking and moving.

He is relaxing on the bed, made modest only by a hand towel over his crotch as his wife Lidia rubs liniment into his legs. The clinical smell reminds me of cold afternoons playing rugby at school. Meanwhile his five-year-old daughter Paloma sits in a corner drawing with crayons. He half-rises to embrace me, speaking in a quiet tone.

'English brother, how are you?'

We talk a little, and Padilla seems distracted and I try to work out the source without asking. Is it the bulls, or an argument that I have interrupted with his wife, or something else?

He shows me the extent of some of his scars, which I had not fully realised before. He has one resembling the old vertical Caesarean section scar, but this one goes from navel to sternum and is jagged and thick, as you expect from the horn of a bull. There is one on the line that divides inner thigh and abdomen – the iliac crest – where the bone has healed wrong and juts out under the taut skin as though someone has inserted half a cricket ball under there.

Padilla calls his daughter over to show me the picture she is drawing, although what it is I do not register.

'Give a kiss to Alexander.'

And she does, shyly. Meanwhile Lidia looks at me with something in her dark and beautiful eyes: sadness, fatigue, worry? The whole situation is too much for me: I am too invested in it now, and it is too alien. I wish him luck with the mantra '*suerte, torero*' (unlike the theatre, this is not bad luck to say) and collect my parents to go down to the arena.

■ ■ ■ ■ ■

The bullring is small, seating a few hundred at most, and with none of the infrastructure which I had assumed was a simple necessity in terms of safety. It is not a place where one would wish to be gored by a bull. How good, I wonder, is the local doctor and how far is the nearest hospital? It is the length of the journey to the hospital that kills the matador as much as the bull's horns.

The people in the stands are raucous and very verbal. My father and I grab a beer from a vendor as my mother remarks on the fact that the audience's age literally extends from one to a hundred, and we settle into the atmosphere. I am still feeling out of sorts. A pair of vultures circle overhead, proving that even the gods have a sense of melodrama.

The matadors enter in an abbreviated version of the *paseíllo*, in their sombre suits, and we notice there are six, one for each bull. They have almost the same age range as their audience, from nineteen to sixty. All in all, it has the feeling of a family affair in small-town Spain. Padilla is not even being paid, all proceeds going to a local Catholic charity.

Across the ring I see Padilla's wife and daughter, who have been joined by a grey-haired man in a dark suit. I recognise him from photos as Padilla's father, a baker from Jerez, where his son apprenticed before he traded that life for this one. It seems a strangely cosy place to risk your life with your family watching.

The first three bulls are not notable. Matadors fight in order of seniority, so José Luis Parada, at sixty years old, fights first and achieves a brave and occasionally graceful turn. Pepe Luis Vázquez, who I have been told can produce tears in the eyes of spectators with the poetry of his work with a good bull, and tears of rage with a bad one, looks so terrified of the bull that the gypsy woman behind me loudly suggests he be put down rather than the bull. Martín Pareja Obregón starts off well, displaying some style, although it seems showy stuff and he has to keep the bull clear of his engorged forty-five-year-old stomach. However, after he gets hit in the kidneys by the bull he spends so much time between passes wincing that, rather cruelly one may say, he loses the sympathy of both the Spanish audience and my own family. It is not that you don't feel for a man hit by a bull, but if he chooses to stay in the ring afterwards, a certain level of stoicism is expected.

However, when Padilla comes into the ring, the audience perks up. There is a rise in expectation, as he is the only *figura* fighting that day. The bulls have been pretty mediocre, but reliable in charging, and if anyone can pick things up the consensus seems to be that he will. He has a certain reputation, which I am still coming to understand. A fighter of difficult bulls, he is known to be brave and has received as much punishment in terms of injury as any matador still alive. He is also a consummate showman with great inner force. And he's been at it for longer than most, and I have seen just how hard he has been training for this season, clocking up hundreds of passes in an afternoon with the *vaquillas*.

However, the gods of the bullfight decide otherwise. When the bull charges into the ring it hits the opposite wall with such force that it cracks its horn at the root. Padilla ignores the accident, which makes the bull unreliable and dangerous, and opens his caping with long passes on his knees from a distance, giving the bull time to accelerate to great speed. Again, this is showmanship, but dangerous nonetheless. And he laughs out loud as he does it. It is impressive to watch, without sadness or great beauty, but powerful. My mother says he reminds her of the opening line of the novel *Scaramouche*: 'He was born with a gift of laughter and a sense that the world was mad.' If ever a man fulfils that description, it is Padilla.

The picador does his job with one light pic, Padilla immediately signalling directly to the president that that is sufficient. And then one of his *banderilleros* picks up his barbed sticks and gets ready to go into the ring and the crowd starts to boo. They know their matador and know he can place them himself. He laughs again, and takes the sticks from his man. It is a set-up; he was always going to do it himself.

Or so it seems. I notice that he is limping slightly and remember the liniment. Either way he has turned the situation to his advantage. The first pair of *banderillas* he places well, firmly and fast. The bull draws to a halt, bewildered and newly infuriated at the stinging pain and the vanishing target. Padilla has been moving fast throughout the fight and making the bull do so as well. They seem almost to be charging each other, and the audience is picking up on their energy.

Padilla cites the bull with the second pair at twenty-five yards, and when it does not immediately charge, he begins to dance a little flamenco, or rather a knowing parody of flamenco. Is this a planned display or is he masking the fact that the bull won't charge? I wonder in hindsight if it is not the latter, carefully removing the frustrating breaks in the action an unwilling bull gives to the display.

The bull charges now, and again Padilla places the sticks neatly. The third set he places over the top of his head, leaning backwards. It would be comic, were it not so dangerous. He goes to the *barrera* and collects his *muleta* and sword.

As he begins the *faena*, the bull is twitchy when its broken horn strokes the *muleta* in passing, probably receiving little stinging shocks from the cracked horn. It cannot be brought close to the body, and it is becoming increasingly unwilling to charge. However, this does not seem to dent Padilla's bonhomie, and he still manages to drag something like a dance out of the poor animal.

Noticeably taller than the other matadors, he seems much more dominant in the ring, much more in control. At one point, when the bull refuses to charge, he approaches it and leans down asking it why. He leans his head between the points of the two semi-circular horn arcs and asks again. The crowd holds its breath. Then, with a flash, he head-butts the bull between the eyes and steps back to receive the inevitable charge. The applause is loud, but even louder when he does it a second time.

When he kills, it is clean and quick: a sword into the aorta, the bull falling, a standing ovation and a sea of white handkerchiefs as he is awarded both ears. He throws his bloody trophies into the crowd, and takes his lap of honour with gusto. When he reaches his family, his daughter Paloma is passed down to kiss her father and then he returns to the centre of the ring, taking a handful of sand from the arena floor and letting it run out into the wind, thanking heaven and earth for their complicity in his craft.

We walk back to the hotel and my parents are excited and alive; Padilla's display has invigorated them, its effect amplified by the personal connection, feeling they know something of the man from my descriptions of him.

However, when I introduce him to my parents he seems withdrawn, drained, completely the opposite of what they had expected. He makes an effort, saying to my father that as the brother of his son, he is his son as well. However, when the bull is mentioned, his face shadows. It was very difficult, he says, disappointing. On those words, he walks away distracted, his mind back in the fight and unhappy to be so.

We realise that it was all show: all that force and energy, the head-butt, the little dance and the laughter. He is a hardworking performer who risks his life to dominate and kill animals, but it is a job. Like an actor working in a long-running play, he must bring freshness to the performance every time, but that does not mean it is refreshing for him.

Going home in the car, we discuss him in comparison with the other matadors we have seen who have been called 'great': Cordobés, Juli, Perera. We agree his performance misses the artistic component of great bullfighting. However, there is a sturdily built craft there, and sometimes comedy can mask art. The human eye always perceives tragedy as more beautiful. This is why so many matadors struggle so hard to achieve it with their overly serious poses, which only work with an excellent bull. With this one they could only have led to boredom or disgust. For this bull one needed a showman like Padilla, a man who fits the old Roman description of what makes a great gladiator, rather than the aestheticised graces of a prima ballerina.

7

El quite

The matador flashes into the face of the bull to draw it away from the horse and the picador's lance, relieving the pressure, testing the damage.

Date: Fri, 20 Mar 2009 02:53:24 +0000
From: Alexander Fiske-Harrison (email)
To: Adolfo Suárez Illana (email)
Subject: Saltillo

My dear friend,
I met Enrique Moreno de la Cova last night who is trying to restore the Saltillo *toros*. I said he should meet Padilla and he would like to invite us all to a *tentadero*. I sent an SMS to Padilla. What do you think? I know the name Saltillo from the old books but nothing else. Tell me your thoughts …
Your brother-in-arms,
Alexander

■ ■ ■ ■ ■

Date: Fri, 20 Mar 2009 09:47:12 +0100
From: Adolfo Suárez Illana (email)
To: Alexander Fiske-Harrison (email)
Subject: Re: Saltillo

Dear brother-in-arms,
Saltillo means danger, my friend. Anyway we will go there. But I

would not recommend you to fight them. I will talk to Padilla.

All the best,

Adolfo

■   ■   ■   ■   ■

Cowardice is a drug. Or at least it is for me. I am sure there are some people who are naturally brave, or perhaps that is just being nerveless. However, for me, there is always the temptation to avoid danger, to stay safe. I fight against it like someone on a twelve-step programme: one day at a time. Inevitably, this struggle with the addictive qualities of safety, which is, after all, a sane and rational state to crave, leads me to outcomes which are not necessarily the best.

Like the time I sat in a London pub with two friends and a woman screamed outside that her bag had been snatched. The urge to sit there, to remain outside of the event in sheep-like safety, was overwhelming. And that was why I got up.

Of course, by the time I was through the door the man was a fleeing figure halfway down the street. Another wave of 'Oh leave it, it's not your trouble, it's only a bag, he's too far away' poured forth from my unconscious in a perfect echo of the voice that tells the alcoholic that one drink won't hurt. So I sprinted. He had thirty yards on me, but he wasn't a fast runner.

We reached the end of the road 100 yards later and I was within fifteen feet of him as he turned the corner. I mentally dug into my muscles for a final burst of speed, knowing it would be the surprise and impact that would determine the outcome of what was about to happen; he hadn't looked over his shoulder once. As I collided with him, he lifted a little into the air, turning, and I grabbed the lapels of whatever he was wearing and took him clean off the ground and into the wall behind him.

'Where's the fucking bag!' I yelled into his terrified face.

He was a young Oriental man. For some reason I thought he looked like a student.

'I was chasing the man who had it!'

I looked down. He didn't have the bag and he couldn't have tossed it without me seeing. There was a pause as we both hyperventilated. The realisation was unavoidable.

'*I am so sorry!*' Luckily the turn had reduced the force of my tackle, otherwise he would have hit the wall a great deal harder. He accepted my apology, but the criminal was long gone. When I got back to the pub, my friends nearly fell off their stools laughing.

Those same instincts were in play now: the conditioned reflex to fight against my natural fear. Despite the above example, this is not an arbitrary war: I don't do bungee or parachute jumps. I require justification. However, I was beginning to wonder exactly what greater good would be served by my getting gored by a *vaquilla*. *Saltillo means danger*. The tone of Adolfo's email was not lost on me. This was not a man, I had heard and seen, who felt fear as other men did. Nor was he one who indulged it or encouraged it in those around him. He didn't mean those words lightly.

Even worse, by the time the day in mid-April was chosen to fit Padilla's schedule, Adolfo was unable to make it. He didn't explain why, but a tiny part of my mind wondered if the prospect of the Saltillos wasn't part of what put him off. As for Padilla, this man had as many responsibilities as Adolfo – wife, children – but fearlessness was his profession, as I had seen. He would never not attend such a challenge. But supposing Adolfo was right, supposing there was a real danger here. Had I just put a friend in danger out of vanity? Had the urge to be connected into the very heart of this world for the sake of a book led me to make a stupid, childish mistake? And if it was a danger to Padilla, then how the hell was I going to survive?

The thoughts bounced back and forth inside my skull as I

looked out the window of Nicolás's car. If I was going to die, there might as well be some half decent photographs, after all. Seville province flew by the window and we crossed into that of Córdoba. He asked me how I felt, and I was evasive. It was not that I didn't want to tell him, but as often as not, when you try to pin thoughts down you actually just create new ones, and they tend to be more negative. As John Stuart Mill said, 'Ask yourself if you are happy and you cease to be so.' Well, ask yourself how afraid you are and I guarantee you'll get more so.

For a little background, I had looked up the breed of Saltillo and found the following. In 1854 Antonio Rueda Quintanilla, first Marquis of Saltillo, purchased the already famous ranch of José Picavea de Lesaca Montemayor. The Marqués spent the next three decades perfecting and 'differencing' the breed from those of his competitors, work continued by his widow, Doña Francisca Osborne, and then by her son Rafael Rueda Osborne around the turn of the century.

In 1918, Rafael sold it to Enrique's grandfather, Felix Moreno Ardanuy, a businessman and mayor of Seville. However, they had already passed their brief but impressive peak by this point. Known for their fine physical 'conformation' yet small size, they were known as 'the sweets of Saltillo' in the early twentieth century. However, as the preferred style of bullfighting began to change, 'difficult' bulls such as these became unfashionable.

The problem Enrique has found in trying to bring the breed back, aside from the expected ones of scepticism and intransigency in a business where conservatism is its very reason for being, is that the bullfight has changed even more since the zenith of the Saltillo reputation and in the same direction: away from difficult bulls. There are many reasons for this that one can point to, but the man at the centre of this change, stylistically and historically, is Juan Belmonte, whose autobiography I quoted earlier.

Belmonte, born in Seville in 1892, is said by the majority of critics to have been the matador who brought about the biggest changes in bullfighting since Pedro Romero moved the focus from nobles fighting bulls on horseback to their servants, who would be called in to dispatch the animals at the end. Belmonte's innovation was to cape the bulls closer to his body than had ever been thought possible, leading contemporary critics to write that you had to see him now because he would be dead next week. How he did this I will explain later, but why he did it is simple. Belmonte was not physically capable of doing it any other way – he lacked the strength or speed to fight by moving himself, so he had to move the bull by making it follow the fabric he manipulated so deftly with his hands.

The results of this change were twofold. First, the physical thrill of watching a bullfight was exponentially increased as both the real and the apparent danger of death for the matador were increased. Second, the contrast between stationary man and the half-ton of charging beast increased the dramatic content of the contest. Where once nimble and brave men scuttled around the ring narrowly avoiding the horned beast in a feat of arms, now the fight was being drawn towards a performance in which an unstoppable force of nature meets an immovable human will.

However, this requires a different type of bull: one who gives the charge readily and easily, and then, once committed to the charge, is directed by the cape or *muleta* without deviation, stopping halfway through, hooking to left or right or any other 'deviant' behaviour. This was a quantum shift, although in terms of physics it was in reverse: back from the random to the smooth, predictable and Newtonian.

Modern matadors, and modern audiences, prefer smoothness to the old *corridas duras*, 'hard fights', although some bullfighters like Padilla or El Fundi have made their living from fighting the bulls that no one else will, like the Miuras. And now the Saltillos.

■ ■ ■ ■ ■

The testing ring for the Saltillo ranch, Miravalles, is a mile or so distant from the other buildings that make up the farm, giving it a wilderness feel. It stands alone among fields on which roam herds of fighting bulls that stand in formation and watch the people, invaders in their desolate domain. And people there are.

As we park the car, we see about thirty people; it seems word has spread about the day. The idea of an audience does not cheer me up. In the middle of this crowd are Enrique, Padilla and another tall lean figure. It turns out that Padilla has brought his friend the matador Finito de Córdoba, whom I last heard of when Padilla insisted we go to his hotel on our wild night out. It is among the laughter, introductions and embraces that he tells us about hiding under his bed to avoid his old friend. He had a big day the next day and knew that if he joined us on our drinking marathon – even halfway through – the next day he would have died.

Finito's looks and manner are in high contrast to Padilla's. Where Padilla is the raffish, battered, but still handsome gypsy with an overdeveloped adrenal gland, Finito looks more like the nineteenth-century Parisian ideal of a poet. He's my height and as sabre-thin as almost all matadors are, with delicate features and curly hair worn shoulder length. His 'look' – and this is a performance art after all – is undeniably 'pretty', but age and experience remove any trace of effeminacy from this. (He must be in his mid-thirties, meaning he will have killed something like 1,000 bulls.)

Most important of all, it is when standing with these two men that the fear starts to drain out of me. Fighting rare and dangerous fighting bull breeds is all in a day's work, at least for Padilla, and when I ask how he is, he just laughs. This is his standard response. Danger, fear, incompetence: these are not possibilities. Of course he has been hit many times by bulls, but that is to be viewed like an earthquake; it is simply not something you should waste your time worrying about.

Meanwhile, Enrique looks excited and anticipatory that his *vaquillas* are to be tested by not just one but two *figuras*, bull-fighters of sufficient note to be termed 'public figures'. Also in the middle of this world of bulls are the number one *aficio-nada* María O'Neill and her friend the blonde wonder Paloma Gaytán de Ayala (offspring of one of the other 'foundational ranches', Santa Coloma). I leave them to chat up their matadors and go to look at the *vaquillas*.

There are six, divided among three pens, and they are much more aggressive than those I have seen at my previous *tentade-ros*. At Fuente Ymbro and Álvaro Domecq's ranch the *vaquillas* were relatively calm when they were together, but here they leap up at people who pass above them on the walkways and when they cannot reach them they turn on each other; luckily their close quarters and thick hides prevent their horns from drawing blood. They are also all considerably larger than the *vaquilla* I faced at Fuente Ymbro, and I have still yet to have a single lesson. I walk back down the steel stairs from the view-ing platform (all but the oldest rings have something of Jurassic Park about them) and go up to Enrique.

'So, which one do you think I should try to cape?'

There must have been some weakness, some fear, some note of pleading in my voice or face because Enrique anwered sim-ply, 'With these? You? No.'

And so that's that. My bullfighting career over in a moment of panic. And I felt happy. Now I could get back to the task of watching and writing. I went into the ring and picked a *burladero* to put myself behind, starting to truly enjoy my sur-roundings. I could even laugh when Finito's *mozo de espadas*, sword-handler, asked if I am related to the matador José Tomás. This was not the first time the resemblance has been brought up – both Álvaro Domecq and Eduardo Davíla Miura said the same thing, although I still had yet to see Tomás fight so it meant nothing to me. Here I return to my diary entry for that day:

'The first *vaquilla* comes in fast and Enrique gestures to Finito, who walks out with the pink and yellow *capote* in his hand. He is an interestingly delicate fighter, once said to be one of the greats although now he seems to be in decline. His style is gentler and smoother in action than Padilla's and he seems tentative. When we come to the second *vaquilla* I see that Padilla himself is more tentative than I have seen him before.

'The cattle are indeed fast and strong, although they seem to me to go for the cape and *muleta* readily and easily. The day is unfolding well and I am again given a sight of the painless (relatively) training side of the world of the bullfight. Padilla now goes to work on his second *vaquilla* and I watch his *banderillero* Miguel start the stopwatch to see if the *vaquilla* has the stamina for a full fifteen-minute fight. Padilla capes and capes, completing dozens of passes in a variety of ways, building up linked series and then turning them into new series in a way impossible with a full-grown bull whose greater strength comes with the price of greater weight and hence less stamina.

'I am admiring this work, lost in contemplation of it, as the fifteen minutes draw to a close. It is then that I hear Padilla shout across the ring, "Alex!"

'And time stands still.

'Surely not.

' "Alex. *Es para ti*?"

'Shit. Well, there's no way out really, is there.

'My pulse begins to climb at an epic rate. Someone hands me a *muleta* and Padilla wanders across the ring to hand me his caping sword. And again it happens, more noticeably this time. All the almost painful worry I had experienced on the journey to the ring in the car, worry equally divided between what the *vaquilla* will do and the idea of caping badly in public because I am untrained, had disappeared when Enrique said I was not to get in front of an animal today. However, this returned a hundredfold when Padilla called my name, and yet when I walk in front of the animal it falls away to nothing. Or rather it is burnt away to nothing by the incredible focus a violent, horned animal three times your body weight brings to your mind. I would like to say it is like walking on stage as an actor, and perhaps it is for the very best, but for me there is always self-awareness in all but a few precious moments of strongest passion in my acting. Other times, my head is stronger than my heart. Here, in the ring, there is no distinction between the two; both are churning in unison – one calculating, the other pumping – in the common cause of self-preservation.

'And so begins my caping. I notice immediately that this *vaquilla* is considerably faster than the one I caped at Fuente Ymbro. Heavier, yes, but with muscle that gives it a greater capacity for both acceleration and change of direction despite the fifteen minutes spent making Padilla sweat.

'My first few capes come off as well as can be expected from someone utterly untrained, better in fact. However, as I relax into the idea I try to bring the animal closer to my body with the inevitable result shown in the photo.

'Being hit by a charging animal in the ring is an interesting experience, although more so in retrospect than at the time. Obviously, parts of your body are moving at a rate which requires taking your brain out of the equation. Your hands grab at horns to prevent penetration. The movable weights of your torso and legs, now dangling from where the animal has caught you, are used in a vain attempt to maintain an upright position so you can fight or fly. The actual impact is not felt, only anxiety over loss of balance. When I hit the ground, though, and the *vaquilla* comes after me with its horns, I find that other instincts kick in, literally, along with the sturdy Tony Mora gaucho boots which have been my preferred footwear for almost two decades as the *vaquilla* comes after me again and I fend it off with a well-placed shove with my foot.

'At that point, Finito steps in and gracefully capes the danger away with his empty hand, Padilla running up in the background. What I cannot explain at all is why both Padilla and I are laughing in the photo; a shared dark sense of humour perhaps? Few memories with any sense of accuracy remain; adrenaline is worse than alcohol for short-term memory loss.

'When I get up again, Finito and Padilla begin to instruct me in the proper use of the *muleta* and I get in a few passes of which even

I can feel proud. I am unaware at the time, but as María says later, you just can't pay for a lesson like that.'

The come-down from that level of anxiety is in some ways worse than the anticipation and turmoil itself. I didn't closely watch the remaining two *vaquillas*, merely stood smoking behind a *burladero*, my eyes pointed at the action but my mind elsewhere. I was aware, though, of both Padilla and Finito stripping down to their shirtsleeves to cape on, the sweat running off them as they got more and more pure in their movements, particularly Finito who developed his *muleta* passes to a level of smoothness, the like of which I had never previously seen.

When it was all over the bullfighters and audience were offered food and beer, and various people came up slapping me on the shoulder and calling me 'bullfighter', but all I wanted was silence and something stronger than beer.

Afterwards, the nucleus retreated back to the palace Enrique and Cristina are restoring nearby at Palmas del Río, although even the uninhibited grandeur of the surroundings, the fine wine and food served at a dinner table that could easily seat eighty people did not move me. Not until Cristina placed a glass of rum into my hand – my right hand, which it would later transpire had suffered a hairline fracture – did anything return to some form of normality. The pain, like the moral hangover when I watch a real bullfight and which I will describe in the next chapter, did not kick in until the next day.

8

El cambio de tercios

Deciding that the bull has been sufficiently weakened, the matador signals to the president to remove the horses from the ring, which he does with a fanfare. The matador gives up his cape, takes a pair of *banderillas*, and turns to face the bull.

Just as there is matter and anti-matter, there are bullfighters and anti-bullfighters. However, unlike with bullfighting, where non-professionals can do it but with none of the skill or beauty of a professional, anti-bullfighting is definitely not improved by professionalism.

My first encounter with an anti-bullfighter was in the London studios of Al Jazeera TV. They'd got in touch with me after word went round the media outlets about my *Prospect* magazine article. They wanted me to talk against him about some fourteen-year-old Mexican matador who was about to fight in the South of France. I explained that I wasn't necessarily pro-bullfighting, I just saw the reasons most often given against it as hypocritical and xenophobic. I was also not pro high-risk child labour and hadn't got the faintest idea who the kid was. They said they understood but they wanted a balancing voice, which I took to mean they couldn't find a soul in England who could speak lucidly on the subject without frothing at the mouth.

Actually, that was unfair of me. I have since discovered that there are one or two English *aficionados* who are perfectly reasonable and likeable, such as David Penton, secretary of the Club Taurino of London, or Sam Graham who sits on their committee, whom I will go out of my way to have a drink with. However, as a general rule, foreign fans of national pastimes have a jealous and possessive streak about their adopted subject which is usually charmless and sometimes downright neurotic. The Spanish on the other hand, fully confident that the bull-fight is theirs, can afford to be more generous with it.

The number of times I have been interrogated, patronised and downright insulted by middle-aged Englishmen who have 'devoted their life to the bulls' I reckon goes into double figures. The number of times this has been done to me by a Spanish bullfighter, breeder or *aficionado* is much easier to estimate: it is zero.

Also, the form these Anglo *aficionados*' love for bullfighting takes always seems more than a little unhealthy. This is usually because it is passionless and numeric, e.g. 'Juan Gomez, "El Numero", was gored 4 times and awarded 61 ears in 1982, up from 3 and 47 on the season before, but 6 per cent and 12 per cent down respectively from his decade average.' This type of *aficionado* I call the the 'blood anorak'. Another type is passion-ate about it in a very different way: 'Have you seen how much weight "El Guapo" has put on? I'm amazed he can get into his suit of lights at all. And don't get me started on the colour scheme he has his team in.' These *aficionados* I shall avoid call-ing anything.

So, for reasons of media-presentability and a different point of view, I found myself walking across London on a warm sum-mer evening wondering what sort of person made their living trying to get a popular activity banned in a European liberal democracy, one with the fifth largest GDP and population in the EU.

What I knew as I walked into the studios was that Jordi Casamitjana was the Campaigns Coordinator of CAS Interna-tional, the largest lobby group devoted solely to bullfighting in the world. Comité Anti Stierenvechten, 'Anti-Bullfighting

Committee', was originally just a Netherlands-based organisation set up to encourage tourists from Holland to Spain not to attend bullfights. Which is fair enough. However, they then decided to expand their horizons to getting it banned everywhere in the world. Which is quite an aggressive policy change. To this end they employed Casamitjana, who was born and raised in Barcelona but whose previous work was in the UK and seemed to consist in trying to close down zoos and pet shops.

Casamitjana is a short man with glasses, a little overweight and losing his hair, and was at the time flustered by being made to rush, as he had nearly missed the interview. He was very polite, speaking rapidly in a Catalan accent as he went into make-up, where I overheard him complaining to the woman about how annoying it was to be late, his driver's fault, etc., and then we were led into the studio.

The presenter was a distractingly pretty woman of Middle Eastern ethnicity, with a clipped international English accent and that bizarre intonation that conveys both authority and neutrality that all news anchors have. They were midway through running footage 'from the field' in Arles, France, and we were quickly introduced, seated and wired for sound as that segment rolled to its conclusion on the giant screens behind us. The presenter introduced us to the audience, myself as a 'writer', Casamitjana as a 'campaigner', and then we were off. I give the transcript of what followed below.

■ ■ ■ ■ ■

PRESENTER: Now, Alexander Fiske-Harrison, if I could start with you, you've obviously gone to many bullfights, you've liked most of them. What is it about them that you've liked?

A.F.-H.: There's something tragic about a bullfight. It's like a piece of theatre – it's even in three acts – and I think it is its artistic quality which mitigates and justifies the undeniable suffering the bull undergoes in the ring. To put it simply: it's a work of art. And I think that as such, some people will like it, and some won't, but I can't see any reason to legislate against it.

PRESENTER: Jordi Casamitjana, a lot of people will agree with that, a lot of people do go and see bullfights and, ultimately, as long as there's a demand, it's unfortunate for the bull, but it's still going to go on.

J.C.: Well, it's not that simple as 'there's a matter of demand', there's a lot of people that liked gladiators. Anything that has been banned there's a demand. Foxhunting there was a demand. Any animal welfare issue is a modern issue that comes from something from the past that was popular, but the majority of the people don't like bullfighting, even in Spain – I'm Spanish myself – 72 per cent of people are not interested at all, 73 per cent in France – which, as we see in this report – is against bullfighting. [It] is a change, [it] is the twenty-first century, so [it is] something from the past really.

PRESENTER: Alexander Fiske-Harrison, in that report we saw there, at least in Arles in the South of France, there were also issues of tourism and money, because it does attract a big audience ...

A.F.-H.: ... indeed ...

PRESENTER: ... do you think that plays a big part in the fact that it's still going on?

A.F.-H.: I think it plays a huge part in it and that leads directly into the welfare issue for me. The amount of money it provides allows animals to be kept in conditions which are infinitely better than are used in intensive farming in Europe, and I think that if one removed the bullfight there would actually be a reduced state of welfare for animals in Europe. Fighting cattle live in large rolling pastures rather than the small corralled farms such as we have in this country.

PRESENTER: Jordi Casamitjana, a lot of people, for example, in this country, disliked foxhunting, and then it's been banned, but is there any sort of EU-wide legislation about animal rights? Is there such a thing as animal rights under EU law?

J.C.: No, there isn't. The Rome Treaty basically said that in issues of animal welfare each country has to create its own legislation, sometimes the EU creates directives, but in the end, in the case of animal welfare or rights – basically welfare – each region, each country in Europe has its own legislation. So bullfighting is illegal in the UK, [it] is illegal in Denmark, [it] is illegal in Germany, but [it] is not illegal in France.

PRESENTER: Alexander Fiske-Harrison, how would you feel if it was made illegal? In a way it's not a very fair match as well obviously between the bull and the man.

A.F.-H.: Absolutely. That's why I approach it as a work of art because it's not a sport, there's no way it could be called sporting, and if it was sporting I would say it should be made illegal immediately from the point of view of human rights: matadors would be dying left, right and centre. As it is, if it was made illegal we would all lose something, and certainly Spanish culture would lose something in particular. But for everyone it has a value, an aesthetic one. And you have to weigh up that aesthetic value against the suffering of the animal just as you do when you order a steak.

PRESENTER: A lot of people may find your views unappealing, it must have made you a bit unpopular sometimes. Have you found that maybe public opinion or the reaction from your friends has changed in the past few years? Do you think that people are hardening towards bullfighting? Or perhaps thinking that it [bullfighting] may be worth it?

A.F.-H.: I think people are increasingly going against bullfighting along with bloodsports, hunting – things like that. There has been a sea-change on that, and I think there are very good reasons for this, but there are also some bad reasons. We've become increasingly distant in our dealings with animals: we buy prepackaged food in the supermarket and we no longer see the reality of how we are actually dealing with the animals involved. I think there's a bit of hypocrisy creeping in here.

PRESENTER: Jordi Casamitjana, let's talk about that. Certainly here in the UK we've seen lots of programmes about battery hens, for example, and mass-farming; what's the difference between having an egg that was farmed in that way and perhaps going to see a bullfight?

J.C.: Well, they're all different types of exploitation, all different types of suffering. There is no suffering that's better than another, there's no exploitation that's better than another. We're not saying that the British animal welfare approach is the right one, each country has its problems. Definitely battery farming is the wrong thing, but one wrong thing doesn't justify other wrong things.

■ ■ ■ ■ ■

And that was all we had time for. As interviews go it is exactly the sort of introduction to a subject that four minutes steered by an unbriefed journalist allows: dull for the uninformed, frustrating for the knowing and infuriating to the entrenched on either side. Casamitjana hadn't brought up a single decent point against the bullfight, and my arguments in its favour were so lightly sketched as to be equally useless.

More interesting was the way that as we exited the building Casamitjana and I fell into polite conversation. It turned out he hadn't read my article and he seemed a little disquieted by why I was there. When I told him I thought I had been gabbling in the interview because I was unsettled by the strange environment, he replied, 'I thought you were an actor, you should be used to it.'

There was something in his tone I couldn't identify at the time, but I saw no reason to follow it up. He'd obviously had someone look me up at his offices and they'd probably come back with the most recent news clippings from the press, which would be reviews of a West End play I'd written and acted in two months before. I remember particularly vividly Casamitjana stopping before we went out of the doors, looking quizzically at me and handing me his card and saying that should I ever want to talk, and hopefully return to being the animal lover I clearly had been, I should give him a call.

The day after the interview I had a look at the website of the magazine where I'd published my article because there had been a lively exchange going on in the comments section. Here is what I found:

Jordi Casamitjana says:
Sunday, 14 September 2008 at 2:40 p.m.

The author of this article, despite his deliberate attempts to appear somehow coming from a neutral position, and he is not, and his perhaps unwilling attempts to misguide the reader with wrong information (although his description of the bullfight itself is not too far from the truth, his explanations about the bull's life and nature certainly are), possibly because he has fallen deeply into the jaws of the bullfighting industry's propaganda machine (which I know very well, since I was born in Spain, I am an ethologist and animal protectionist, and I am currently specialised on the subject of bullfighting), seems to focus his main thesis on the concept of 'Art'.

He seems to believe that all is justifiable in the name of art, and the aesthetics of a bullfight is a currency one can actually exchange for animal suffering and human degradation.

Such currency is obviously worthless, and to prove it imagine the following: imagine a bullfight that is exactly as the one the author describes, but instead of a bull a child has been used (better a teenager, since the bulls in bullrings are actually teenagers, dying at four years old when they can live up to twelve years or more). The aesthetic value would be exactly the same, with the same music, customs, dances, colours, and of course the same 'conceptual' aspect of live [sic] and death, drama of suffering, struggles of life, ancient tradition (children's sacrifice was indeed a tradition once, was it not?), and so on. Imagine that such teenager was actually kidnapped as a baby from his mother, and fed and kept in a relatively hassle-free environment for the purpose of being sacrificed in the ritual spectacle when he would reach a certain age. So far, we are having here the exact same situation, but with a different species as the victim. That being the case, not only nobody would ever dare to describe the event as art, but of course the perpetrators of the event would be immediately jailed for life (and so the kidnappers and keepers, perhaps known as 'breeders'), and their 'intellectual' supporters as the author would be, at the very least, put in a 'children abuse register' of some sort. And yet, we are talking here about the same 'aesthetic' value, because one cannot claim that the 'drama' involved in torturing and killing a child is less powerful than the one involving a bull instead.

Why we have such a different social response to two events that are virtually the same? Because 'art' is not a philosophical event, is a social event in itself, and although aesthetics do play some role in it, in the end a work of art is a social convention base [sic] on giving artificial worth to an object or performance that somehow 'speaks' to an audience, and, most importantly, it remains within the basic acceptable rules of the society of that audience. If such rules are broken, all aesthetic value is worthless, and the object can now be classed as rubbish or the performance as a crime. To accept bullfighting as an art it has to fit into the basic rules of the twenty-first century world society (we do not longer live in isolation in separate tribes, so art now is an universal concept and therefore the society that judges it is the 'world' society, not a small tribal one), and it certainly does not. Not only bullfighting is considered as an abomination by the majority of people in today's world, but it is actually banned in the majority of countries in the world, and is no longer supported by the majority of people of the countries where it is still performed (so, not even the 'tribe' where it was born likes it any more).

If aesthetics cannot really justify torture, then the authors [sic] is left only with one thing. He seems to be confessing that he enjoys witnessing torture, and therefore the pleasure he experiences can only be described as morbid, sadistic or even perverse. And as we all know, people whose behaviour grant any of these adjectives are very good in 'rationalising' their feeling, and they like to get together with others of similar disposition so they can create their little worlds with their special rules, language and values, where they can indulge their interest undisturbed. Are they evil? No, I don't think so. They are also victims, sometimes of their upbringing, sometimes of their genes, sometimes of their traumas. In this case, they are all victims of the social disease I call 'tauromachy'. Certainly, if we all help and it is in everyone's interest to do so some can be cured. Impossible? Not really. Even a prominent 1980s bullfighter, Albaro Munera 'El Pilarico', is today a strong anti-bullfighting campaigner and he now describes what he used to call art as brutal murder.

I would imagine that it would not be too late for the author to return to the times when he was an animal lover, before he was contaminated by this disease, and be free to use his many talents to a full potential for the greater good.

Now, my response to this at the time was outrage, and Casamitjana and I exchanged enough words to take up fifty pages of this book and eventually led him to threaten me with legal action.

However, although only by two years, I am older and wiser now. I will say this, though. Far from having 'fallen deeply into the jaws of the bullfighting industry', at that time I spoke no Spanish and had yet to meet any *aficionados*, English or otherwise, and was basing my views on a few books by non-Spanish authors and what I could find on the internet, which was largely anti-bullfighting. In fact, the real basis of my argument was my own knowledge of animal behaviour and ethics, and what I had seen in half a dozen fights. As for Casamitjana being an ethologist – he has a bachelor's degree from the University of Barcelona in zoology, no more, no less.

However, it is when we get to the point where he says that bullfighting and 'torturing and killing a child' are 'virtually the same' that I give up. Is eating meat virtually the same as cannibalism? Or pest control as genocide? I was unsurprised when I found out some time later that he is a vegan who is also against the keeping of pets. Not a wise choice, I would say, as a lobbyist on the perfectly defensible position that bullfighting is cruel. The question is, how cruel is it?

Well, Casamitjana is partly right. If it was done to a human it would be very cruel indeed. However, it is not humans we are talking about, it is cattle, and cattle lives are very different from human lives. It is worth being reminded of this.

The average life expectancy of cattle in the meat industry is eighteen months, because we like our meat nice and tender. In the US, 34 million such cattle were slaughtered in 2008, and 78 per cent of those were factory farmed. And how humane is that death? The following is from Jonathan Safran Foer's excellent 2009 book *Eating Animals*:

> Let's say what we mean: animals are bled, skinned and
> dismembered while conscious. It happens all the time, and
> the industry and the government know it. Several plants
> cited for bleeding or skinning or dismembering live animals
> have defended their actions as common in the industry and
> asked, perhaps rightly, why they were being singled out.

The reason for the horrifying cruelty is simple: this is an industrialised process with tight deadlines and even tighter profit margins. So, although the bolt gun that shoots a metal rod into the animal's brain is meant to kill it outright, 'sometimes the bolt only dazes the animal, which either remains conscious or wakes up as it is being "processed"'. Processing involves the animal being hoisted into the air by a chain around a leg so its throat can be cut. As one slaughterhouse worker put it, sometimes 'they'd be blinking and stretching their necks from side to side, looking around, really frantic'. From here, the head is skinned and the legs below the knee are removed. Some are still awake at this point, as the interviewee continued: 'As far as the ones that come back to life … the cattle just go wild, kicking in every direction.'

So, what is the life of a fighting bull in comparison? It lives on average five years on wild pastureland, not eighteen months in *corrales*. And its death? It is taken to the ring, where what I have described in some detail above occurs. From the moment the matador enters with the *muleta*, by Spanish law the bull must be dead within fifteen minutes.

The biggest contrast with the slaughterhouse death described above is this, though: fighting adrenalises the animal in an aggressive manner, and, given that this particular breed has been selected for generations for its fighting ability, there is a good reason to believe that this actually reduces suffering in terms of pain. What is more, by replacing terror with rage, by allowing a fighting instinct to be both aroused and maintained, psychological suffering is reduced as well. For while any extreme emotional state will actually reduce pain due to hormone levels, as the American animal scientist Temple Grandin has pointed out time and time again to the meat industry, fear is a form of suffering in itself, just as much as pain is. Anger, on the other hand, while not a pleasant emotion to witness, is not *itself* a form of suffering.

This argument that bullfighting is no worse than meat-eating from the animal's perspective is an old one. However, modern farming techniques have come to the point where bull-fighting is actually better in terms of welfare.

Just as old are the counter-arguments: The first is the old moral chestnut that two wrongs don't make a right. To which the obvious reply is that if you banned bullfighting you would create two entirely new wrongs. First, the breeding ranches would be turned into farms for beef cattle, leading to the massively diminished animal welfare I have just described. Second, the landscape of the farms would be destroyed to accommodate this change.

It is worth understanding a little about the importance of that landscape. Here is how it is described by a European Commission environmental study on Mediterranean ecosystems:

> *Dehesas* are typical ecosystems in western and south western parts of the Iberian Peninsula. They result from ancient methods of exploiting the landscape, which are well adapted to Mediterranean ecological conditions. Structurally, *dehesas* consist of open woodlands originating from past dense Mediterranean forests, which were thinned in order to favour grazing activity … A very important characteristic of *dehesas* is their high ecological value, with a combination of nature conservation with natural resource exploitation. Simultaneously, *dehesas* give shelter to a great diversity of wildlife species (some endangered and extinct in many other parts of Spain), which are preserved in these areas of human intervention.

The harsh economic reality is that if the bullfight is banned, the breeders will have no choice but to convert their land to normal agricultural use or sell it to those who will. And bull-fighting ranches make up one and a quarter million acres of *dehesa*, between a quarter and a sixth of the total in Spain (depending on how you classify *dehesa*).

However, this is a slightly facile answer to the charge, 'Two wrongs don't make a right.' The real answer would be, 'How can you dare to say this?' If you live in a developed country, you live with mechanised death factories whose products – both carnal and financial – pervade every strata of your life and economy. From gelatine capsule coatings to leather goods to petfood. To even attempt to pass judgement on welfare standards in the world of the Spanish bullfight is the moral equivalent of an antebellum Southern plantation owner protesting about worker conditions in Chinese sweatshops.

The same goes for the repellently dishonest reply that meat animals are killed for food and bullfighting ones for entertainment. The reason this argument is so repellent is the blatant self-deceit. As populations in the developed world struggle with obesity (to say nothing of a financial crisis and a climatic one, on both of which the meat industry impinges), does anyone really believe that a person walks into a fast food restaurant and buys a hamburger for reasons of nutrition? Or that commissioning producers at television channels are flooding our screens with cooking programmes because of a moral imperative to feed us? Food today *is* entertainment in the West.

Sure, at a basic level we need it to survive. Just as at a basic level as a species we need sex to survive, but I've yet to hear someone argue that internet pornography is a biological necessity. The basic level for nutrition is a couple of thousand calories a day – £1.50 worth of pasta from Asda – some vitamin and mineral supplements and a little care to ensure that the eight amino acids the body can't synthesise are obtained elsewhere. Once you have that inside you, to then eat a burger actually has a negative nutritional value, in so far as it is bad for your health (infinitesimally so, but still bad nonetheless). Even if we ended up needing some cattle farmed and killed, the numbers would still be a tenth of what they are today. And I am not calling for vegetarianism here. I am not criticising what we do. I am just bringing it to our attention to remind ourselves that our moral high horses are in fact broken-down old hacks.

Now, these arguments certainly convince me that banning the bullfight may not be a great idea – certainly not one to run at headlong – in so far as I happily eat meat (although I have a great deal more respect for a steak than I did before I began this book). However, there are some people whom they do not convince, and the reason for that failure is always the same: idealism. And not just any sort of idealism, but blind idealism, the sort on whose altar some people are willing to actually harm animals. The sort that breaks cages only to let non-native species either die painfully because they aren't suited to the climate or out-compete indigenous ones, wreaking havoc on the ecosystem.

Indeed, one former friend of mine, who no longer speaks to me for this very reason, once said to me, 'I don't understand why we can't just leave animals to live out their lives in peace.'

Ignoring the glaring question of where exactly they were going to do this, i.e. who was going to donate the land, I asked, 'Do you really think the natural life is one of peace? OK, I can't talk about cattle, because they are domesticated and the ancestral form is extinct. The ones we have now wouldn't last five minutes against a landscape with a proper number of wolves and bears. But what about African buffalo? Have you seen how they live in the wild? From birth to death they are slowly being eaten alive by disease and parasites, they suffer extremes of heat and cold, starvation and thirst, and, provided one of those doesn't kill them, they can look forward to being taken down by a lion or hyena. What is more, because a buffalo is so big and the horns so dangerous, invariably the predators begin to eat it while it is still alive, starting at the opposite end, often beginning with the genitals.'

Needless to say, this was not something she wanted to believe, but that doesn't alter its truth.

No, that is not a good argument against the bullfight. But that is not to say there isn't one. There is. Why is anyone willing to tolerate watching an animal damaged and damaged and damaged again, and then killed, no matter the beauty of the dance that leads to it, no matter the courage of the man doing it, no matter how much less horrific it is than something else we all facilitate behind closed doors?

That is a good question, and one I ask myself time and time again. However, what we are questioning there is not the animal welfare, but the virtue of the audience for wishing to watch it. And liberal democracies do not pass new legislation on virtue. There are members of the audience at a bullfight, I know, who watch for the violence, the blood and the death. They are not many, but they are there. However, in the words of the first Queen Elizabeth, who taught England tolerance: I would not make windows on to men's souls. And that is all I will say for now.

9

Al cuarteo

The matador cites the bull and then runs in a curve towards it. The bull adjusts, also tracing a quarter-circle, until the two arcs collide. The matador drives the *banderillas* into the bull's shoulder, momentum driving him beyond the horns.

T he historic origins of the bullfight, like its rights and wrongs, are one of those areas of research where ideological agendas obscure the truth to the point of invisibility. Trying to find out how it actually started is like trying to discern the racial origins of the Teutonic peoples in 1930s Germany, or the health effects of smoking in 1950s America. In situations like that, it's not about someone eventually 'getting it right', it's about the correct theory being broadcast with a voice sufficiently loud to dwarf the misleading chatter of vested interests.

This is because the bullfight – like most other things in modern Spain – is perceived as a matter of political identity. Where it comes from tells you what bullfighting is, which in turn tells you who you are for loving it. So some link it to bull-leaping frescoes of pre-classical Greece, the most famous depiction of which is a wall painting from the late Minoan kingdom on the island of Crete. In this image, athletes are seen somersaulting over charging bulls' horns, head on. (*Recortadores* perform similar feats in the rings of Spain today.) This view gives the bullfight the dignity of linking it to the most ancient of European Mediterranean societies, although the link is to a period 1,500 years before the birth of Christ as well as being 1,500 nautical miles from Spain – a long way from the modern fight.

Others link it to documented dealings with the bulls of the pre-Roman inhabitants of Spain, the Celtiberians, who stampeded the long-horned cattle into invading armies, leading, by repute, directly to the death of the great Carthaginian General Hamilcar Barca, father of Hannibal, in 229 BC.

Another school claims it derives from the gladiatorial traditions of ancient Rome, although the cattle used then would most likely have fled from the gladiator, as breeds other than the fighting cattle of Spain are not so eager to charge. (I will deal with the breed issue later.)

A related argument links it to the great competitor of Christianity in the early Roman Empire, Mithraism. Immensely popular with Roman legionaries, its central figure, Mithras, supposedly slew a bull with a sword, and one of the ceremonies of its initiates was to perform the same feat.

All these histories have the obvious appeal of showing a tradition of great antiquity, and, in the case of the latter two, linking Spain with the might of Imperial Rome, but proving any continuity through the Dark Ages is a literal impossibility. The fact is that there is no hard evidence for the priority of any one of these theories, or any of their multiple sub-branches. What we do know is that the bull has long been a symbol of masculinity in nature, and an irresistible invitation to combat for the men of any society that promotes warrior virtues such as courage and physical skill – which is, in effect, any pre-industrial society. So, just because people were doing it somewhere else on the Med a long time before doesn't mean that is the reason it is being done in Spain today. An analogous situation exists in societies that are surrounded by a wilder and less pastoral landscape. The hunting of lions with spears has a long history in Africa, but no one would suggest that the ancient Egyptian hunt actually had a causal link to the present-day one performed by the Masai in Kenya.

Even the medieval history of the bullfight is seen through a

glass very darkly. The Moors – a generic term originally signifying both the Arab knights and the North African Berbers they
led at the orders of the Caliphate in Damascus – conquered
Spain and Portugal in AD 711 and progressively lost it over the
next seven centuries. These Arab knights would have been
gifted horsemen, and it seems that they invented a form of
bullfighting from horseback to show both courage and eques-
trian skill.

However, quite a few ardent supporters of bullfighting
would *far* rather it was linked to the Christian Visigoths than
the Muslim invaders. So it comes as no surprise that some claim
that the first man to fight a bull from horseback with a lance
in an enclosed arena was the great El Cid, the eleventh-century
knight famous for his work in the reconquest of Spain from
the Moors. It seems likely that this belief is as mythical as the
Cid's own religious fervour. The Cid was in reality a successful
mercenary of noble birth who served more than one Muslim
king with the same loyalty he did their Christian counterparts.

In this knightly jousting of bulls, the actual killing of the
animal was often delegated to a servant on foot, who would
sometimes use a piece of cloth as a lure to line up the animal.
Two influences then came into parallel play. The first was that
the crowd were more impressed by the actions of the man on
the ground, the matador or 'killer', than by his mounted master. The second was that the ruling House of Bourbon, who took
over from the Habsburgs in the early eighteenth century, didn't
like bullfighting, adding an actively discouraging force against
the nobility indulging in the spectacle.

This led to the creation of a new breed of working-class fighters: the first being Joaquín Rodríguez Costillares, who was born
in Seville in 1729 and is believed to have been the inventor of
the most basic pass with the cape – the *verónica* – and the most
common method of killing, the *volapié*, 'flying feet', when the
man charges the bull with his sword to deliver the killing blow.

It was in the Maestranza of Seville that Costillares had his greatest triumphs and began his rivalry – the first in a long history of rivalries between matadors – with the great Pedro Romero, born fifteen years later in Ronda, who invented the *muleta*, the smaller red cape, and the method of killing *en recibiendo,* which involves waiting for the bull the charge the matador.

By 2009 the Spanish bullfight had become a sprawling, some would say bloated, beast, with a record 1,345 bullfights the year before (including the *rejoneo*, the modern horseback fight, and the *novilladas*, the 'novice fights'). Although there are smaller fights and fairs almost throughout the year, the season of the big fights starts with Seville, opening with the Resurrection itself – the Easter Sunday bullfight.

Seville's Semana Santa, Holy Week, is an event of international proportions. Over a million people from all over the globe descend on the Andalusian capital to block the non-existent pavements of its historic centre in quiet – but stubbornly immovable – contemplation of the Glorious and Sorrowful Mysteries. Between them pass the great processions. In 2009 sixty set out from the churches of the different *barrios* of the city to the cathedral, some numbering as many as 5,000 penitents dressed in the robes of the Inquisition.

The processions – bearing ecclesiastical candles after sunset – follow and lead the vast gilded effigies of the martyred Christ and his endlessly suffering and virginal Mother, which, weighing between one and two tons each on their sacred litters, are brought to life with the swaying movements of the broad-shouldered faithful who carry them at the sedate pace of the divine. Some of these brotherhoods have trodden this path for seven centuries.

As a result of this massive influx of people, tickets for the Easter Resurrection Sunday bullfight are absolutely impossible to find, featuring as it does the two foremost bullfighting sons of Seville, Morante de la Puebla, whom I had yet to see, and

El Cid, whose epic 2007 Seville Feria fight led to the magazine article that led to this book. So I sit that one out and read the following day's newspapers, which describe the fight as a fail-ure, due to the cattle of Zaldueno not living up to their reputa-tion. *El Diario de Sevilla* has the headline, 'The Bulls Crushed Expectations.' To be honest, the next one isn't much better, but at least I see it, courtesy of a ticket sent round to my house by María O'Neill, wife of Tristán Ybarra, neither of whom I had seen since the *tertulia*.

I arrived at the main gate to the bullring at 6.15 p.m. Called the Gate of the Prince, it is a large piece of Spanish baroque finery dedicated to a son of Philip V who died in infancy. My entrance was just to the right, a discreet little door leading up a grand marble staircase into a balcony of seats just behind the president. A little far away from the action, but when the rain started to pour down, and the uncovered seats below became an ocean of umbrellas, I was glad of the comfort. (Bullfighting is one activity where rain doesn't stop play.)

I took my seat and leafed through the programme: the bulls were from José Luis Pereda, of whom I had never heard. Nor had I heard of any of the three matadors. I was still learning. Here is my diary write-up at the time:

'The first bull, Paleto, looks heavy at 1,223lb, with the distinctive "*color*", colouring, a medium brown with pale patches around the eyes. Whether it is his weight or his temperament, I don't know, but he won't charge: neither the men with their pink and yellow capes, nor the horse with its armed picador atop in the first act. He seems afraid of the lance, and yet he ends up receiving an overly large number of pics as a result.

'Despite the blood, there is a terribly black humour in the situation. This bull, which has vast, wide-ranging horns like an African buffalo, seems too intelligent to charge at the threats he is expected to: the *burladero*, "hide", wall, the capes, the horse, anything. Instead he goes after individual men, forcing them to flee the ring, dispersing the *banderilleros* who are trying to place their *banderillas* – coloured, barbed sticks – in the second act like so much chaff.

'However, the fight is bad, partly because of this. It is messy, without either art or a sense of real danger for anyone but the bull. In the third and final act it is a strong animal and does not die easily, leaving one with a sense of sadness, and anger at the lack of technique in the fighters. When the crowd whistles the dead body of the bull – an odd habit for a deeply Catholic people who claim the bull has no soul, as well whistle a nail that bends under the hammer – I write in my notes, "The bastards!" Oddly, the matador, Curro Díaz, a thirty-four-year-old from Linares, remains totally unacknowledged.'

It seems odd now that I could be so cold about the animal, but I was already immersing myself in my subject. I sometimes wonder if it is actually a sense of the reader's sensibility – playing to the gallery – that prevents professional war correspondents being equally nonchalant given that they witness more conflict than most soldiers. Or perhaps they are indeed just more humane.

'The second bull, a light 1,082lb animal of the same colour and breed called Arabe, comes in fast with good horns although still hesitant. However, when it commits to the charge it rapidly hits top speed, allowing the thirty-year-old Miguel Abellán from Madrid to perform a neat series of *verónicas*, sweeping the large pink and yellow cape over the rapidly charging bull's face, although in the last it takes the cape from the matador's hands. When the horse enters the ring it goes for it without hesitation, pushing the heavily armoured and mounted horse across the ring, taking two pics easily in its stride. It is still at this point, as my notes say, "young, fit, feisty". However, "this matador is obsessed with dominating, and he can". A proud fighter, he refuses to be opportunistic or overly adaptive to the animal, instead insisting it is fought in territory of his choosing, in the manner and way he wants.

'The *banderillas*, often for me the most boring part of a bullfight, are quickly, neatly and efficiently placed. The matador, whom I now realise I have seen many years before but cannot remember if he was any good, takes up the *muleta* – the smaller, red cape – for the final act and dedicates the bull to the entire crowd, which always receives a happy response, and tosses his *montera*, the traditional hat, into the centre of the ring (it lands the right way up, which indicates good luck). He then leads the bull into the centre of the ring and begins to cape it closer and closer to his body, circling the bull round him, frequently changing hands to the more difficult left and then back again, giving his *faena*, the display, a rather unique figure of eight shape with the danger of death at its nexus in the centre. However, the bull, so lively to begin with, is tiring rapidly.

'The matador goes in for the kill, but misses with the sword and then fails with the first attempt with the *descabello* sword – a differently bladed sword with a crossbar near the point designed to sever the spinal column and drop the bull as though poleaxed. On the second attempt the bull falls.

'The third bull (Islero, 1,004lb) comes in looking like a cross between the two earlier bulls and starts to make sounds – vocalising, as biologists call it. The sound is strange, not distress, but certainly not happiness. Worry? A call to arms? I do not know, but this is no cry for help – the bull charges straight across the ring and plunges his horns into the wooden wall of the *burladero*, looking for the man behind it. The matador then drops to his knees for a *larga cambiada de rodillas*, the long pass on the knees. It is very impressive-looking, letting the bull charge the person – who cannot run, being on his knees – and then flinging the cape around the head in a manner that sweeps the horns away from your head as they pass.

'This bull is interesting. Intelligent, but its intelligence is not of the kind the Spanish like to call cowardly (meaning it doesn't fight the way they want). It commits fully to a charge, showing aggression and boldness, but as its horns hit the cape, finding no substance to its opponent, it digs its rear hooves into the sand, allowing it to turn hard back on the matador with remarkable agility for such a large animal.

'When the picador's horse comes in it charges it without hesitation, and despite the picador's lance in its shoulder it strives against horse and rider pushing them yards across the ring. As it does this it cries out again and its cry has a much more aggressive tone. However, the crowd doesn't like all this chatter. I wonder at the time if this is because the sound has a humanising effect. Again, I note the contradictory stance of the crowd, and the fact that they don't like that contradiction being highlighted. Given the bull's behaviour, I doubt that it is undergoing high levels of suffering, but the possibility that it might be is not something the crowd wishes to contemplate. They like their bulls doughty, dangerous and dumb – in both meanings of that last word. The sound disturbs me even more.

'The matador, César Giron, a twenty-five-year-old Venezuelan, is good with the *muleta*, bringing the bull's head low in sweeping passes. This low pass is good for several reasons, the main being aesthetic. It is the chorus in the strange song of domination that lends whatever art to such movements there can be. It also tires the bull for the kill, and shows its strength. At the end, he kills it on the second attempt and, despite the speed of the event, it calls and calls and calls.

'At this point, I decide I need a break from the blood, and step down to the bar of the ring to grab a beer. When I return, the first matador of the day is entering the third act of fighting his second bull, Alberco, the smallest of the day at 1,080lb. I had heard the applause from outside and realised I had picked the wrong moment to leave. Sure enough, this time he works the bull close in to his body with the *muleta*; too close, as it transpires, and the bull hits him hard. Immediately, having found the solid mass that has been so notably absent every time it has charged a man before, it aims at the fallen body of the matador with its horns, but he evades the horns by rolling his body quickly out of the way. As some of his *banderilleros* cape the animal away from him, he is helped up by the rest and appears not just shaken but disoriented. Despite this, he insists on continuing, to the applause of the crowd, and brings the bull even closer, raising the expectation that the now wiser bull will catch him again. However, it does not and he kills well and cleanly.

As a result, the crowd is ecstatic and out come the handkerchiefs, waving in a sea of white. I think to myself: where are the tourists and the first-timers at this fight? The matador is awarded an ear of the bull he has killed and does a slow lap of honour around the ring, receiving a standing ovation from each section of the stadium in turn. This man is not a great fighter, but his bravery undoubtedly warrants something.

'After this, however, both the bulls and the other two matadors go from bad to worse. Miguel Abellán's urge to dominate a bull which is interested only in returning to the ranch from whence he has come merely presents itself as overwhelming cruelty. And for the first time I see a bull trying to remove the *banderillas* from his shoulders with his own horns. He is feeling them; his lack of aggression, adrenaline and whatever else comes into the equation of pain renders the fight infinitely worse to behold. The final bull, fought by César Giron, is so boring and painful to watch I give up entirely and head to the bar.

'A little later, I meet María's husband Tristán Ybarra outside the Gate of the Prince. He's been sitting in seats with his brother-in-law Enrique Moreno de la Cova (the breeder of the Saltillos) in the front and we head round to the favourite bar of the *aficionados* of Seville, La Bodeguita de San José, a Virgin-Mary-bedecked dive with a long bar and the most efficient and harassed-looking staff in the city. Within a single visit these people will have memorised my favourite drinks and tapas and yet still never smile or say hello.

'At the bar a bedraggled-looking man with wispy hair on head and face and a beaten-up army jacket is being interrogated by acolytes for his views on the fights. He is Pedro Romero de Solis, a professor of sociology at the University of Seville and a renowned *aficionado* of the bulls. We talk, and although I agree with his view about the bravery of the bull with the singing voice, when I ask why it sings he says the sound signifies nothing. I wonder if this is part of the mechanism which allows him to psychologically push to one side the suffering he witnesses or whether he really doesn't care. Tristán, who trained originally in biology, is not allowed that luxury, and I speculate with him whether or not such a brave and aggressive bull was not some form of leader within his herd and thus was calling for reserves in the battle he so valiantly fought. I also wonder whether the finely tuned ears of the subsequent bulls in the ring – who being from the same breeder would have been from the same herd – could hear this call from where they were being held prior to their own deaths. It is not an idea I enjoy.

'We are joined by María and soon head off on a post-fight jaunt through Seville, stopping for drinks and tapas around the town, that ends as all such evenings do, in a blur. One memory that sticks in my mind most strongly is eating some excellent steak in a tiny restaurant called La Sal, whose owner they know. As we eat we talk, rambling through the Rioja, discussing my own fumbling attempts in the ring. Thinking about the bull who cried out, I put to them the idea that perhaps a great number of the theories matadors, breeders and aficionados alike believe to be true of the bull are not so. I mention the autobiography of the great matador Juan Belmonte, referencing the passage where he says about his beginnings in the ring in 1913:

> At that time there was a complicated system of 'territories of the bull' and 'territories of the bullfighter', which in my judgement was quite superfluous. The bull has no territory, because it is not a reasoning creature and there are no surveyors to lay down its boundaries. All the ground belongs to the bullfighter, the only intelligent being in the game, and it seemed natural to me that he should keep them.
>
> Those who saw me defying what they considered to be cosmic laws threw up their hands and said: 'He's bound to die. If he doesn't change his ground he'll be killed.' I didn't change my ground, the bull took a long time to kill me. [He died six days before his seventieth birthday, by his own hand.]

'I go on to suggest that some of the theories bullfighters still believe are hangovers from that unscientific age. However, this is not to belittle their craft. If one is running the consistent risk of death – and deliberately increasing it to the greatest extent one can in order to create drama – one will rely on anything one can. Equally, these proto-scientific theories have yet to be replaced by anything better.

'The most important of these theories, though, is that of the charge. Belmonte says quite clearly that a bull in the open will always run away, whereas I had been told by various *aficionados* that the fighting bull, the most aggressive animal in the world, should be treated in the field like a shark in the sea.

'The young Belmonte, from a poverty-stricken background with no access to the bullfighting world, used to swim across the river from his hovel in Triana with friends to cape bulls in the fields, using nothing more than moonlight and a lantern. The moon gave them the general layout of the land, and they would group together to single out one animal. Then, when it seemed ready for the charge, the lantern would come out and Belmonte would stand by its light, blinded beyond a distance of a few feet, and wait for the fury to plunge in from the darkness. One can see how this would develop into his signature style of stillness. There is no margin for fleeing if the bull is upon you at speed when you first see it, you must already have attached all its rage to the cape before you've even seen it, so that when it looms, rushes you and disappears, it does so without skewering you. However, what is particularly pertinent in his description of this was how difficult it was to get the bull to charge in the first place; how carefully the young men had to round it up and make it feel hemmed in before allowing it a way out towards the one lit object in the field – Belmonte. I have started to see myself that although some bulls undeniably enter the ring with the simple urge to charge and destroy all in their path, some first seek to establish that there is no other option, no matter how cursory the enquiry is before they default to aggression. I make a note to investigate this further.'

My notes end there but my memories do not. Haunted by the crying of the bull, I asked María, that most devout of *aficionados* of bullfighting, how it could not disturb her. Her answer echoes just as loud as the bull: 'They have no souls.'

■ ■ ■ ■ ■

It is an irony that the first attempt to ban the bullfight was by a pope, back in 1567, the mid-point of Spain's Golden Age. Pius V gave the Pontiff's seal to an edict stating:

> Divine Providence granted us the responsibility for caring for the Lord's flock and with deep concern we are so compelled by relevant pastoral duties to at all times deviate all the faithful of our congregations from imminent perils to the body and from condemnation of the soul.
>
> Verily, although the abominable use of the duel, introduced by the devil to also gain condemnation of souls through the cruel death of bodies, was forbidden by a Decree of the Council of Trent, up to now in many cities and places, so as to demonstrate their strength and courage at public spectacles, many individuals have not ceased engaging with bulls and other wild animals, frequently resulting in the death of men, in mutilation of members and endangering souls.
>
> Therefore, considering such spectacles which are removed from Christian piety and charity, in which bulls and wild animals are challenged in circuses and plazas, and desiring to abolish such cruel and base spectacles of the devil and not of man, and to take measures for the salvation of souls as far as we are able with the power of God – to each and every Christian prince, in any kingdom or enjoying any high position, whether ecclesiastical, civil or imperial, proclaimed by any name by any community or republic in perpetuity, by means of our constitution valid for the future, on pain of ipso facto excommunication and anathema, we interdict and prohibit the carrying out of spectacles of this nature in their provinces, cities, lands, castles and places where spectacles of this kind are realised, where bullfights and similar sports with other wild animals are permitted.
>
> Ecclesiastical burial will be denied to anyone who is killed as a result of participating in such bullfights.
>
> And all venerable patriarch brethren, primates, archbishops and bishops and other high Church officials, by virtue of the holy obedience and on pain of divine

judgment and eternal interminable condemnation, shall
adequately divulge and seek to obey our letter in their
own cities and dioceses, on pain of incurring ecclesiastical
punishment and censure ...

What is notable is that the justification for the ban is that
it endangers, physically and metaphysically, the men who take
part rather than the animals – for they have no souls. And this
from a pope who was a one-time inquisitor, who restored the
powers of the Inquisition to kill and persecute heretics, intel-
lectuals, Jews and prostitutes. He also encouraged greater ruth-
lessness in Philip II's bloody repression of the Netherlands,
sent troops to aid Catherine de' Medici's similarly bloody dealings with the Huguenots and excommunicated and declared
'usurper' England's own Elizabeth I, promising heaven to any
who would assassinate her.

Of course, the ban was never enforced in Spain, and within
less than a century and a half the Vatican had so watered down
this unenforceable law that it merely prohibited the clergy from
entering the ring. Churches famously used charity bullfights
to raise money for construction and repairs. In 1893 they even
altered the time of the Corpus Christi Mass in Madrid so that it
didn't conflict with the farewell tour of the matador Lagartijo,
'fearing the competition from this retired colossus of the bullring'. No souls, indeed.

10

De poder a poder

'From power to power', the matador cites the bull with *banderillas* and then begins to run away at an angle. The bull charges after, and the two lines curve and intersect like the outline of a horn, at the point of which the matador strikes.

The next fight I saw – two days later – was notable more for the circumstances than the fight itself. María O'Neill's brother-in-law, Enrique Moreno de la Cova, called me and said, 'You come and sit with me in the front row tonight. Come to my house at half past five.'

So I duly pitched up at his rather grand town house – around the corner from my apartment, which was feeling smaller and darker each day – and we walked together down the street. Enrique is an interesting conversationalist, always trying to catch the salient point of a topic, trying to 'cut to the chase', but without being curt because there is an underlying streak of good humour. He also has a certain humility, which is why it was from his wife, Cristina Ybarra, that I had heard of his various feats of physical prowess in his youth. I asked him about them as we walked.

'Cristina told me that when you went to work in banking in New York in your twenties, and all the new employees were asked in a round table what they did in their spare time, you said, "I fight bulls." Is that true?'

He smiled and nodded. The smile, no doubt, from remembering the looks on the faces of the next generation of Manhattan's financial elite.

'What sort of bulls did you fight?'

He waves the question back into the ether, saying, 'Oh nothing, only small ones, in village festivals. My father didn't want me to devote my life to it so I never went any further. It is addictive, this "life in the country", with the horses and the bulls and the bullfighters and the long evenings ...'

There is something there. A regret? We walk on in silence for a while, and I understand another facet of the man who has been pouring his fortune into restoring a long defunct breed of bulls. (By defunct, I mean in their pure form. Almost all the bulls fought in South America are of Saltillo blood.)

'Cristina also told me you were once bet that you couldn't outrun a galloping horse. I hear you won the bet.'

He smiles again. 'I raced him twenty metres. I won. I raced him thirty metres, I won. I raced him forty, I didn't. It took him that long to get his legs in the right order. He was *de pura raza*, a thoroughbred.'

I was wondering if I would fare so well – 400 metres was my distance in the school team – as we entered the Maestranza, this time by the Gate of the Prince. I doubted it.

■ ■ ■ ■ ■

Inside we pick up a couple of 'gin-tonics' as they are affectionately known in Spain and copiously drunk (bizarrely, Spain has the highest per capita gin consumption in the world). Enrique seems to know half the people who pass the bar, and introduces me in incomprehensibly rapid Spanish, from which I pick up words like 'journalist', 'writer', 'brave', and I nod at the right moments and smile, and try to look either studious or courageous according to the adjective in use. Then we head into the ring.

I have sat in various parts of the Maestranza, from the cheap seats high up in the sun on my own, to good ones midway down in the shade with my family, but Enrique's seats are special. The front row, the *barrera*, 'barrier', seats are the best in any ring, whatever anyone else tells you. And Enrique's are in the part of the ring where you just can't buy them, because everyone there buys them as season tickets and some of these have been in families since the ring was built. Which is why there are photos of a younger Enrique sitting in the same seat next to the greatest post-war matador Antonio Ordóñez, who had the season ticket next door. There are also photos of a very young Enrique sitting with his father. The late Ordóñez's seats to my left are taken by strangers now, but to Enrique's right are his elder brother, Felix, and his wife, who hold the season tickets adjacent. Just behind us is the breeder of that day's bulls, João Folque de Mendoza from Portugal, with his elegant wife Mercedes and daughter Inés. Enrique waves to them, promising to introduce me later.

After the pomp of the entry parade, the matadors enter the *callejón*, the 'alleyway' that runs between the *barrera* and the *tablas*, the 'wooden boards' that contain the bull. Here I see all the paraphernalia of a Grade I bullfighting plaza. Here is my write-up from the day:

'The alleyway is filled with journalists, the matadors and their teams, publicists, managers, and all the accoutrements of a large industry at the meeting point between the worlds of culture and of sport. Most remarkable of all is an elderly photographer scuttling up and down, nimble and lean with a weathered face topped by a white baseball cap with some writing on it. I look more closely and read, "CANO 18–12–1912 ALICANTE", which turn out to be his name, date and place of birth.'

The photos I had seen of Enrique and Ordóñez, of Enrique and his father, of Orson Welles and Ernest Hemingway in Spain, were all by Paco Cano. He had been a trainee bullfighter himself, although of a rough and ready sort. He had first caped a steer that escaped from a slaughterhouse into his father's shop, and his debut in the ring was as an *espontáneo*, a 'spontaneous', who jumped into the ring impromptu from the audience and started caping a bull during a fight. Anyway, he had hung up his suit of lights for a Leica in Madrid during the Civil War, and hadn't looked back. His most famous and terrible photo is of an event that hangs over the bullfight like few others, the death of Manuel Laureano Rodríguez Sánchez – Manolete.

'When the matadors had completed their *paseíllo*, their walking-in ceremony, we got an intimate look at the exchanges of words and changes of mood which they undergo before and between the entry of their bulls. The remarkable thing is the apparent lack of fear, even of the performance aspect of it – being in front of an audience – let alone fear of who they are going to share a stage with. It seems so strange to someone familiar with acting in theatres that there is no backstage for these men, no privacy, even their preparations are under scrutiny by the crowd and the press.

'The bulls today are known to be a tough breed, as in one which creates *corridas duras*, "hard bullfights", which leave little room for expositions of the post-Belmonte art of close-fighting, but require great courage, skill and endurance to complete. The first sign of this was the very first bull, a 1,113lb black beast called Lumbrero, meaning the fiery one, who charged into the ring like an explosion, crossed it down the diameter, and rather than striking the wood of the *burladero*, the hide behind which the *toreros* take shelter, going straight over the top with his horns, striking the first matador, El Fundi, directly in the face.

'Fundi collapsed in the small space as though struck with a sledgehammer (a less risky weapon than the point of a horn backed with a half-ton of galloping momentum), and there was the immediate question of whether or not he was still alive. Helped to his feet, it was clear from the bleeding on his face that he was fine (in bullfighting terms) and that the horn had neither hit the eye nor the throat, instead the dense and planed bones of Fundi's cheek, before skating off.

'Fundi is a matador who has been fighting the dangerous and large breeds like the Miuras and Palhas for longer than any other matador, even Padilla with whom he often shares an afternoon. He certainly had the air of a pugilist about him: compact, broad-shouldered, moving with economy and determination, not showing fear but instead a certain care and respect for his opponents. It was like this that he entered the ring, with the addition of blood dripping down his face. An epic sight, and it led me to hope I would see great things. However, two things conspired against El Fundi that day, one being the fact that he is the ideal body shape for a gladiator – strong, compact, hard-boned and a low centre of gravity – but absolutely the wrong shape for bullfighting. His bravery and technique cannot for a second be doubted, but there is nothing elegant about his movements: the arms are too short to sweep the capes long, the legs too bandy to conflict with the horizontal line of the charge, and the body too much like the bull's in shape to offer a stark contrast between man and beast. And these bulls were beasts, which is the second thing that worked against him. Heavy (between 1,100 and 1,300lb), with short charges, reluctantly given, making the matador dance to avoid the horns and then insist with the cape to invoke a response.

'El Fundi's first bull not only hit him, but also caught the second matador, Sergio Aguilar, in the chest as he tried to take him off the horse, although without shedding the man's blood. Aguilar was then knocked down and hunted across the ground by his bull. The third bull did have some style and long charges in him, but the heavy-jawed matador, Salvador Cortés, was so insistent on his own greatness as he fought him that awarding him an ear seemed somehow wrong, but the president did it anyway. From there, things went downhill into tedium.

'It was then that I realised a terrible truth. Once you have got over the initial astonishment at the nature of the event, and if you can stomach the blood and suffering (which, just as it does for surgeons and soldiers, gets easier), then bullfights can actually be monotonous. Yes, there is the terrible poetry of death, but it's the same poem. I actually found myself sitting in the ring making notes about the weather. Admittedly they were notes about whether the particularly heavy rains the year before meant that the bulls had had an ease in finding water and pasture which prevented them from building any muscle while reaching the required weights and that that was why they were reluctant to charge, but it was the weather nonetheless. After we left I was actually glad Enrique did not fulfil his promise and introduce me to the breeder and his family, as I simply would not have known what to say.'

I remember a little later that night getting a phone call from my old flatmate, the actor Hugh Dancy, who offered an interesting analysis.

'I imagine bullfighting is like Shakespeare performances. You sit through a thousand terrible versions – you know I once watched someone do *The Tempest* in an interpretation so dire that Ariel actually walked on dressed as a box of Ariel soap powder? – Anyway, all that shit, and then you see a great one. And without the mistaken innovation of the dross, you would never get the gold.'

Only an actor could come up with that analogy. However, if part of the justification of the suffering is the art; then what happens when there is no art? That, I can't answer. Not yet.

Of course, while sometimes the bullfight – like theatre – lacks drama, sometimes it has too much. When I got back home that night I looked up Cano's photos of the death of Manolete, and remembered what I had heard about him.

While it is true that the death of bullfighters often gives them an immortality they would not have earned from their skill alone, the greatness of Manolete is not in doubt. The greatest since Belmonte, and the greatest to die in the ring besides, perhaps, Belmonte's great friend and rival Joselito, 'El Gallo'. Manolete was born in 1917 in Córdoba and the first

paragraph of his entry in the *Encyclopedia Britannica* tells you
a lot.

> His great-uncle, a minor-league bullfighter, was killed by
> a bull of the dreaded Miura breed. His mother was already
> the widow of a matador when she married his father, also
> a bullfighter, who went blind and died in poverty when
> Manolete was five years old.

He started aged seventeen, and by the time he was thirty he
was a phenomenon perhaps greater than Belmonte. His stylistic
innovation was a terrifyingly dignified stillness – emphasised
by his long limbs, gaunt face and tired, gypsy eyes – while passing with unusual closeness the furious thunder of the bull.

His wealth and celebrity were unique for the time, and as a
result he fought more often than he should and started drinking heavily to cope with the two-handed stress of facing an
audience and facing Death simultaneously. The practice of
horn-shaving was said to be relatively common in those days
compared to today, although he asked for it more than most
so that he would be hit less often and be able to fight more. In
interviews not long before his death he spoke only of his wish
to retire, to rest, that the crowd demanded too much, too many
bulls, fought too well, for any single man to live for very long.

The day before his fight he visited his elderly mother in
Córdoba and then drove the 73 miles to Linares. He fought that
day alongside the up-and-coming young matador Luis Miguel
Dominguín, who was trying to claim Manolete's crown, and
the older matador Gitanillo de Triana. The bulls were Miuras,
and in the first four, Dominguín took an ear, but no one else
achieved anything. For the fifth, in walked Islero at 1,090lb. It
was the 1,004th bull of Manolete's career, and it was as tricky
as Miuras always are. It would stop mid-charge and could turn
within its own body length. He caped it briefly before turning it over to the picador, then it scared the hell out of the

banderilleros before Manolete came out again with the *muleta*. His agent, José Camará, shouted from the *callejón*, 'Manolo, I don't like him. Keep the cloth low and finish him off quickly.'

Manolete did not. He passed the bull low a few times, and then he performed some of his trademark *manoletinas*. His sword-handler, Guillermo, shouted from the *burladero*, 'Take it easy, Maestro.'

Again, Manolete did not. Instead he went in for the kill in the most honest, direct and truthful manner possible. A slow advance, carefully placing the sword in the killing spot, and as he slid it in, the bull raised its horn and equally slowly lifted the matador into the air until distressed skin, tissue and muscle parted and he slid down on to the horn before the bull began to spin his body on its point. It is this exact moment that Cano caught on his camera, along with a second one of Manolete's team carrying him semi-conscious from the bullring. It is these photos that made Cano famous. And Manolete even more so.

Manolete didn't die immediately. His body was going into shock from the blood loss and the wound – in fact, there were three wounds within one, as he had bounced on the horn. He was given two blood transfusions in the infirmary and then moved to the municipal hospital. He was operated on and given a third transfusion at midnight, and said to Álvaro Domecq Díez (whose son I spent the day with at their ranch, Los Alburejos, the drawing room filled with photos of the father and Manolete together): 'This is a bad feeling.'

A few minutes before five in the morning he was given the last rites. It was only later, after he was dead, that his lover, the actress Antonita Lupe Sino, was allowed in to see him. She had once said of his fans, 'They'll never let him go until they see him dead.'

The next day the Spanish press ran the headline, 'He Killed As He Died, And He Died As He Killed.' For the bull was killed at that moment just as surely as the matador, and the crowd, unaware of the severity of his injury, had awarded Manolete both ears and the tail for his courage and his art. The *New York Times* went with the headline, 'Manolete, 30, Dies After Fatal Goring By Bull; All Spain Mourns Her Greatest Matador.' And all Spain did. Twenty thousand filed past his body in his Córdoba house, and National Radio played only funeral dirges for two weeks afterwards, at the orders of General Franco.

11

El tirabuzón

'The corkscrew'. The man leans against the wooden barrier citing. The bull charges. The man runs in a circle. When it is on him, he passes between it and the barrier and turns to run backwards. It follows and the man places the *banderillas*.

There is a special route that can be taken around Seville in a horse-drawn carriage that takes in the main part of its historic monuments. It begins at the cathedral, in the shade of which the horses stand, while their drivers haggle price with tourists. It goes past the Palace of the Alcázar and its gardens, through the heart of the Arenal, past the Plaza de Toros, along the river with its Tower of Gold, around the perfect green labyrinth that is the María Luisa Park and finishes in the splendour of the Plaza de España. I remember taking one such ride with my family in 2000, and all along the way my older brother – the one who traded the Army for banking by way of a history degree – was pondering a single question: whatever happened to the great wealth of the Spanish Empire? At the end of the tour, having digested some of the most beautiful distributions of space, stone and greenery in western Europe, he sat with a look of realisation on his face that I mistook for admiration. Then he said, with a mixture of disgust and disbelief, 'The fools, *they spent it!*'

Cold to the beautiful and passionate about the material, he is always an insightful travel companion. They did indeed spend it, because whatever Spain does, it does in excess with an almost drunken fervour. Spain's expenditure of its American treasure alone – for which Seville long held the sole licence – was heroic enough to drive inflation in Europe through a six-fold increase in the century and a half between the *Niña*, *Pinta* and *Santa María* sighting the Bahamas (1492) and the peace of Westphalia, which ended the disaster that was the Thirty Years War (1648). Spain shipped 190 tonnes of gold across the Atlantic in that period and spent it on pretty buildings and ugly wars, including the Great and Most Fortunate Armada, wiped out by Britain in 1588. Given that the average price of gold was £3 per fine ounce over the period, adjusted for the increase in average earnings, this is worth £45 trillion today. And then there is the sixteen and a half *thousand* tons of silver shipped in that period, valued at almost six times that.

Any nation that can spend £300 trillion in a century and a half on war, architecture and courtly opulence is a good place to attend a national party, and the Feria de Abril in Seville is definitely that: from all over Spain they come to the great fair-ground in Triana, on the other side of the River Guadalquivir, a mile long and half a mile wide, with 1,000 marquees. While Holy Week still holds to its original religious purpose, the veneration of Catholic idols, the same cannot be said of the Spring Fair. What is now a million people drinking, dancing and eyeing one another in that singularly Mediterranean way actually began as a livestock market. In fact, it was founded by Tristán Ybarra's great-great-great-grandfather, José María Ybarra.

One person flying in to celebrate it was my girlfriend Sam. She and I had met when I was a cast member in my play *The Pendulum* in a tiny theatre in the West End the previous summer. Despite the bizarre turn my life had taken since then, she had taken it in her stride and given me her full support, despite the fact that she was a true urbanite – an interior designer by profession – and had never seen a bullfight in her life. Since my move to Spain I had flown back to London a few times to see her and we spoke every day on the phone. Now, however, she was flying out to join me for the first time. So I met her at the airport and to make her feel at home I took her straight to an Irish pub, Flaherty's, where James, the bartender from New York, mixed us Cosmopolitans until we both decided to swim a lap of the Seville cathedral fountain fully clothed.

The next day we visited Cristina Ybarra (Tristán's sister) at the sprawling house she and Enrique share around the corner from where I was living. She had said she might have a *traje gitana*, a 'gypsy dress', from her own childhood that might fit Sam for the *feria*. Indeed she did: a lovely old handmade dress that fitted like a light blue glove, combining so well with Sam's cornflower eyes and violently red hair. I will always remember her standing in the courtyard of my house in that dress to pose for a photograph, looking more beautiful than I care to admit. Especially given that those few days were, unbeknownst to us, the last we would spend together in that way.

We went to the *feria* that day, and Sam loved her dress, and the streets between the *casetas*, the colourful tents of the *feria*, were filled with people on horses, the men in *traje corto* with short jackets and Córdobes hats, and women in their flamenco dresses like Sam's riding behind them. (I asked Sam whether she would want to ride behind me next year if I got a horse, and she said she wanted her own horse and to trade in her *traje gitana* for a *traje corto*. I agreed with her: to ride behind a man seems to imply ownership, an imbalance between the sexes. And between the classes as well: your gypsy mistress may ride behind you, but your wife has her own horse.)

There is something affecting in the sight of horses riding up and down pedestrian thoroughfares. It conjures up strange images and associations: a sense of history, of nobility, but also of inequality and the backward. Of course, the illusion of a previous era is broken by the tourists stopping to photograph it all.

Either way, though, there are few sights more appealing

than a family of horsemen in their Sunday best riding up to a *caseta* to hail some friend, who strolls out cheerfully with a bottle of chilled sherry and glasses for all so they can drink and chat from the saddle with passers-by. Or perhaps they will hitch their horses to a post and come inside, boots sounding hard on the wooden floors, with the chink of a spur-chain, sometimes becoming louder should they decide to dance a *sevillana* or two.

After a long siesta, I showed Sam Casa Matias and introduced her to Curro and Matias and a stocky old ticket tout named Manni, who respectively supplied us with rum, flamenco and tickets to that day's bullfight. Sam had been reading up about bullfighting on my blog and in the copy of Hemingway's *Death in the Afternoon* I had given her, and decided that she needed fortification before watching.

Manni had supplied us with good tickets, which he said belonged to the doctor who attended some of the bullfights as locum. Apparently, when he was working he had seats much closer to the action.

'So he can get to the bullfighters more quickly?' I asked.

'Yes, but more importantly, so he can count the number of trajectories of a wound if the matador goes up on the horn. You know, bounce one, bounce two, bounce three. Then he knows to look for each one and clear the dirt out to prevent infection,' Manni replied.

When I translated this for Sam, she turned a little pale and ordered another rum.

■ ■ ■ ■ ■

When we got to the ring, they were indeed good seats for a first fight: in the shade, halfway up so Sam could get the overall spectacle, not too much of the viscera, and yet still see the detail of the bullfighters' work (for the curious, in Seville this is Tendido 5, Fila 3). As my particularly short write-up of the day says:

'The fight that day was between Finito de Córdoba, Morante de la Puebla, Sebastián Castella and the bulls of Jandilla. Finito, despite my having a personal liking for him after the *tentadero* I attended, where he not only taught me how to cape but intervened when the *vaquilla* tossed me, performed the worst of the three. Morante, whose *capote divino*, "divine cape", is being so praised this season, was very good, although he does not exactly have the most handsome "line of the body" when he does so. He did however take one ear and I was beginning to see something unusual in his style, although perhaps I was just beginning to see differently in general. Castella gave nothing to the bulls and they gave nothing back.

'At the end of this perfectly functional but non-memorable *corrida* my girlfriend's conclusion was "Wow." In the great division among spectators between those whose sympathies attach to their fellow humans and those to the animals, she had fallen firmly on the side of the human. It was she who pointed this out to me, and she went so far as to suggest that my vacillation between the two positions left her better qualified to write about bulls than me.'

I took no notes outside the arena, although I do remember this. After the fight we met up with a gypsy friend called Juan, along with his daughter and her trainee bullfighter boyfriend José, whom I had met before and didn't much like. Although he was flatteringly ingratiating, I assumed it was because I was writing a book. Along with them were some other nephews of Juan's and a young Argentinian man called Diego. Diego spoke perfect English and had something in his manner and style that drew one towards him immediately. He was intelligent and I'm sure had as many secrets as the rest of us, but they weren't secrets that came between him and other people – he had an open spirit. He wore a jacket wrapped tight to his thin physique, but cut from cheap cloth. He also wore a slightly dirty cravat tied raffishly around his neck. It was clear what he was: 'So *cantaor*, *bailaor* or *guitarrista*?' I asked, using the Andalusian flamenco terms for singer and dancer rather than the general, Castilian ones: *canter* and *bailarín*.

'Guitar, my friend.'

And we fell into deep conversation about flamenco. Five years before, a newspaper had sent me to Seville to do a travel piece on flamenco and I had spent a few very happy days – or rather nights – trying to find out everything I could about it without speaking Spanish or playing an instrument. Which basically meant reading Federico García Lorca and trawling the tourist flamenco spectacles until I had found the only decent one in town, at Los Gallos, 'The Cockerels'.

However, the finest flamenco I had ever encountered had been at four in the morning at El Rejoneo on the banks of the river Guadalquivir, when some performers from Los Gallos had joined up with their gypsy friends after hours, and all were lost to the world on cheap brandy and cheaper cocaine, dancing for their pleasure and their resentment and producing something incredibly dark and moving.

'Yes. Sometimes it is like that. *Duende*.'

'*Duende*. Yes. The dark spirit. I once read it is the wind that crosses the graveyard, comes in through the window of the bar, and possesses the performer and makes the hairs on the audience stand up like a dog's.'

'*¡Ja! Escritor* ... writer, you are funny. But what do you know of the guitar?'

I didn't want to say that I began by loving the dance, then the guitar, but now saw only the song as the true flamenco.

'Paco de Lucía.'

'Ah. You aren't just words, then. He is the best. Do you want to come to the *feria* tonight with the *torerito* ('little bullfighter') and us? It will only be *sevillanas*, which have no soul and were invented so secretaries could dance, not true flamenco, but it will be fun.'

He was referring to the very reduced and formalised version of flamenco, for which there are four carefully choreographed dances, called the *sevillanas*, which are the mainstay of the *ferias* of Andalusia.

I said yes and we went back to Paco de Lucía. This guitarist, when you watch him play, which I had only done on film, not only had a technical brilliance which appeared to divide the left thumb and fingers of the left hand into two completely different voices, but he also poured the whole of the rest of his mind and body through those conduits into an extremity of emotion and pain. Flamenco is the song of a lost people, the *gitanos*, the gypsies of Spain, modulated through the influence of other displaced peoples, the Sephardic Jews and the Moors.

As we talked I noticed that the trainee bullfighter, José, was looking at Diego with a look of anger, because he did not speak English and so couldn't join in our conversation. The two young men, superficially similar – Hispanic colouring, lean, early twenties – could not have been more different. José was in dressed jeans and a polo shirt, both freshly pressed, cleanshaven and hair immaculate – like an advert for Abercrombie & Fitch's Seville branch. Diego had a louche and easy manner and style – and it was definitely a style – that spoke of a man knowing what looks good, but not going so far as to try to impress.

We headed down to the *feria* ground with its long streets – all named after bullfighters of old, Belmonte, Joselito, Manolete – down towards the rowdier end, where the neat *sevillanas* were occasionally punctuated by the raucous sorrow of the *cante jondo*, 'the deep song', of real flamenco. Diego led us into a tent, where he was greeted with enthusiasm by everyone there. José, I noticed, was not so happily met. However, he carefully arranged the seating and launched into a pitch that surprised even me in its vehemence and scope.

'You are the only Englishman in all Spain who understands bullfighting!'

'Um, well, no.'

'And you are a famous writer, respected in the country.'

'That really isn't tru—'

'I want you to be my manager.'

'What?'

'Yes. You know the people, they respect you, you manage me, you get me fights, you watch, you write your book about me.'

'Um, José, with great respect, that's just not a possibility.'

'Don't say no, Don Alejandro. You can introduce me to people, you can help me. That is all I ask, do not say I cannot ask!' And this last statement had a hint of a threat in it.

This back-footed me. I have no issue in dealing with aggression, but this was in a crowded public venue I did not know. Sam was dancing with Diego at the time, so I tried to come up with a compromise that would dilute the situation and my refusal to commit.

'I will talk to my friend Enrique, who owns the Saltillos. Next time he has a *tentadero* you can come and fight and others can see how good you are and I am sure it will lead to good things.'

'Exactly! Precisely. Now you are my manager. The first English manager in the history of the bullfight.'

He shook my hand firmly, then embraced me. He got up, smiling, and walked into the part of the *caseta* where everyone was dancing. I was just happy he had gone.

Diego's brother, who was seated with us, then launched into a complicated and interesting exposition on the links between bullfighting and flamenco, which rested on the fact – as far as I could work out – that many bullfighters had married flamenco dancers and that this is because the bullfighter is the most masculine animal in Spain, whereas the female flamenco dancer is the most feminine animal in all of Spain. Which has its merits as a view, or seemed to after all the sherry.

As we were immersed in this, Diego came in with Sam, whom he introduced to his brother as he took me outside by the arm.

'My friend, you seem to me like a good person, a good man.'

'Thank you, Diego.'

'I think you should know that José is not a good man.'

'I agree. He can be annoying.'

'No. You do not understand. He is bad inside. Like bad food. All day he sits on Juan's sofa saying, "Arrange me a bullfight, I am a bullfighter," eating his food, screwing his daughter, going to bars with Juan's money for what he calls publicity. There is nothing good in him.'

'I'll admit, I didn't like him from the first time I met him.'

'I am glad. You talk to him for your book, good. You should know about people like that, but you must keep them far away. He is in that room saying tomorrow you will introduce him to a breeder who will pay him a thousand euros to fight his cattle.'

'*What?*'

'Exactly. And he has borrowed money off the owner for drinks which he will repay with money from "the great English writer".'

'The mother-fucker!'

'Be careful of that one.'

'Careful! I *never* said to him I was going to get him money. Where is that little c—'

'*No!*' he took my arm. 'Not here. People don't like him, but he is the lover of Juan's daughter, and him they like. Me and my brother can't stand him, but we are from Argentina and we don't count in Seville. You will have your revenge when he has to pay his debts tomorrow and cannot. Come and forget about it, have another drink.'

So we did.

■ ■ ■ ■ ■

The following day – Sam was less nervous about the fight, and much more excited – we went to see Francisco Rivera Ordóñez, El Juli and José María Manzanares fight the bulls of Daniel Ruiz from seats high up on the sunny side which give you all of the spectacle and none of the detail. It turned out that two of the bulls of Ruiz did not meet the standards of the attendant vet for entry into the ring and so were replaced with those of the *finca* of Gavira. This is a very important point to note: the bull *must* enter the ring in good condition. Otherwise it is rejected, and the cost is to the breeder.

Again, the fight was good but not amazing. Which surely is the point in a bullfight – that it should amaze. Fran Rivera was brave, hurled into the air in front of us as he killed the first bull, which then angled to catch him on its point as he landed. Luckily for him it misjudged and he landed between the horns, 'without major consequence' as *El Mundo* put it. Although in any other public spectacle in the civilised world, you would not return to the ring. Which he did. (This being a matador whose father, Pacquirri, died in the ring when he was ten years old.)

Sam, who did not even jolt in her seat for Fran's tossing, found the skill of El Juli particularly to her liking. And when he took an ear for his efforts and did a lap of the ring she stood and clapped, clearly as moved by his handsome face as by his skill with the *muleta*. Manzanares' first bull and Fran and Juli's seconds were all animals who did not want to fight, and it was a sorry display as a result. Then Manzanares drew a true fighting bull and managed to get two ears from it. Sam was delighted. At this point, I finally came to understand her lack of sympathy for the bull. Although she fully understood and sympathised with the arguments against the bullfight, she actually disliked animals. At least, those of the more violent temperaments, partly explained by the fact that she had been badly thrown by a horse when she was a child.

■ ■ ■ ■ ■

However, when we returned for the third and final fight of the series (El Cid, Sebastián Castella and Daniel Luque versus Puerto de San Lorenzo), which was truly uninspiring, she finally saw – and I felt somehow good that she did – the terrible brutality that can happen in the ring. The young matador Luque killed worse than I have ever seen a matador kill before or after. Here are my notes on him alone:

'Not only did this "matador" (never has the Spanish word for "killer" been more misapplied, and never so in need of being regulated and withdrawable) have to go in three times with the killing sword, but then, when the bull was clearly insufficiently wounded for death, his use of the *descabello* sword to sever the spinal cord was execrable. I lost count of the number of times he stabbed the poor animal – twenty, thirty? [the critic from *El Mundo* counted seventeen] – by then its neck began to resemble a dish you might serve on a plate. Somewhere around the twelfth strike, the animal began to vocalise – or to lose the tepid biological terms, cry out. For the first time in my life watching bullfights, I had tears in my eyes: of anger, of disgust, of sadness. When it finally died, I asked my girlfriend if she wanted to leave, but now, her perspective on bullfights changed for ever, she felt she had a duty to see it through. I left for the bar and returned a little while later for the final bull, and the same matador, and although he killed well and won an ear, it did nothing for me. After that, though, Manolete could have risen from the grave and killed with the grace of Michelangelo and I wouldn't have been moved.'

Of course, that was exactly what I was going to see a few days later in Jerez, but I am getting ahead of myself.

■ ■ ■ ■ ■

The next day I took Sam to the airport and she wished me luck with my continued research. She had had a glimpse of how strange my world had become, and how uncomfortable it could be for me. She also realised, as did I, what different worlds we were now living in. And I was not even close to fulfilling my remit to write about one year of bullfighting in Spain. I returned to the Seville Spring Fair, but not exactly light-hearted. And the reason for that was not only my failing relationship, but also the way the bullfights seemed to be going. The argument in favour of bullfighting simply doesn't run if they are ugly and boring. Like I said, the cultural relativists' argument that just because it's Spanish it should be allowed to exist doesn't wash with me at all.

I saw two more fights in Seville – the last two on 2 and 3 May – because of the amazing generosity of a British *aficionada*, Madeleine Rampling; she had come to see them with a mutual friend who was then called away to a funeral, so I was substituted as someone who could give her a commentary on the bulls. Sitting next to Mads through those two fights was a vicarious thrill because of her constant enthusiasm. A lady of a certain age, with a warm heart and open arms for everything from stray cats to bullfighters, her energy restored some of my faith in the *corridas* I was watching in apparently endless array. It was with her that I saw the cowardice of Javier Condé, Condé the clown as some *aficionados* call him, who won't cape a bull within a mile of his body, and the emotionally empty grandstanding of El Cordobés, unacknowledged son of the most famous matador of the 1970s who fought under that name.

The next day, though, we saw my friend Padilla, who took an ear from the largest and most unwieldy Miura I have ever seen – 1,428lb, or 648kg, or almost 102 stone. To Mads, the greatest highlight of all was the raised eyebrow and smile he gave me in passing, brother to brother. Mads, whom I have not seen since, I remember with fondness.

12

La dedicación

The six *banderillas* placed, all bullfighters leave the ring. The matador takes up his *muleta* and sword, salutes the president and then walks to the barrier to dedicate the bull to a member of the audience: a lover, a friend, or an inspiration.

'The town of Jerez de la Frontera, once the frontier between the lands of the Moors and those of the Christian kings, and from where sherry takes its name, is a far less grand affair than Seville. There are fewer inhabitants and those inhabitants are poorer. And yet it is still richer than Sanlúcar de Barrameda down the road, and consequently looks down on it, while Sanlúcar looks upon its marginally richer, marginally bigger brother as lacking in authenticity and manliness. Such is the way in Spain.

'This is not to say that Jerez doesn't have lovely parts to it, little idylls of unreconstructed Spain. They just don't seem to be the parts I find myself in.

'I arrive by train in the middle of May – the train networks of Spain having a comfort and efficiency that much richer Britain seems unable to provide. On the journey I call the journalist Giles Coren, who I know will be in town on a press junket for *The Times*. I had thanked him about the article on my late brother, and he had told me he would be there and suggested we meet up. So I drop my bags at his hotel and stroll in the sweltering heat in jacket and tie into the heart of the Feria del Caballo, the Horse Fair. The *feria* resembles Seville but on a far smaller scale. The great sherry houses – Sandeman, Gonzalez Byass, Domecq, Osborne – all have grand *casetas*, but the average is far rougher than their Seville counterparts.

However, the quality of the horses in the streets is notably superior. Sherry and horses are the main industries here.

'At the grand Gonzalez Byass tent I see Giles and the other journalists, tipsily effervescent in the sun and definitely not dressed for the occasion. I remember Giles as a vaguely familiar presence from my childhood, whom I have seen only once in the twenty-one years since my brother's funeral, when he took me out to lunch in 1998.

'This time Giles appears not to have aged, although his neat features are roughened by a hangover and two days' stubble. He seems to look like the slightly shabbier brother of the man in the photo that accompanies his *Times* articles, especially in his jeans and a paisley shirt among the groomed and suited Spaniards of the *feria*. Next to him is the explosively eloquent Tom Parker Bowles, stepson to a future king but today food critic for a magazine. The two of them are on ribald form, as are the other three journalists present, all being shepherded by two young PR girls on a well-lubricated culinary tour of Jerez.

'Stories are swapped about the night before which are unrepeatable, and the sherry flows in *feria* style. I introduce them to various local personalities whom I have met in Seville, and slope off at some point to meet María Del Rio, the tall young niece of Álvaro Domecq who is managing the hotel I am to be staying at that night. I have met María once before, and again I am struck by how the inner workings can overwhelm the outer appearance of some people, her prettiness almost swamped by the alternating anger and sadness that seem to run through her.

'I rejoin the journalists and it is somewhere around this point that once again recollections become hazy. Giles, Tom and I, having entered into the sort of competitive drunken anecdote-exchange that can be such fun for oneself and such a pain to surrounding tables, are soon rounded up by the PRs to attend the bullfight. I remember a hilarious walk and Tom insisting on buying everyone cushions to sit on in the ring. They had all been supplied tickets by their hosts, whereas I had my own, so we separated briefly. I rejoined Giles at the bar after a couple of bulls and we fell into conversation about my late brother while pretending to watch the bulls from the steps.

'The fight itself I did not note. Meeting your dead brother's best friend is always going to overwhelm the day.

'We return to their hotel for further drinks, and then they are marched off for a formal dinner to sample the local wares further while I decide to head out of town to my Domecq-family hotel, the Viña de Alcantara, some time after midnight.'

■ ■ ■ ■ ■

'The next day I wake up in pitch darkness with a sense of dislocation so complete I could not have said my own name. I realise am moving too much, too often, phrases that are true of my alcohol consumption as well. Getting out of bed, I make out the cracks of light around the window and open the shutters on to a little poet's garden bright with morning sun. I wander out into the grounds – a combination of close-cut lawns and free-flowing woods – and then further out into the vineyards belonging to the family which run Tio Pepe: handpicked grapes for brandy to the right, machine-picked rows of vines for wine to the left; sherry being a combination of the two. I slowly prepare myself for that night's fight.

'The programme that night is the bulls of Juan Pedro Domecq facing Morante de la Puebla, El Fandi and José María Manzanares.

'The *cartel* [the line up of matadors to fight that day] begins with the *sevillano* Morante, the divine cape. However, with bulls that so quickly lose their spirit, and Morante's lack of finish with the *muleta*, the audience is left unmoved despite the collectively high blood-alcohol levels. He also shows a liking for what *aficionados* of the bullfight call *adornos*, unnecessary ornamentation to a bullfight like touching the bull's head at the end, something which lowers the dignity of the bull, and thus of the matador who does it. It neither suits Morante's style nor shows his true skills.

'Next comes El Fandi, whom I had seen as a novice in my very first bullfight, a fight which left my family and me in awe of his athleticism and courage for performing the *larga cambiada de portagayola*, "the long exchange at the cage-door".

'What strikes me this time is his gifts with the *banderillas*, he being the only matador other than Padilla that I have seen place them himself this season. Fandi's footwork and body are lighter – he fights the regular bulls, not the heavy ones Padilla fights – and it gives a prettier picture but also a lessened sense of danger. Fandi postures more as well.

'For all this finesse, though, the lack of beauty in his capework diminishes the initial interest he can inspire in the spectator. There is nothing profound in his *toreo*, "bullfighting technique".

'After Fandi comes José María Manzanares, a tall, good-looking matador who is proficient with cape and *muleta*, and yet one whom I cannot bring myself to like, nor can I understand where this dislike comes from. He is perfectly good, and his broad shoulders and placement of arms and legs actually give him a certain swaggering, piratical elegance, but his intensity does not fit him. It is as though it comes from the wrong place within him. He seems to insist on his own greatness too much.

'Next comes Morante's second bull, and here one truly sees the "divine cape" which has made him so notable this season to *aficionado* and critic alike. The power of the *verónica*, the basis of the large cape, is that in the very first moments of the fight there is an apparent conflict between the slow, steady control of the matador's two hands and the rampaging speed of the bull's two horns. The true art of it lies in making the bull seek the lowest point of the cape, stretching his neck down, which slows him further so he does not trip nor catch his horns in the sand of the arena, and then drawing him slowly round. On reflection, its visual power lies in the illusion of causation: it seems as though the matador is leading the bull, making him attain and then maintain the speed the matador dictates with the suppleness – not the strength – of his wrists.

'The basis of the *muleta* is the *natural*, the simplest manoeuvre, performed with left hand, the sword hanging out of the way in the matador's right hand behind his back. However, after the fatigue of twenty minutes charging in the sun and the damage of the pic and the sticks to the bull, the appearance is far more of the matador dragging the great beast round his body, another sort of conflict which transmits another emotion altogether, and one no less strong.

Morante was quite rightly awarded the ear for his performance this time.

'Fandi then performs some quite impressive acrobatics and embellishments in the ring, including caping on his knees, which does not move me at all after Morante's classical purity (a contrast which I had not noticed before but was to witness the next day *in extremis*). He is awarded two ears, which shows exactly what the crowd wants on the Friday night of a boozy *feria*, and it goes further downhill after that with Manzanares.

'I leave the arena and meet up with the hostess of my hotel, María Del Rio. We stroll together through the evening towards a bar where she says she "has family". En route, we encounter the heavy figure of Álvaro Domecq, who seems far more genial and kindly on meeting me with his young niece – and he has watched a bullfight and clearly had some sherry – and we watch laughing as he compresses his stout body into his tiny old car and winds off down the deceptively straight road from the ring. Then we walk onwards through the streets to a small bar packed with men dressed in unusually well-cut suits for Jerez. I am soon introduced to the first round of Domecqs of the evening: Álvaro's first cousins – and fellow breeders – Juan Pedro, Fernando and Salvador Domecq. There I also bump into a friend from Seville, "Tilda of the smiling eyes" – as María O'Neill and I call her – who is there with her brother, and fighting bull breeder, Curro Núñez Benjumea. They are both children of the great Joaquín Núñez del Cuvillo, owner of the first ranch I ever went to, with Nicolás, and met my first ever bull, the pardoned Idílico, who lives there to this day.

'Everyone is talking rapidly, some in Spanish, some in English: I am writing a book, I must meet Juan Pedro who is writing a book (and happens to be responsible for about 80 per cent of the fighting cattle DNA in existence in Spain), and his cousin's brother's wife's cousin José is … and so on. It is an impossible density of information and I realise that rather than try to conduct any form of interview, I should save up introductions for future research in more depth, a policy which serves me well. I will end up in the ring with many of their cattle myself within twelve months.

'Soon the sherry begins to turn sour in our mouths and hunger is the overwhelming urge, so María and I move on to to the grand Gonzalez Byass *caseta* in the *feria*, where we are joined by María's brother, Gonzalo, a wild thing revelling in his youth with vicious pleasure, and another whole round of Domecqs whose first names are exact replicas of their parents'.

'However, singularly the most interesting conversationalist there in a mixture of his bad English and my bad Spanish is the grandson of the greatest matador of all time, Juan Belmonte. We become immersed in a long argument about the virtues of stillness in the bullfight – an innovation of his grandfather taken to its logical and near-lethal conclusion by José Tomás, whom I have still yet to see. We speak late into the night about the various conflicts inherent in the bullfight and what feelings they transmit to the audience – stillness versus speed, force versus object, strength versus skill – and I briefly realise that no one has talked to me in far too long about the bull and what he feels. I feel myself slipping into the taurine Spanish night. I end it by dancing what I think is flamenco in a small *caseta* accompanied by the clapping hands of my new friends.'

13

El derechazo

The matador takes sword and *muleta* into his right hand, placing the handle halfway along the stick supporting the *muleta*, the blade at an angle, the point into the fabric, doubling its size, and calls the bull into the simplest pass of all.

The next day I joined my photographer Nicolás Haro and his wife Carla at her family's house in the botanical gardens down the road in Sanlúcar de Barrameda. I had bought us three tickets to see the fight that night in Jerez, in a billing which included El Cid, my friend Padilla – the Cyclone of Jerez – and the legendary José Tomás, all against the bulls of my friend Tilda's father, Joaquín Núñez del Cuvillo.

Carla's mother, Gerarda de Orléans-Borbón, who introduced me to Nicolás, had been a regular attendee at bullfights in her youth. In fact, her grandfather built the bullring in Sanlúcar, but had gone off the bullfights out of a particular sympathy for the bull. Geri described to me how, after a simple operation on her back in an English hospital, she contracted the bacterium MRSA in its necrotising fasciitis form, the 'flesh-eating bug' of newspaper horror stories. Not only did it very nearly kill her, it caused her the most agonising pain. She survived, but says that to now see the bull with the sword in its back, as the *banderilleros* flash their capes in front of it to make it turn so that the blade will sever a major blood vessel within and hasten its death, was now almost unbearable for her. It is perhaps the strongest and most truthful argument against bullfighting I have yet heard because of its undeniable purity of motivation – sympathy.

On arrival, Nicolás, Carla and I found Jerez full, far fuller than the *feria* had made it on any other day, and all the people in the streets were clutching cushions for the bullring. The draw of Tomás in the town was overwhelming, as the sevenfold increase in ticket prices indicated it would be. Three weeks before the fight I had been unable to buy tickets at all, and had had to buy them on resale from a website, and even then it was still a fortnight's salary (if my book advance counts as a year's) for bad tickets high up in the sun in a provincial ring. Those close to the action in the shade were changing hands for a thousand euros each.

All this was for a matador I had never seen fight, not even on television. In fact, I try not to watch bullfighting on television, as without the ambience of the arena it really does just look like a man goading a dumb beast into charging him. Unless you can feel the physical threat of the bull, which does not exist on screen (who would stand and watch the events in the street that are depicted so glibly in most Hollywood movies), all one sees is the control of the situation the matador exerts. However, Tomás has refused to fight in a televised corrida since March 2000. Which, of course, only serves to increase his mystique. As do his other actions, like fighting in small rings because only they will give him the proportion of the box-office he regards as fair. So, in the end, he takes far less money than he could, turning down hundreds of thousands of euros for one afternoon in Madrid, because he believed it was worth more. Just as he returned his Gold Medal for Fine Arts to the King – one of only four ever given to matadors – because he thought the next matador to receive it, Francisco Rivera Ordóñez, was not good enough and was given it for reasons of favouritism and nepotism (I shall go into this more later).

However, what I had heard about him fighting was almost

unbelievable. He divided the *aficionados*, which is not hard – these people with their tribal loyalties love division almost as much as they love bullfighting – but the reason I had most often heard is that he fights with *'demasiado sangre'*, 'too much blood', and by blood, they mean his own. Even a cursory glance through the press clippings of his bullfights shows his face and body drenched in blood like something from a Jacobean tragedy. I understand how those, especially in Madrid, who 'aestheticise' the bullfight don't like to be confronted with such *memento mori*, such visible reminders that their heroes are mortal.

But suddenly and for no stated reason, at the height of his powers at twenty-six years old, Tomás retired from both bull-fighting and public life (the latter being a small change, as he famously shunned publicity). Then, just as suddenly, he reap-peared in Barcelona five years later in 2007, saying only that 'living without bullfighting is not living at all', and causing that stadium's first sell-out in decades.

And his return heralded a return to a form if anything more dangerous. When he fought in the Feria de Jerez in 2008 with the same bulls I was to see exactly one year later, he nearly died when the tapering horn of the bull entered his neck deep enough to leave a wound larger than the orbit of his eye, caus-ing lacerations to his jugular. And yet still he fought on oblivi-ous, killing the bull and saluting the crowd with an ear before going to the infirmary. He returned to take two more ears from the second bull.

As a phenomenon, the general view is that he is either a genius or a holy fool. His first manager, the former *banderillero* Antonio Corbacho, was said to have passed on his fascination with bushido, 'the way of the samurai', to the young Tomás, who took its principles to heart, especially that of facing death with honour to the point of holding it in contempt or simply ignoring it. We would see.

As Nicolás, Carla and I entered the bullring, we said a brief hello to Padilla, but his focus was intense. This was the town of his birth and he was fighting on a ticket with a matador whom the entire taurine world holds in awe if not always respect. We took our seats, which were in the burning sun, despite the price of the tickets, and settled in to watch Padilla fight first, as the most senior bullfighter (he became a full matador in 1994, Tomás in 1995 and El Cid in 2000.

Padilla opened in classic Padilla style, caping on both knees, placing his own *banderillas*, and yet the crowd gave their local boy only light applause, everyone waiting with baited breath for Tomás, for the myth to be made flesh.

And my God it was. He opened the caping with the fresh galloping bull with six *verónicas* on one knee, immediately outdoing Padilla's showier *largas cambiadas de rodillas*, 'long exchanges of the knees', with their classicism. This was quickly reflected by the crowd's *olés*, which as always began on the second pass (it is the series that is congratulated, not the first pass, which may be accidental), and increased in volume until he performed a *remate* which turned and stopped the bull in its tracks for the finale, eliciting immediate applause.

Then, after the first lance wound by the picador, Tomás took the bull away from the horse for a *quite*, a series of passes between pics, in the centre of the ring. Here he performed five *chicuelinas* and his 'art' began fully to show. Perhaps two inches shorter than my six foot (I know because I literally bumped into him once at Barcelona airport), he is almost painfully thin and narrow-boned, making him appear taller than he is without the effect of dwarfing the bull, as happens with larger fighters. So the turning on the spot required by the *chicuelina*, in which half the cape is flapped to the bull and then the body rotates as the bull passes, appears to draw cape and bull into a terrifying collapsing orbit timed so the horns brush the cape at exactly the moment it encases the body, rendering it immobile.

After this series, the crowd reached the crescendo of *olés* on their feet, so their applause for the *remate* which stopped the bull – a *revolera* with the cape spinning round his waist at a perfect horizontal – was a ready-made standing ovation.

However, it is as we move to the final act of the drama, to the *muleta*, that I really see why people describe him as the 'phenomenon' and themselves as 'Tomásistas'. He begins with a manoeuvre I have never seen, the *estatuari*, the 'statuary' (as in the art of making statues).

Standing in profile to the bull with his feet together, the sword held directly out in front of him horizontally, with the *muleta* hanging down from it, he glances sideways at the bull some twenty yards away. He gives the *muleta* a small shake, and the bull, having decided the *muleta* is a threat, commits to a charge at a full gallop. Tomás then does not move again, trusting that the bull has decided the *muleta* – one of whose edges flows down along his legs – is the real target. Not looking at the animal, he literally is a statue as it hits the yielding cloth and passes harmlessly through. Bewildered, the bull turns on the other side and, now ten yards away, stares at the man and the cloth. Tomás shakes again, and this time it charges harder and faster, twisting its head in the cloth, seeking to destroy its opponent, the movement putting its own flanks out of alignment so its hindquarters smash into Tomás's legs, knocking his feet apart. This he corrects with a small shuffle as the bull turns again, this time seven yards away. He sends a thrill of movement through the *muleta* and the bull charges again, this time rearing its head upwards as it passes through, rather than side to side as before. It is trying to find the main body of the enemy that is mocking it with this lure. Again Tomás does not move an inch, waiting for the bull to turn, which it does. He remains still for a second longer this time – the bull is breathless from the great efforts involved in accelerating its muscular bulk to its top speed.

Then he moves the *muleta* again, and again the bull comes

through, rearing, both forehooves coming three feet off the ground. As it turns this time, Tomás shuffles forward to find the right place to cite it from, because now it is a mere three feet from him. As the bull reaches the cloth, he lets the fabric fall from the sword entirely into his left hand, so it goes down to the ground, forcing the bull to foreshorten its charge and stop while turning, allowing him to merely stand and stare at it for a moment, before he calmly walks away to allow the bull to catch its breath.

He begins again a few moments later and enters into a series of passes with the *muleta* in the left hand, sword in the right behind his back, which are so classic in their form, so pure, so wounding in their seriousness – and I know that this will never come across in prose, but their *sadness* – that the three of us are on our feet applauding at the end of each series with the rest of the crowd. Nicolás, who dislikes bullfighting, who adopts stray dogs and cats, along with his wife Carla, who is so gentle and humane, who studied poetry and the arts at university in England and America and has three beautiful children; there is not one of us who is not bewitched by this man's artistry and courage.

Although courage is not the word for what he does, nor is contempt for death. As he fights he has a studied seriousness, a focus, which is perfectly weighted for the task at hand because it is on the task, not on its possible repercussions. When the pass calls for his focus to be on the *muleta*, he focuses on the *muleta*, not on the bull galloping towards him. Only when the bull is almost touching the *muleta* does he widen his gaze to the two to achieve *templar*, the matching of one's own rhythm to the bull's so it never reaches the elusive cloth; but, equally, the cloth never goes so far in front of the bull that it seeks another target.

However, it is not just in his actions that Tomás achieves a perfection of technique (and I do mean to say perfection, this is not hyperbole), but in his 'being'. He is not a handsome man, he is too thin and spindly, and yet the suit of lights with its braided shoulders and short jacket gives the rotation of his torso above his waist an elegance of line which other matadors with more athletic proportions lack. The long thin legs are grounded in feet perfectly held together or angled, dancer-like, against each other. The grace is not sexual – there is nothing homoerotic here – but the aesthetics of a perfect form fitting function. He does not have the body of a sportsman or a fighter, because you do not fight bulls (although in English I have to use that verb, in Spanish the verb is *torear*, which simply has no translation because we do not do it). He has the body of a man trying to create the greatest elegance possible with the bull, the cape and his own body, a shifting tableau designed to strike the part of the mind which perceives beauty just as the other part which recognises risk adds a sort of background music of danger.

In fact, in order to describe properly what he does so well, one really has to describe what he doesn't do. For example, the aesthetic of the bullfighter is largely based on being upright and rigid. It shows pride and immovability in the face of the massive streak of darkness that is the charging bull. However, so many bullfighters achieve it by locking their joints, by overdoing it, by 'insisting' on themselves, as I have written before. Tomás just *is* upright. He has good posture, however, his muscles are loose, his physique relaxed, a dancer at rest trailing a cloth in the dust to draw pretty geometrical shapes. Meanwhile, swirling around him, occasionally knocking into him, is a 1,212lb bull moving at a gallop, frantically trying to find him, kill him, take out the threat, destroy the frustration.

And these are not the short series of passes I saw in Seville, these are nine or ten passes long, every single time the horns and body of the bull grazing across his body, so that his lavender and gold suit of lights becomes redder and redder from the blood of the bull. In fact, so precise is his passing of the bull that in any other circumstance it would be obscene, for when it passes him, the bull brushes past his crotch, so that the genital area of his suit is black and sodden with bull's blood, and yet there is nothing ridiculous or grotesque about this. As an old drama teacher used to say to me, 'Anything, no matter how laughable, that can be justified, can be done or said on stage. You just have to *earn it!*' Maybe, one day, he will see José Tomás and smile at his own wisdom.

Back in the ring, Tomás lines up the bull and flies over the horns with his sword, totally disregarding his own safety. Although people always talk of the perfect kill as a matador going over the horns, there is always a point at which he must deviate to the side to avoid the rising horn-points as the bull realises something deadly is now looming over it and stabbing it between the shoulder blades. However, Tomás, by resting his entire weight on his sword through his wrist, allows his entire body to pass between the horns, and then uses the bull's reflex to rear upwards to push him back out from between the horns. Incredibly, he finds safety through a total and complete disregard for his own life, where even a momentary hesitation or weakness would leave him gravely injured.

Now I understood what people were talking about. *Now* I saw what they meant when some said he was the best that had ever lived. They weren't claiming they had watched three centuries of bullfighting on foot, or even one century of bullfighting for art, they were saying that when you watch Tomás fight you have the sense that you simply couldn't imagine anything better, that there simply couldn't be anything better.

Tomás took two ears, but we continued to wave our scraps of programmes – we had no white handkerchiefs – with the rest of the crowd to demand the tail for a full minute afterwards. It was not given.

El Cid fought the next bull and I hear he won an ear. The

trouble is, that is not what I remember, nor do Nicolás and Carla, because all throughout his fight we were talking about Tomás: about the closeness of the bull, the elegance of the line, the perfection of the style, the fact that there was simply no denying it – it was art. Cruelty was forgotten, hesitation and self-doubt had equally flown out the window. We were besotted. And not as part of some general crowd hysteria or bloodlust. Far from it, this was three people trying to talk over one another about what they had seen as *individuals*, felt as individuals, and adored as individuals.

When Padilla, whom we knew, returned to the ring, we did look up from our haze and it was then we saw the terrible consequence of incomparable greatness on those around it. When he had left the ring after the first bull, it was clear Padilla felt unhappy, perhaps even a little betrayed by the people, *his* people. However, he had known they were there for Tomás and hadn't minded, but when he saw how much they adored this man from Madrid it hurt. Then when they gave an ear to El Cid, who is from Seville, Padilla decided to do what he did best: defy death.

There is something awful in watching a friend twist his pride and his undeniably great courage into a single corrupted knot and risk his life out of something as small-minded as jealousy. Padilla went into the ring to impress, and in doing so, and in contrast to the images of Tomás still replaying in my mind's eye, he came across as reckless and artless. He brought the bull so close to his body that it was constantly buffeting him. On any other occasion one might have wondered at the incredible skill that allowed him to make the horns merely graze his body rather than penetrate, but there was no beauty in the movements, and there was only petty ugliness in the motives. Every audience member seemed to be thinking the same thing simultaneously: 'Padilla, we forgot about Padilla!' And he took his revenge on our nerves, forcing us to the edge of our seats with his ludicrously dangerous caping, staring up at the crowd rather than at the bull with accusing eyes, the jilted lover standing at the cliff's edge.

For fifteen terrible minutes he fought a bull in the English sense of the word, giving it an even chance, tearing the fabric of his jacket in a dozen places, blood running from small cuts on his legs and torso, and miraculously not being seriously injured. And this made it worse, because he *is* capable of fighting that close, as close as Tomás, closer perhaps. However, Padilla is a man without a strong concept of art, and without anything but the rough-hewn natural elegance of the gifted craftsman. What was more, he was now being given sympathy and solace where he wanted only accolade. One man in the crowd shouted at him, '*¡No! ¡Basta!*' ('No! Enough!')

To which he snarled back, '*¡Soy Padilla!*' ('I am Padilla!')

He killed furiously and well and was given an ear, one felt, almost as a sop to his vanity. He took it with a look of helpless rage, lapping the ring in a perfunctory manner, not even looking up as he passed us.

Despite this, as Padilla slipped out of the ring, everyone forgot their guilt and their allegiances and once again stared at the Maestro, wondering how he would top his previous performance.

This bull came in with a reluctance to charge which led Tomás to abandon his pre-picador caping, and I leant forward, wondering how this artist would deal with the eternal problem of a bad bull. Between the two pics the bull received, Tomás again tried to display his skill with the large cape with *chicuelinas*, but the bull was too easily distracted. Certain members of the crowd started to whistle and call out '*Es un toro manso*', literally 'It is a tame bull'. The whistling signifying that they wanted the bull replaced; after all, the Maestro was clearly on incredible form and the crowd had spent a fortune on their tickets (Jerez has the highest unemployment of a city its size in all Europe).

Although the matador never himself signals directly that he is unhappy with a bull, for that would undermine the symbolic authority of the president, I have many times seen them spit, swear, shake their heads, stare at the ground or the heavens, and generally make it pretty damned clear that they are unhappy with a bull. Whether they want to actually change it, or are just setting up an excuse in case they fail to fight it well, I do not know. (How many times had I walked off stage after a performance probably as good as any other, met a friend round the corner in the pub, and opened with the line, 'What a terrible night!')

However, Tomás did none of these things. Even as he performed the flawed *quite* – taking the bull from the horse after the first pic, attempting the *chicuelinas*, completing the series, returning the bull for the second and final pic – he seemed to be evaluating and calculating. He kept changing position, finding the bull's preference to charge threats appearing in the left side of its field of vision. He would wait patiently for the crowd to quiet down so the bull was drawn to him as the sole threat present in its mind. And he gave the bull time to breathe and relax, so that when it did finally commit to the charge, it had the wind and the will to do so fully.

Even after his assistants placed the *banderillas*, he continued in this task, showing a knowledge of the bull and a patience that I had never seen in the ring before. The amazing thing was how unpredictable the bull's behaviour was as he did this – forcing Tomás to get close before it charged, and then leaping forwards without warning, hooking its horns from side to side. And yet his calm never slipped, and his concentration never wavered. In fact, he seemed to almost be downplaying the danger and the drama other matadors heighten and boast of, unpicking the problem with a steady hand, utterly ignoring the danger the bull presented, but never ignoring the bull itself. In fact, one could say that while his focus was entirely on the bull, his intent was not, it was on what he could make of the bull. This was an artist working with difficult materials in the shadow of death, and ignoring it, focusing merely on the work.

The stopping and starting nature of this sort of caping removed the flow of the earlier bull, but it was fascinating to watch, like seeing a master painting over a moth-eaten canvas, riddled with holes. And yet there were moments, great long series of passes of eight or nine *naturales* with the left hand, slow and deep and sad and profound.

And then, to show the crowd that this was still a lethal art-form he was working in, Tomás moved in front of this complicated, unpredictable bull so that he was less than three feet away and erected the cape sideways from his body, like the *estatuario* but facing the bull rather than in profile, and performed the terrifying trademark of his slain hero Manolete: the *manoletina*.

The bull charged and reared haphazardly through, again and again and again, and yet Tomás barely shifted his feet and was barely more than a few inches from the bull's horns, but was not touched by it once, despite the fact that he appeared not even to look at the bull. It was mastery: pure, clean and utterly honest. He killed with exactly the same cleanliness, and again, despite the paucity of the bull for fighting purposes, was awarded both ears of the bull.

And again, I do not remember what El Cid did, but he managed to get two ears from a crowd revelling in the great feast of art and danger they had dined upon. He and Tomás were hoisted on to the shoulders of the crowd, along with the farm manager from the ranch of Núñez del Cuvillo, and the president ordered the main gate opened so they could leave the ring victoriously.

We left, ecstatic, enthralled and exhausted, into the night, to drink with Nicolás's crazy friends in Sanlúcar and talk about 'the bulls, the bulls!' And I had forgotten about Padilla, my friend, and his embarrassment, and I had forgotten about the suffering of the bulls. For that is the conjuring trick great drama performs: it makes you identify with the protagonist, and to hell with everyone else. Which is fine when you deal in fictions, but what is it when the stakes are real?

14

El pase de pecho

He rounds off his series of passes by turning his back to the bull, trailing the sword-widened *muleta* behind him, and when it charges, he draws the bull round and past him, its head rearing at the head past his *pecho*, his 'chest'.

Ernest Hemingway is without doubt the greatest writer in English on bullfighting as it was in the early twentieth century. Hemingway was also a man whose life and literature resemble his subject matter in their odd combination of courage and deceit, of truth and its avoidance. The heart of bullfighting is tricking the bull into charging the cloth rather than the man, the lure rather than the predator. Even beyond that, though, it is born of the sort of pride that encourages lies. Bullfighters are among the bravest men I know, and yet sometimes even they exaggerate the dangers, poeticise the blood. Like the matador who claimed to me that a bull he killed was 1,550lb, when I know it was only 1,400. All I could think as we spoke was why he needed to add that extra ten per cent or so, when it was already one third larger than those killed by other *toreros*.

Hemingway was a man of astonishing literary skill, with an impressive war record and physical prowess, and yet he was riddled with insecurities – social, sexual, intellectual and artistic – which no number of wives, Nobel prizes or lion hunts in Africa could hope to quiet. So it should be no surprise that he wrote his first detailed account of a bullfight in April 1923, without ever having seen one.

Europe at the time had reopened its doors after the Great War, and cash-rich Americans flocked over to see what had survived the conflict and to admire what was left of the history. The twenty-two-year-old Hemingway, newly wed and with an infant son, had arrived in Paris as a foreign correspondent in 1921 for the *Toronto Star*, although he had already made up his mind to become a 'writer' rather than a journalist. It was there that he met his artistic mentors, like the poet Ezra Pound, who would help him refine an already economical use of words learnt in journalism, resulting in a style he used so well at the beginning, and unwittingly parodied so terribly later on.

(I remember pasted to the wall of the philosophy faculty at Oxford were a series of 'in the style of' answers to the immortal question, 'Why did the chicken cross the road?' Some were ineffective in-jokes, such as the one attributed to the Parisian existentialist Jean-Paul Sartre: 'In order to act in good faith and be true to itself, the chicken found it necessary to cross the road.' The one for Hemingway was genuinely inspired. It read merely: 'To die. In the rain.')

The other defining feature of Hemingway's writing, which also betrayed him – or was betrayed by him – in later life, was an aesthetic notion he learnt as an ambulanceman on the Western front, a notion he described as 'grace under pressure'. This is the ability of certain unusual people to act with almost inhuman integrity and courage in the face of the sort of danger that makes other men break, and the tragic heroic beauty that is associated with witnessing such events.

This can have a simplistic, Hollywood leading man connotation, but anyone who has read Hemingway at his best, and understands what he witnessed in the Great War, realises that this idea goes much deeper. For example, on the day of his arrival in the theatre of operations, aged eighteen, a dynamite factory staffed entirely by women had exploded and Hemingway was part of the team assigned the task of picking up the bodies, or rather their constituent parts. The images with which he was left he described with a touching and horrifying exactitude in the story 'A Natural History of the Dead'. He found it 'amazing that the human body should be blown into pieces which exploded along no anatomical lines, but rather divided as capriciously as the fragmentation in the burst of a high explosive shell'.

His greatest mentor during his time in Paris was the modernist writer Gertrude Stein. It was she who steered him on to the great French and Russian novelists, which made up for his lack of university education. She also saw the potential in Hemingway's concept of 'grace under pressure' and told him he should go to Pamplona, where the locals run with the bulls through the streets in the morning, then watch their favourite matadors dance with them and dispatch them in the evening.

So Hemingway drove down from Paris in June 1923 and entered the anarchic celebrations of the Feria de San Fermín, where wine, urine and blood flowed freely in the streets, and you started drinking the moment you woke in the morning, sitting in bars watching those who would brave the streets to run in among the half-dozen bulls and their accompanying half-dozen steers, as they stampeded the half-mile from the old train station to the bullring.

Hemingway was entranced by what he saw – booze and unsophisticated excess combined with rural masculinity and courage. Then he saw the *corridas* and it was then that he finally saw the matadors fight, standing their ground and making the classical manoeuvres in carefully structured series with the intention of moving the emotions of an audience, all this *despite* the half-ton animal trying to kill them as they did it.

It was two years later in Pamplona that one bullfighter in particular struck him as exceptional. Niño de la Palma had become a full matador – taken his *alternativa* as they say – only a few weeks before in Seville. Hemingway befriended him and followed him to Madrid, where he was to have his status as a matador confirmed in Spain's capital city, fighting on the same *cartel*, 'billing', as the then thirty-three-year-old Juan Belmonte. He described the fight in a letter to Stein in Paris:

> He did everything Belmonte did and did it better – kidding him – all the adornos and desplantes and all. Then he stepped out all by himself without any tricks, suave, templando with the cape and smooth and slow – splendid banderilleros and started with 5 Naturales with the muleta – beautiful, complete faena all linked up and then killed perfectly.

Hemingway's first novel, *The Sun Also Rises* (published under the draft title *Fiesta* in the UK), was originally written as a short story about that *feria* in Pamplona under the real name of Niño de la Palma, Cayetano Ordóñez, and concerned that 'lost weekend' in which Hemingway facilitated the young matador's love affair with Lady Duff Twysden, to the fury of one of his enamoured friends. In the finished, fictionalised version she became Lady Brett Ashley, and Cayetano, who was from Ronda, was renamed after that city's most famous matador, Pedro Romero.

Cayetano didn't go on to flourish in the way so many expected after that first year, because, as Hemingway put it in *Death in the Afternoon*:

> He was gored severely and painfully in the thigh, very near the femoral artery. That was the end of him … The next year … his actions in the ring were a series of disasters. He could hardly look at a bull. His fright as he had to go in to kill was painful to see and he spent the whole season assassinating bulls in the way that offered him least danger … It was the most shameful season any matador had ever had up until that year in bullfighting.

What is easy to forget is that recuperation from even a near fatal wound nowadays is expedited by drugs countering infection, pain, consciousness and memory itself in such a way that the psychological damage is minimised, and even then many are cursed with the effects of post-traumatic stress disorder. To lie sweating in a 1920s Spanish hospital for weeks with only morphine, ether and cheap brandy to addle your brain, while gangrene-causing bacilli and white blood cells war across your body, generating febrile nightmares of being swept into the air by a malicious boulder of darkness intent on your destruction: that is the true testing of the mettle of a matador.

Despite his fall from grace, Cayetano remained a well-known matador and breeder of bulls. And, as is the way of such things, his sons followed him into bullfighting, and one son, Antonio Ordóñez, not only displayed the promise of the father, but realised it in its fullness. Antonio was also married to the younger sister of the matador Luis Miguel Dominguín.

Luis Miguel González Lucas, 'Dominguín', was a matador who had divided the *afición* where Antonio would unify it. His father was a famous matador of the era of Belmonte and Joselito, Domingo González Mateos, who fought under the name Domingo Dominguín. All three of his matador sons took their father's name in the ring but it was Luis Miguel Dominguín who became the star, through naked ambition and an undeniable talent which some say pressured Manolete into the reckless fighting that led to his death in 1947 (at which Dominguín was present). Two years later, in a gesture shocking in its arrogance, he crowned himself 'number one' with a raised finger in Las Ventas in Madrid. There was no one who denied his talent, but his showy style and use of various impressive tricks in the ring lost him many fans, Hemingway included.

His life outside the ring was no less vibrant, maintaining close friendships with notables of the time, including both Franco and Picasso, despite the fact that the former had declared the latter an enemy of the state. However, the only thing that ever eclipsed his bullfighting fame was his romantic life, in which he was linked to actresses from Lauren Bacall to Brigitte Bardot, Zsa Zsa Gabor to Ava Gardner. It was Hemingway who introduced him to Gardner in 1953, while she was filming *The Barefoot Contessa*. Gardner was at the height of her powers at the time, had just been nominated for an Oscar, and was two years into an over-publicised firefight of a marriage to Frank Sinatra.

According to famous anecdote, having lured Gardner into bed, DomInguín got up, dressed and moved towards the door. Gardner asked him where he thought he was going, to which he answered, 'Where am I going? To tell everyone!'

There is also a story about the time Sinatra came to Spain to get Gardner back, accompanied by a pair of his 'Italian-American friends'. Even then there were rumours that Sinatra used his Mafia connections to get his own way, with Hearst newspapers running the story that the Chicago boss 'Sam the Cigar' got Sinatra out of his binding contract with the Dorsey Band by putting a revolver to band-leader Tommy Dorsey's head and offering him a choice between giving up Sinatra or his brains. The incident even came up in the film *The Godfather*, with Sinatra thinly disguised under the name Johnny Fontane.

Sinatra found out where DomInguín would be fighting one day, and followed him to a taurine bar after a successful *corrida*. Flanked by his *soldatos*, Sinatra approached the Maestro, who was sitting, elegantly dressed, with a glass of sherry. Sinatra said, 'Do you know who I am?'

DomInguín looked at Sinatra and the two men behind him, and then stood up, the world's tallest matador facing its shortest crooner.

'Yes, Mr Sinatra, I know exactly who you are. In this place, you are no one.'

As he said this, half a dozen of the Maestro's team who were sitting drinking at the bar also stood up, each with a knife on their belt as was the way with such men in those days, and each with the violent confidence of having already faced death that day, survived, and had a couple of strong drinks after.

Sinatra and his men left in silence. To quote *The Godfather*, a matador 'ain't no bandleader'. Of course, the truth of this story is unconfirmable.

Dominguín, having killed 2,300 bulls and become a millionaire several times over, retired in 1955 aged twenty-nine and married the film actress and former Miss Italy, Lucia Bosé. However, when in 1958 people were talking of his brother-in-law Antonio Ordóñez as perhaps the greatest matador since Belmonte, and at least since Manolete, Dominguín declared his intention to re-enter the ring the next season to teach Spain a lesson: he, Dominguín, had retired by choice rather than necessity and could still outfight any young pretender to the throne.

This incendiary combination of rivalry, family, fame and bullfighting had such potential for 'grace under pressure' that *Life* magazine commissioned Hemingway to follow the two matadors around Spain and write about their duel in the rings, sometimes with a third matador present, sometimes just the two going *mano a mano* with three bulls each.

The magazine had asked Hemingway for 4,000 words, but through a combination of intense inspiration and failing powers to edit his own output he wrote more than twenty-seven times that. In the end, they published 30,000 words in three instalments in 1960, and a longer version was published posthumously as the book *The Dangerous Summer* in 1985.

Hemingway followed the consensus in stating that Antonio Ordóñez was the better matador, both in the technicalities and in the overall style, which was deeply classical. Not that both didn't perform brilliantly; for example, in their *mano a mano* in Málaga – always an important ring – they were awarded ten out of twelve possible ears, along with four tails and two hooves. Of course, both matadors were gored as a result of the contest, Dominguín almost fatally so.

Hemingway´s clear favouring of Ordóñez, however, was as much to do with his adoration of the young matador – which at times borders on the homoerotic in his writing – as it was the younger man's superior *toreo*. There is also a clear masculine rivalry with the prouder and older Dominguín, a challenge to Hemingway's ego which he couldn't defuse by playing the patrician.

After publication, Dominguín remarked that Hemingway was 'a commonplace bore … a crude and vulgar man' who 'knew nothing about fighting bulls'. One assumes that this was not a view he held when he stayed with Hemingway in Cuba in the early 1950s. Antonio Ordóñez, on the other hand, claimed his literary patron was more knowledgeable about bullfighting than any other non-Spaniard and most Spaniards too. The truth, in my opinion and those of most *aficionados* who have read him, lies somewhere in between. He claimed more than he knew but knew a great deal, was partial to those whom he liked, or felt he should like, and described it all with the literary voice of an angel. As another famous American *aficionado*, Orson Welles, remarked about Hemingway in an interview on the BBC:

> He was a very close friend of mine … but we never discussed bullfighting because we – except on the subject of Ordóñez – we disagreed profoundly on too many points and he thought he invented it, you know. He really did think he invented it. Maybe he did.

And although this last was delivered tongue-in-cheek, since the man who made *Citizen Kane* had actually trained as a bullfighter in Seville for four months, fighting in pay-as-you-go *corridas* under the name El Americano (I have no idea how large the bulls would have been), I think we can take his overall statement as having some weight.

■ ■ ■ ■ ■

Antonio Ordóñez and Hemingway remained close friends until the writer's suicide in 1961 (Orson Welles was also a close friend of Antonio). Antonio's daughter Carmen, a woman of strident beauty and emotion, married the twenty-four-year-old matador Francisco Rivera, 'Paquirri', when she was only seventeen, only to divorce him on their fourth wedding anniversary. Paquirri's star went on to rise and be snuffed out while still in the ascendant by the bull Avispado in 1984.

The couple had two sons who fulfil the tragic-heroic Spanish ideal of the bullfighter to the point of stereotype. Having suffered first their parents' divorce when young, and lost their father to the bulls not long after, they were sent by their mother to be educated in North America in the hope that they would avoid a similar fate. Francisco Rivera Ordóñez returned first, training with his grandfather, who became his first manager. Fran, an impossibly good-looking young matador, soon married the daughter and heir of the largest landowner in Spain, the Duchess of Alba, a title which can descend in the female line (although I have no idea about her other seven duchies, eighteen marquessates and God knows how many others). They had a daughter, Cayetana.

In 2002 Antonio Ordóñez died, a few weeks later Fran divorced his wife, and a few weeks after that, so did his younger brother Cayetano. Carmen Ordóñez, whose life had always been both unhappy and unstable – and publicly so, not least because of her endless charitable work with the poor of Triana, where she still has a status second only to the Madonna – went into a steep decline, frequently ending up in various rehab clinics until she died of a heart attack two years later, aged forty-nine. A few weeks after that, her other son, Cayetano, left his home in Los Angeles, where he had studied media and film, and came back to Spain, in order to become a matador as well.

With that background, and the modern Spanish media, it is little wonder that the spotlight shines so brightly on these matador brothers as to obscure the details. Their skill in the ring, and the horrors they have undergone within it and beyond, are either unheathily inflated, or totally ignored by those who would focus on the fact that both currently date former Miss Spains and that Cayetano – if anything better-looking than his brother – is the face of Armani in Spain. As a result, their fame has spread far beyond Spain, and before I saw either in the ring I had seen the *60 Minutes* documentary about them called 'Blood Brothers' on CBS.

So when *The Times* commissioned me for a short interview with a matador – any matador – in their 'A Life In The Day' slot, which has covered everyone from Nelson Mandela to Muhammad Ali, I got in touch with Cayetano's press people and lined up an interview to coincide with his fight in Sanlúcar de Barrameda. When Nicolás and I set off from the Botanical Gardens on one of his ageing BMW motorbikes (he won't enter the ring with a bull, but he rides like a maniac), I knew more than was normal about the subject of the interview and knew exactly how I wanted the interview to go.

We arrived at a four-star concrete bunker of a hotel in the centre of town, where Cayetano had taken a room for the day, and were met in the lobby by his *mozo de espadas*, his manager and other members of his team. I left Nicolás to explain what I was doing in Spain as a small crowd gathered in the lobby, expecting, like me, the arrival of the Killer.

When he arrived, with a beaming smile and vigorous handshake, I was struck by two things. The first was that he was shorter than I expected – average height by Spanish standards, but still shorter than his appearance in the ring and on television had led me to believe – and that he was very, very good at dealing with journalists.

'This place is crowded, my friend, shall we move out to the swimming pool to talk?' he suggested in English, with the accent of California. Which we did, and I laid out my dictaphone and pad as Nicolás – playing his role with aplomb – explained in Spanish to Cayetano and his people that I was actually in Spain to write a book rather than 'mere journalism' and had faced the fighting cattle on ranches, including Saltillo, which raised even Cayetano's eyebrows.

'You have faced Saltillo?' he asked, and when I nodded, he continued, 'How did you find them?'

'Difficult.' He laughed at this.

'Every bullfighter must find the right bull for him. Your friend Padilla – I admire him for what he does, but what he does is fight Miuras, like your Saltillos. For me, it is the bulls of Domecq, especially of Fernando Domecq.'

I explained that I had met Fernando in Jerez, and his extremely pretty daughter María. He smiled at this.

'Yes, she is, isn't she? You know, you remind me of a story my grandfather Antonio once told me. He had a friend who was a philosopher and he wanted to get into the ring to face the fighting cattle for the experience, like you. My grandfather arranged it at his farm, a *tentadero*, and was very impressed that the philosopher seemed so fearless as he watched the cow he was going to face attack the padded horse, the fighters, the walls, everything. Then it came to his turn to enter and he turned to my grandfather and said, "So where's the padding?" "The what?" said my grandfather. "You know, the body armour you wear to go in." "*Hombre*, you go in as you are." At this the philosopher turned pale and started to sweat, then he said, "No, that will not be possible. I wish to have the experience so that I can write about it. I have to be alive to write!" You did well, Alex.'

From there we segued into the interview, and I found him helpful, intelligent, fluent and open. I explained that I felt like a fool asking him his daily routine when what defined him was the work in the ring – and the work his forebears had done and suffered to be done to them in the ring – but if Mandela and Ali could handle it, I guess he could too. He took it in his stride speaking of training the body and the mind – especially the mind – for what to expect from a bull, and then how to craft that expectation into a form that fits the performance the matador might wish to give. He also dwelt at length – far greater length than *The Times* required – on the sensations the bull induced, of the warmth a great bull could inspire in him, of his sadness at killing.

'It is like a friend at that point. You do not want to kill it, but you have to, and that is your tragedy, your sadness. But it is *your* bull, only you can deliver death to it, for only you have risked your life to face it. And then, that, the moment of the kill, is the most important moment of all. For fifteen minutes the bull has been charging you, and now you must charge it with the sword. This is the only moment the matador himself charges the bull.'

I looked at my watch then and realised that we had been talking for over two hours, and that he was already late to dress for the fight. I apologised for keeping him for so long – his manager and *mozo* were pacing up and down nearby, neither following a word of our English therefore totally unable to steer the interview as they would normally – and as we said goodbye he turned back.

'Thank you for the interview, it was good. Are you coming to see the fight?'

I replied that we had tickets.

'No, you must see it properly, you must come with me in the *callejón*, then you will really feel the fight. See you at the *plaza*.'

So, an hour or so later, Nicolás and I went to the ring on his motorcycle, his wife Carla and other friends of hers going separately to enter the family box next to the president's (her great-grandfather had built the ring). The crowd outside the ring was three times what I expected, one third being people with tickets, the other two-thirds being the screaming young female fans of Cayetano. José Tomás may draw the *afición*, but the women of Spain are firmly in the hands of the Rivera brothers and, nowadays, especially the younger one.

We fought our way to the main gate and then had to stand among the heaving mass of Andalusian femininity as they waited for a glimpse of their hero. Despite the fame of the other two more senior matadors working, El Fandi and Manzanares, we knew when Cayetano had arrived by the shrieks of delight deafening us. Luckily, while his team formed a moving circle of arms around him as the girls literally threw themselves on him, Cayetano spotted us in the crowd and came over to grab us and take us through the door.

I must admit to feeling rather humbled by the whole thing, which is not to say I was star-struck. The crowds and the adulation were impressive, yes, but I could sense the incredible concentration Cayetano was trying to achieve – maintaining an internal equilibrium, while being gracious to an aggressively affectionate mob, while also thinking about what he had to do. And despite this, he was going out of his way to be generous and make sure that the impenetrable gate that keeps performers of his level apart was held open long enough to include myself and Nicolás, both figuratively and literally (every security guard along the way tried to close doors on us, and every time Cayetano would turn back and demand it was reopened). I could see that he was fighting against his own instinct to ignore everything around him, and was grateful for it.

We reached the inner sanctum, the *plaza de cuadrillas*, where he and the other two matadors and their teams were assembling. Padilla walked through – he lives in Sanlúcar and no one would close a door on Padilla – giving all present a hug for luck. Then Cayetano walked into the small chapel all bullrings have, to prepare himself (I watched through the window and was oddly touched watching Fandi help Cayetano arrange his tie, a matador of ten years' fighting assisting one of two). Then they all came out and lined the walls, waiting for the signal for their entrance ceremony, the *paseíllo*. With long experience of being backstage in an environment where reputations but not lives were on the line, I took my notebook, found an empty piece of wall to lean against and tried to become as unobtrusive as possible.

However, Cayetano, either because he dislikes the loneliness that importance always brings, or through some natural affability, came over and began to crack a series of very funny jokes in English, none of which, sadly, I remember. Midway through his routine, though, he looked up into the ring with a serious face and, fixing his gaze on some distant object, said, 'That! That is what I hate.'

I followed the direction of his eyes, and could see only the flag of Spain fluttering above the ring.

'The flag of Spain?'

'No, the wind that makes it fly. The wind, that is what kills you.'

And that, in a single moment, showed me the entire difference between backstage at a theatre and a bullring. Only in the latter can a man whose father died in such a place look with dismay at the possibility of his own death, admit dislike, and still walk on to that stage. Which he did, as Nicolás and I were ushered by his manager, Curro Vásquez, his uncle and a former matador of note, into the *callejón* until we were at the other side of the ring, the crowd behind us, and nothing between the bulls and us but the thin wood of *las tablas*, 'the planks'.

The feeling within the *callejón* is a strange one. A ring of journalists and members of the bullfighting world stand behind miniature hides, which are there in case the bull leaps the planks; it's an uncommon occurrence, but when it happens the bull simply charges headlong down the alley and those who aren't behind a hide have no choice but to vault into the ring or be gored. Walking back and forth with boxes of *banderillas*, capes, swords and anything else they might need are the teams, their masters meanwhile leaning against the planks, some stretching – usually ones whose style is more athletic like Fandi – others merely striving to attain focus like Cayetano. All of this goes on under the steady gaze and commentary of the audience, who are just a couple of feet away. There is no privacy for the bullfighters now; every gesture and facial expression – in the smaller rings like this one, every comment passed – is scrutinised by the *aficionados*. Cayetano looked impenetrable and impassive, a statue awaiting its call to movement.

The first bull entered, and it was for El Fandi. Having seen him work a few times now, and seen Tomás work his magical art, I realised how emotionless Fandi's style was. Everything was done for spectacle, without any deep appreciation of either the bull or the danger, the two other protagonists in this theatre.

His caping began with little to recommend it. Despite this, because of the proximity of the matador to us, everything was heightened. When the bull charged in our direction, we felt a genuine part of the action. So much so that Nicolás's photographs had to be taken in between his natural urge to duck every time the bull hit the planks in front of us. And when the picador lined up his horse directly before us and cited the bull, which charged into him so hard he was knocked back three paces until he hit the wood of the planks, we both flinched. Up this close – and when I say I could reach and touch them it is no literary conceit – the two beasts were like dinosaurs fighting. Amazingly the horse, as always, left without even a limp.

(When one does the physics it does make sense. Body-armour works by blocking the projectile so it does not penetrate and spread its force over a wider area. A modern rifle bullet has around 500 calories of kinetic energy, and as long as it is stopped by the armour, injury is limited to bruising when that energy is dissipated over the entire torso of the man. A bull has about 2,000 calories of energy, divided over two horns, and a horse's body is ten times as large as a man's, hence injury is so rare. In fact, even falling over is uncommon.)

Fandi again embarked upon his showy placing of the *banderillas*, running backwards to place the third pair almost matching the pace of the charging bull. Then, this former national-level skier upped his game even further: while running backwards he placed his hand, palm forwards, on the space on the bull´s forehead between the horns and, locking his arm straight, used the bull's momentum to augment his own. The bull, feeling the presence of a real, tangible opponent against its head, accelerated and Fandi began a backwards sprint in a circle around the ring, being pushed by the bull.

Impressive as it was, when he moved on to the *muleta*, his work was showy and soulless, his body a well-made puppet driven by a fearless athlete's brain. What did impress, or rather burn itself into my awareness, were the sounds one heard down in the *callejón*: the bull's relentless breathing, the horrendous tearing sound as a *banderilla* freed itself from its leather shoulders during a pass, the gruesome slick sound as the sword slid into place. The bull fell quickly, its battle over; the matador took his bow and an ear.

We watched Manzanares perform well, and with soul, but I still couldn't bring myself to like his style; his imperious posture seemed somehow out of place in the ring, based on vanity rather than grace, a notion of power rather than one of elegance.

As Cayetano prepared for his bull, Nicolás and I became more excited and more nervous. We had just been talking to him and knew he felt fear, unlike Padilla. This fear was a flaw, but a tragic one, which in theatre is what allows the audience to sympathise with the hero. He walked into the ring with a face set with an aggressive determination, and the young women in the crowd upped the overall frequency of the cheering by a couple of octaves.

He began well with the *capote*, not like Morante, but with a clear technical proficiency and a wider variety of passes than most matadors use. Not just *verónicas*, but a pass I had not seen before, like a *verónica* performed in reverse, with the bull sweeping under the cape from behind as it is flicked slowly away from the man like someone laying a large, heavy cloth over a nearby table.

The most striking thing was the fearlessness of the manoeuvring, despite Cayetano's earlier words. I realised that in getting to know him a little, and in coming to understand how he thought, my perspective on his fighting had been completely changed. Which is not to say that I had lost my objectivity – good bullfighting is about being 'moved', and there's nothing objective about an emotional response – but my emotional response was tempered by knowing this man. I felt the magnitude of the danger more keenly than I did for the other strangers on that *cartel*.

After the picadors and *banderilleros* had done their bloody work, Cayetano walked into the ring and went over to a place in the audience where I spotted the former mother-in-law of his brother, the Duchess of Alba, who was smiling. I assumed that he was going to dedicate the bull to her. However, as he stepped on the rail which runs around the *tablas* to allow beleaguered bullfighters to more easily vault out of danger, another figure further back stood up. A man in his fifties, with shoulder-length, wild grey hair and stubble over a hard face. He wore a tightly cut black jacket of coarse cloth and was clearly from the world with which the bullfight will always be linked, one far removed from that of dukes: flamenco. It was the great José Mercé, himself from a long dynasty of gypsy singers in Jerez.

All the while, the bull was having his attention held by the waving hands of a *banderillero* at one of the hides, and then Cayetano turned around and sat down on the foot rail, his back to the planks, and waved the *muleta* in front of him, calling to the bull.

'¡*Toro! Toro!*'

The bull, angered by the pain of the *banderillas* and having recovered its breath, flicked its head in his direction, lowered it and charged headlong at the figure against the wall, who had no escape open to him. As he came close, Cayetano moved the cape again, allowing the bull to distinguish the cape as the focus of its anger, and it passed harmlessly through, rearing as it went, and then turned hard to find its target again. Still seated, feet apart, his back against the wall as though relaxing in the evening sun, Cayetano flicked the cape again, and again the bull bore down on him, again deviating at the last minute. Then Cayetano stood and began caping in earnest, *derechazos* with the right hand, *muleta* spread further by the sword placed inside, his body straight, feet apart, everything classically ordered and fearlessly executed. This was good – very good – bullfighting. Then he switched to the left and brought the bull closer and closer, his capework again excellent and ordered, the emotion being projected to the audience as much by his facial expression and line of body as by the bull itself.

At the end of this *faena*, he walked over to change his aluminium caping sword for the steel, and then lined up the bull directly in front of me. I watched the incredible focus on his face, thinking of his words about how this was the only moment the matador charged the bull. His body was in three-quarter profile to the bull, then he slowly swept the sword up from behind him, over his head, and then down in front of him, aiming it like a gun. With his other hand he placed the *muleta* on the ground so that the bull focused down. Then he swept it up and ... and did not move an inch. The bull lurched forwards towards his unprotected body, the sword point taking it between the shoulder blades, and it drove itself along the blade, Cayetano stepping to one side at the very last moment so that the horns brushed past his legs. He was left standing, a figure of graceful stillness, while beside him, facing in the opposite direction, stood the bull, sword hilt standing proud of its shoulders, blade buried deep down within its chest. Cayetano waved his men away as they ran in with their capes, and within ten seconds the bull fell to its knees, then its belly, and then rolled over in the dust. Cayetano caught my eye and smiled. He was well aware that after his speech about the moment of truth being the matador's only charge, he had subverted my expectations, and that of the cheering crowd's, by killing *en recibiendo*, the old style of Ronda, the town with which his family was synonymous. He was awarded both ears.

Because I was standing in the *callejón*, constantly moving out of the way of *banderilleros* running to and fro with the implements of their craft, my notes from that day are incomplete to the point of skeletal. However, of the remaining three bulls, the next one stood out as a true exception to the rule. This was a bull that won the bullfight, if such a thing is actually possible within the essentially artistic – as opposed to sporting – logic of the Spanish bullfight.

When he came out he was clearly a strong bull and Fandi played him with the large cape longer than he normally did, the *capote* not being his favoured weapon. The bull was then extraordinarily strong against the horse, not flinching for a moment when the lance struck it, pushing up on to the lance, using the crossbar locked into its shoulder to drive the rider off-balance, just as its horns first of all removed his stirrup, before then going lower and slipping under the horse like a pitchfork. It then lifted horse and rider into the air and toppled them clean over before it was distracted away by the *banderilleros* with their capes.

Fandi placed his *banderillas* again with his usual flair, but this time he didn't try any more tricks but instead seemed somehow eager to get to the *muleta*. He knew something about this incredibly powerful bull that neither I nor the rest of the audience could.

He began on the right with feet apart, then to the left, then feet together on the right, then on the left, then he began again. Pass piled on pass, all well done, lacking art, but focus was now on the bull. Every bull I had ever seen after four or five *tandas*, series of passes, would be almost finished, tongue lolling, breath roaring out of its mouth and nostrils, ready for the kill. This bull looked exactly as it had when he had begun. It was not tiring. Nor was it 'playing up', trying to find the matador with its horns under the cape, deviating in the directness of its charge or hesitating in its willingness to do so. The bull was running 'as though on rails', in Hemingway's phrase, and this train had one hell of an engine drawing it. Eight *tandas* became nine and the crowd started to change. First of all one or two white handkerchiefs came out, then it spread through the crowd. By the tenth *tanda*, the entire crowd had their handkerchiefs out and Nicolás was smiling with delight.

'They are asking for an *indulto*, they want the bull to be pardoned.'

At this point Fandi let his *muleta* drop down by his side and the bull, only two feet away, duly stopped its charging, its focus remaining on the limp cloth. Then he looked up at the president in exactly the same manner as thousands of gladiators had looked up to Caesar over the still living form of a defeated opponent, and waited to see if he would be condemned to death or spared.

The mob bayed for mercy, the matador indicated he followed their opinion with a small gesture of his hand and an inclination of his head, but the president merely rolled his fingers, giving the universal gesture of 'carry on'. Carry on and we shall see.

And so Fandi began again, but now there was a change in the temperature of the *plaza* and in the approach of the matador. He was fighting to save the bull's life, to display its virtuoso ability to dance with him according to his steps, his movements of the cape, now increasingly complicated, the crowd pleading en masse to the president to show magnanimity. The *tandas* rolled on, we knew the matador was not at risk now (although, of course, he was), and we knew eventually the president would have to give in. This bull, Aviador from the *finca* of Santiago Domecq, was the perfect *toro de lidia*, indefatigable in pursuit of its prey, incorruptible by pain, unchangeable by experience. The audience chanted a shorter version of their usual three-syllable acclamation, '*To-re-ro*'. Now they chanted just two: '*To-ro! To-ro! TO-RO!*'

And the president yielded, flopping an orange-coloured cloth over his balcony, demanding the reopening of the *toril* gate.

Fandi, delighted at being given permission not only to take the crowd's acclaim for showing the bull's talents and his own, but also to concede to their wishes, could now cape the bull out of the ring – no easy feat – without needing to cross its horns with his sword and expose himself to the ultimate risk in the ring. However, he had other ideas, tossing to one side his sword, lining up the bull with the *muleta*, and charging forwards with an empty hand over the horns to touch the bull's hump of muscle with his fingers, to show that he could have killed and had not, mercy and proof of potency in a single flourish. He then led the bull from the ring and through the gate with a series of perfunctory, but no less cheered for being so, passes. Fandi was awarded two ears and a tail from some other animal that had not fared so well with which to tour the arena for the crowd's applause.

Manzanares cut two ears on his next bull and Cayetano another on his. So at the end, the *feria* audience, driven wild by excellent bullfighting and an excess of *manzanilla*, the Sanlúcar version of sherry, poured into the ring and took the matadors on to their shoulders, as the president demanded that the great gate on to the street was opened for them. The matadors took a lap of the ring so that those dignified enough to stay in the stands could applaud. Nicolás and I wandered into the ring to observe more closely, and Cayetano steered his supporters in my direction and came over to shake my hand, delighted his ordeal was over, the ordeal being not the risk of death, but the possibility of failure.

■ ■ ■ ■ ■

Later that evening Nicolás and I met up with Cayetano and his manager, Curro, in a bar for a drink. They invited us to join them for dinner, but it was clear that the invitation was given contrary to what he wanted and needed after a bullfight. So he was both surprised and relieved when I turned it down, saying that I had what I needed for my book.

'And the article?'

I had forgotten about that and said as much. He looked even more surprised about this, and we exchanged mobile numbers as they left to dine upstairs while Nicolás and I took tapas at the bar. A few minutes later I received a message on my phone: 'You truly are a writer not a journalist. Come and see my fight in Ronda, my friend. Then you will see something really special. *Un abrazo*, C.'

But first I must go to Pamplona.

15

El natural

The matador takes the muleta *into his left hand, keeping the sword in his right which he places behind his back. With the smaller* muleta *he approaches the bull again, and draws it ever closer, ever nearer.*

The train from Barcelona to Pamplona is old-fashioned for Spain and even has a long bar complete with bar stools, where I can sit with tapas and a beer as the arid hills and tall thin trees sweep by the windows. Catalan country gives way to the ancient kingdom of Navarre, and its capital, the city of the running of the bulls, Pamplona.

Sitting on the train in early July, all I can think about is the day before, when I had been in a very different place, at the very heart of the British Army on Salisbury Plain, where I had learnt a very different perspective on bullfighting.

Courtesy of a contribution to the Army Benevolent Fund, I had been asked to spend a day with General Sir David Richards, then Commander-in-Chief of the Land Forces of the United Kingdom (now Chief of the Defence Staff). Some of the day was spent driving prototype desert vehicles, using their vast simulators to test my identify-and-kill skills on filmed sequences from insurgency areas and testing the limits of the Challenger Mark II main battle tank.

All great 'boys' own adventure' stuff, but infinitely more interesting were the chats I had with the C-in-C and his subordinates: from meetings with major-generals down to lunch with some lads fresh back from the war zone in Afghanistan.

When I arrived in the office of a lieutenant-general, he apologised for the delay – an Army delay, meaning under two minutes – but the office was running at unusual speed to deal with the fact that a record number of British servicemen had died earlier that day in Afghanistan. The main incident, which had killed five men at once, involved a secondary attack with Improvised Explosive Devices (IEDs). The lieutenant-general, whose role that day was really to explain the structure of Land Command to me, happily leapt up and explained with devastating clarity with a whiteboard and marker the threat his men faced and its infinite upgradeability. In answer to my question as to whether better armour on personnel carriers was required, he said: 'You could give me a main battle tank and in the end it would make no difference, because they would just use a larger charge. I need local intel and troops on the ground who can tell me where the damn things are placed, not to take an area for an hour with casualties on both sides, then retreat claiming victory and leaving the locals to the tender mercies of a vengeful Taliban. I need more soldiers. The US marine corp alone is larger than our entire army.'

However, what struck me most was the calm manner with which everyone – and I include the rank and file I met – dealt with the death of comrades and the risk of death to themselves. It contrasts a great deal with the way people talk about matadors, and sometimes the way matadors talk about themselves, even though no *torero* has died in the ring in Spain since 1992.

Despite this, the most interesting thing was not the bravery, but its absence, or rather its absence from discussions about training. The troops are so heavily conditioned by exercises and simulations that one has the impression that when a vehicle is fired upon, they are out of the vehicle in a defensive perimeter, calling in air-cover, and then on the offensive themselves, before consciousness has time to voice its thoughts (this is not to say that great courage does not exist, but that is what goes beyond the training, and not something to be relied upon).

Of course, the matador does something very different. He must not only stand fast and use his training with the bull, but he must dance with it, linking a series of passes with the cape into a deliberately chosen *faena*, which contains within its graces an exquisite and esoteric death. Art is the order of the day, not assassination, although it all too often stoops to mere butchery (and lack of bravery, lack of skill, lack of taste – all these are the reasons for this).

Sadly, the soldiers' operating-manual conditioned reflexes are predictable, and so it appears that that morning, when the first IED took out the soldiers' vehicle, they deployed into a nice-looking patch of ground – one with cover or some other advantage – and it contained a carefully placed second IED which finished them off outside of their vehicle's armour.

Oddly enough, I spent quite some time explaining what I was doing to these men of action, who seemed to find it as interesting as I did their unique career choice. The only one who struck a bum note was a mid-ranking desk officer in his late forties, who began by asking me if I'd ever thought of a military career. So I mentioned that courtesy of my brother's time in the 2nd Royal Tank Regiment, I had joined the Army Corp at school, and even got as far as being selected for special training at Sandhurst, but in the end undergraduate and postgraduate study got in the way and before I knew it I was twenty-six and too old.

The officer raised an eyebrow and said, in the tone of one offering consolation for being born a lesser man, 'Ah, yes, as Kipling said, "Every man thinks meanly of himself for not having been a soldier." What do you do now?'

What I thought was, 'I refrain from correcting misattributions, you pompous ass – it was Johnson, not Kipling.'

What I said was, 'I'm training as a bullfighter in Spain.

Tomorrow I'm back to Pamplona to run.' And I must confess that I smiled at the look on his face.

However, this is short-lived, as only fifteen minutes after that I began to receive text messages from concerned friends asking if I was all right. In a relatively unusual incident, a young man – at first rumoured to be British – had died running the bulls in Pamplona that day. To say that I found this unnerving is to understate heroically. All of a sudden I was confronted by the realities of the taurine world, and this was a part of it about which I knew absolutely nothing. What was more, one of my two promised companions on the run, Adolfo Suárez Illana, had sent me a message wishing me luck and apologising for not being able to come with me. However, he said, Padilla would be there to offer advice, assistance and jump in should need be.

■ ■ ■ ■ ■

When I finally arrive in Pamplona it is at the height of what seems to be a Rio carnival-style street party, although, strikingly, everyone is in the same uniform – white shirt, white trousers, red neckerchief and red sash. These bull-running festivals used to be far more common, and there are still a fair few in Spain, although even the next most famous, San Sebastián de los Reyes, is infinitely smaller. They also happen across the border in France, in towns like Dax and Bayonne. In fact, they happened in England until the mid-nineteenth century. This is an account of the most famous one, in Stamford, Lincolnshire:

> About a quarter to eleven o'clock, on the festal-day, the
> bell of St Mary's commenced to toll as a warning for the
> thoroughfares to be cleared of infirm persons and children;
> and precisely at eleven, the bull was turned into a street,
> blocked up at each end by a barricade of carts and wagons.
> At this moment, every post, pump, and 'coign of vantage'
> was occupied, and those happy enough to have such

protections, could grin at their less fortunate friends, who were compelled to have recourse to flight; the barricades, windows, and house-tops being crowded with spectators. The bull, irritated by hats being thrown at him, and other means of annoyance, soon became ready to run; and then, the barricades being removed, the whole crowd, bull, men, boys, and dogs, rushed helter-skelter through the streets.

(from *Chamber's Book of Days*)

This run was banned after protests by the Society for the Protection of Animals in 1839, the year before Queen Victoria's matronage turned them into the RSPCA.

Of all bull-runs in the world, though, Pamplona is the most famous, and for one reason alone, the writings of Ernest 'Papa' Hemingway. This even though it is generally accepted that he never actually ran. By generally accepted I mean by everyone except Hemingway himself. While researching this I came across a front-page story by Hemingway in the 20 July 1924 edition of the *Toronto Daily Star*, with the wonderfully self-referential headline 'Bull Gores Toronto Writer in Annual Pamplona Festival'.

(I asked his grandson, the writer John Hemingway, about this and got the following pithy response: 'Well, excuse the pun but I think that there was a lot of bull in my grandfather's dispatches to Toronto in the '20s. *Un abrazo*, John.')

Returning to that night in Pamplona, I leave my hotel nearby and walk out the ground of the run. It is a half-mile of streets with three corners, all of which are now packed with drunken revellers. I ignore them, trying to see how I am going to deal with the next morning, looking at the height of the bars on the windows and the height of the heavy wooden barriers, like a climber looking for a route of ascent or a burglar looking for a point of entry. I see some likely spots, but I have no idea as yet how the crowds will be in the morning. I speak to my father and mother, neither of whom stoop to trying to talk me out of it although they indicate that they might prefer that, especially since Padilla has told me he won't be running with me. The bravest of *toreros* telephoned me on the train to say that an injury he received to his shoulder in a bullfight in France means that he won't risk running in the morning even though he has to fight the same bulls that evening. I am truly alone.

Well, almost. I do meet up with the American *aficionado* Robert Weldon – a young man of imposing height and knowledge about this taurine world – who has been running for the first four days of the festival. He takes me to a place on the slope of the calle San Domingo which he has run from each time and then tells me I can have it; he says he has no intention of running with the infamous Miuras on the Sunday of the *feria*, when the number of people in the streets has doubled to over 4,000 and most have been up since the night before in the bars.

I get home at about half past twelve – the run is at 8 a.m. – but I do not sleep. Instead, I sit down in all seriousness and write my will. It is ridiculous and melodramatic, I know, but that is how I am thinking at the time. Not that it would be legally binding, but I'm sure my parents would follow it to the letter. The cash in the bank and my few shares to my surviving brother, everything else to be offered to my friends as keepsakes, my love to all, especially my girlfriend Sam. I save it as an unpublished draft on my blog, then write the password in a letter underneath the contact details for my father and put it into an envelope marked '*en caso de emergencia*' on the desk of the hotel room. I finally fall asleep close to three in the morning.

By the way, this is not to say I am in some form of panic. I am just trying to size up my chances in a totally unquantifiable situation, covering every angle, dotting the unknown 'i's and crossing the mysterious 't's.

Three hours later I wake up just before my alarm. I shower

and slowly dress in a carefully selected version of the traditional dress for the day. A twofold white cotton shirt and a flexible white denim trouser – nothing that inhibits movement, but tight enough not to be caught on a horn unless I am, and thick enough that protection against minor slashes is given. I tie the red bandana around my neck in reverse, so it appears like a cravat and thus mimics the blood of San Fermín, in whose honour this festival is and who had his throat cut, and tie the red sash around my waist, wrapping it twice so there is no slack to catch. I am aware it is not advisable to wear belts with bulls, as people are often caught by that first, and then when they don't fly off the horn, the bull goes to work on them. However, I figure the nod to tradition outweighs the risk. I decide against wearing something different from the mob so I'll stand out in photos. That's not why I'm here. Then I walk out into the streets of Pamplona.

At the entrance to the Town Hall square section of the run there are hundreds upon hundreds of people milling, moving, edging from foot to foot and emitting a combined stench of urine, alcohol and vomit that is nearly overwhelming. The one thing they do not stink of is fear. Fear itself has no smell, despite what the novelists say.

I find my spot in the street with an hour to go and overhear an Australian man say to his sylph-like girlfriend, 'I'll look after you.' The astonishing naïvety of the remark annoys me. What is he going to do? Pick her up and throw her over the people stacked four deep and the six-foot fence behind them? While running? Because anything else he tries with a 1,400lb Miura running at thirty miles an hour won't nudge it even one degree off course. If he wants to save his seven-stone girlfriend, who won't stand a chance of dictating her own trajectory among panicked twelve-stone men, he should get her out now, and if he's stupid enough to talk like that he should probably follow suit himself.

I decide to get away from them, ducking under the fence and heading away from the course to a small church where Robert told me the hardened runners gather – some Spanish, some Americans who have been doing it for as many as thirty years. In this little enclave of calm, I watch the men greet each other briefly with cordial handshakes and short sentences, confident and focused, not indulging in nervous small-talk, each parting with the word '*suerte*', 'good luck'. Their confidence is contagious.

I run a little, testing the torn meniscus in the cartilage in my right knee which I can't have operated on until I finish this book and which runs the risk of locking. Then I stretch like I used to in my high school athletics team for the 400 metres and begin slaloming between traffic bollards at a half-sprint. By half past I'm dripping with sweat and adrenaline and as ready as I will ever be. Am I nervous? No. Not now. It is beyond the time for that. There had been moments the night before when I thought, given that no one knows me here, I could say I had done it without doing it at all. Or I could not do it and no one would judge. At least not in any way I would care about. But in that odd way the mind has – or at least my mind – having committed to a course of action, I will go through unless I can find a justifiable way out. And for this one I can't; even though they're Miuras, even though it's the weekend crowd, even though everyone else has bailed out on me. I walk down the hill and take my place and wait.

As the time approaches, the streets thicken with people, then seem to clear. I later discover that this is an artificial density, as the final section of the run is closed until ten minutes to eight. I find myself alone in a section of street that has a crowd on steps behind the barrier watching like an audience. I find it very odd to be walking on what feels like a stage at a time like this.

With five minutes to go that feeling fades. That is when the false breaks begin: all of a sudden a group of people will get the jitters and run up the hill, convincing other people – ones with untrustworthy watches or untrusting minds – that the bulls have been released early. I have no idea if they leave the course or decide to stay further up, but they don't return to my space, my little island.

The minutes pass slowly. Incredibly slowly. In fact, I can safely say that no period of time in my life has ever passed that slowly. This is firing-squad stuff. The background noise and movement of the runners escalates, so that when the clock tower bells chime the hour I do not hear them. However, I know my watch is good so I am not exactly surprised when a rocket explodes in the air. I am certainly fully awake though.

Then come the joggers, people laughing off their fear and embarrassment, but having made the very clear decision that they want to be further away from whatever is about to happen. When the second rocket goes off a few seconds later, they accelerate and I have to turn sideways to let the rush past. Then I bend my knees a little and lean my shoulder downhill as Robert advised, forcing people to part round me because this is becoming a stampede. And then the bulls turn the corner at the bottom of the hill and the thin blue line of police holding the people and the bulls apart breaks off to the sides and the mass of people shatters and flees like a medieval rabble under a heavy cavalry charge.

■ ■ ■ ■ ■

Of the many things I have seen researching this book, again and again the phrase 'never seen before' springs to my typing fingers, but this really was a sight that very few people in the modern era will see: a populace put to flight through its own streets, as though a siege has been broken, a city wall breached. As the bulls cleared their path up the hill and I attempted to hold my ground, people were running past screaming, grabbing at me, diving against the wall, which was now thick with people trying to make sure they were not the front line. As the bulls got closer – it seemed like ten feet away, but I would calculate from the images I have seen it was twenty – a clearer space in front of them enveloped me and I turned and started to run.

When I was in the athletics team at school, I had it drilled into me that you can think you are sprinting flat out, but then you look inside yourself and find an extra reserve of speed. However, this was not one of those times. I had enough adrenaline in me that I don't doubt for a second that I have never run faster and that if I hadn't warmed up I would have done a lot more than ended up with a strained Achilles tendon and aching hamstrings.

However, the bulls were much, much faster. By the top of the hill – maybe fifteen yards away – the front ones were passing me, the relatively harmless but massive steers between the bulls and me, but then I spotted one fighting bull, chewing his way through the people to my rear, his horn visible behind the falling man behind me.

As he neared me, and the mass of people in the square began to push me and themselves towards his horns, I decided enough was enough and pushed myself back into the crowd on the side, arms out to hold back the falling people around me. The Miuras had passed, but I was not finished.

I jumped back into the middle of the street and went back to sprinting in an attempt to follow them, out of the town square, along calle Mercaderes and into one of the most dangerous parts of the course, the corner of calle Estafeta. As I reached it I was confronted with the sight of a fallen grey and white Miura, a *suelto*, a 'loose one'. He was getting back on to his feet, facing in the opposite direction to the now vanished herd, facing me. At his most dangerous – fresh, massively strong, and with no idea where he was or what to do – he was swinging his great horns back and forth looking for prey and I slammed on the brakes on the cobbled street, thanking God for the grip on my Nike trainers, and went into speedy reverse. Soon there were people between the bull and me and I knew I was safe. Then he moved in the right direction and a gate was closed behind him to keep the crowd on my part of the course safe. As I walked over to the railings to catch my breath a man was pulled out by paramedics from behind the barrier, blood pumping from his neck. (A little later someone pointed out a large bloodstain on my shirt and I can only assume it sprayed out from him.) The wound was evidently bad, but he was holding the bandages to his own throat despite being on a stretcher, so I assumed he was relatively OK. According to the newspapers, after a four-day spell in intensive care he was.

Walking back from the corner, a sudden scream went up through the crowd, entirely in English, saying, 'More bulls.' This one I was ready for, having been forewarned by Robert. It was the giant steers, three of them in a row, charging through the street to clean up any loose bulls that might still be on the course. As people leapt to either side, I continued near the middle of the road and applauded them as they passed. I may have been awash with fear and confusion a few moments before, but I was damned if I wasn't going to have a little flourish.

I walked back to the hotel and called my parents and girlfriend to say I was alive, before heading to a bar where I was told the American runners all met up to confirm the number left standing. It had been a bloody day: two in intensive care, two other serious gorings, a dozen minor injuries from human or bovine feet. As I introduced myself to the men I had seen so calmly warming up before, I discovered that not one of them had been injured, despite the fact that I had seen them leap in closer to the bulls than anyone else. This may in part be explained by how long they have been running for. One of them, a retired English lecturer from New York, called Jose Distler, has been running since 1967 and has been the subject of numerous documentaries since. As one of them, a man known as Beef, said to me when I said I didn't know anyone there.

'Welcome. These guys are your friends for life.'

Despite that welcome, after one drink I decided to abandon them for some English and American first-time runners who were as hopped up on survival as I was, and we drank from 8.30 a.m. until I fell on to my bed at 4 p.m. I had had enough of embellishing stories and drinking odd Navarese cocktails for one day. I even slept through Padilla's bullfight, but to be fair, he hadn't turned up for mine.

■　■　■　■　■

I took the next day off, letting my torn muscles heal, but decided to run again the day after that, the final day of the *feria*. This time I took up a position in a doorway halfway along the calle Estafeta. Since most people either like to run on the corners, the beginning, or at the end where they can enter the bullring, I found myself in a relatively clear spot (doubtless helped by few people having the strength to run on the last day). The bulls were Núñez del Cuvillo and this time I got it right, getting into the street and starting jogging about twenty yards ahead of them.

Then, when they cut out the intervening people and reached me, I put on a burst of speed to match that of a bull running at my shoulder, and I did, I achieved *templar*. In bullfighting, the term means to match the speed of the bull's charge with the cape, and some say it even means to moderate the charge by doing so. In bull running, it means to match not only your speed but the rhythm of your run to an animal's.

It was a strangely moving experience running side-by-side with a bull, close enough to touch, although I had been warned that that was frowned upon. His head heaved up and down from the ground as great muscles contracted and relaxed to shift great weight at a speed equal to my sprint, even though he had already sprinted almost half a mile uphill. He was pure brown in colour and apparently totally ignorant of my existence at his flank, his whole being determined only to keep with his herd and get clear of this mass of humanity. The kinship I felt with him was purely physical, locomotory, experience, but it was still more than superficial.

Later that evening I watched the one and only bullfight I will ever see in Pamplona. The party atmosphere from the streets was magnified in the ring. Not one, but six bands were in operation, each one from a different fan club celebrating. The fans themselves danced and shouted and swore and drank, half the time with their backs to the sand. The matadors valiantly tried to get their attention by fighting, but the bulls were so distracted by the noise – and being run through the streets that morning – that they were almost impossible to make charge. It was an ugly, barbaric thing. And then the bull I had run beside came in, and although he was fought well, he refused to die, despite the sword being within him. As the crowd cheered and booed, swayed and screamed, he walked over to the planks and began a long slow march around the ring, holding on to life as though with some internal clenched fist, refusing to give up, refusing to die. I had run next to this great animal, had matched myself to him as best I could, and in doing so felt some form of connection to the powers that propelled him. Now I watched them all turned inwards in an attempt to defy the tiny, rigid ribbon of steel within his chest, and having been blinded by no beauty, tricked by no displays of courage or prowess by the matadors, I just saw an animal trying to stay on its feet against the insuperable reality of death. I left the *plaza de toros* with tears in my eyes after that. And there was nothing good in all that place.

That night I went out for dinner with Robert and he, the

true *aficionado* who had no inner moral qualms about the bull-fight, and I the doubting writer who was once again riddled with them, both agreed that amazing and historic as Pamplona was, we wouldn't be back again for the bullfighting, for there was none there.

16

El trincherazo

As with the *pase de pecho*, the matador performs a move beginning with his back three-quarter turned, but rather than the long arc, it is a short sweep, pulling the horns down to his feet, forcing the bull into a hard turn.

It was a perfect early September evening as my bus wended its way through the glacier-slashed mountains down towards Ronda. I felt fresh and vigorous, my mind recharged from a visit to London for a dear friend's stag night that had lasted three days and involved me at one point going into a field and riding a strange horse under the moon without saddle, bridle or head collar – a story for another book.

Ronda is perched precariously on a landscape sliced in two by some vast tectonic knife. This is the town Hemingway described in his Civil War novel *For Whom the Bell Tolls*, which I was rereading on the bus. This is the ravine in which the local conservative Nationalists were hurled to their deaths by the drunken mob representing the honour of the Republic, who then had even worse terrors inflicted on them when the Fascists took it back in the name of old Spain.

It is also the town from which bullfighting had its birth, because this is where the first matador of the modern bullfight, Pedro Romero, was born, and this is where Spain's oldest bull-ring stands.

Despite its antiquity, I am here to see Ronda's youngest son, Cayetano Rivera Ordóñez, whom I had last seen in Sanlúcar de Barrameda; we have been in touch by telephone ever since. I could not claim close friendship, but we had been trying to meet up for some time and one or other of us was always unable to make it. However, with Ronda he left nothing to chance, arranging tickets for the sole, sold-out bullfight of the *feria*. Then, when it turned out that every hotel in town had been booked up months in advance, he sent me a message saying, 'Don't worry, I have arranged everything, you are with me.' I had no idea the *feria* in Ronda was such a big deal, nor what a great favour Cayetano was doing me.

The *feria* of Ronda was begun by Cayetano's grandfather Antonio Ordóñez in 1954, in honour of the 200th birthday of Pedro Romero. It comprises a single *corrida* with full matadors, although there is a novice fight the night before and a horseback fight the day after. However, it also has one other difference from other *ferias*: that the matadors should wear uniforms in the older manner of Romero's epoch, depicted in the paintings of Goya, hence the full name of Feria Goyesca de Pedro Romero. Antonio's original outfit was designed by Pablo Picasso himself.

When I arrive in town I quickly take in the sloping streets, whitewashed buildings, the pretty parks and the predominance of statues linked to bulls and the fighting of them, before getting in a taxi and asking for the Hotel la Fuente de la Higuera. We drive out along the hills outside Ronda and keep turning right until we are on dirt tracks. We then arrive at a pretty little boutique hotel set into the hillside, looking out over the ravine back on to Ronda. It is half past seven and I am greeted effusively in flowing English by the German owner, Tina Piek, who leads me to a lovely open suite which opens on to a private terrace looking up into the hills, with a huge bed draped in mosquito nets, before telling me that Cayetano and his girlfriend Eva are resting in their room.

I unpack and set off into the hills to run off the lethargy

and grime of travel, stunned by how green the landscape is, the mountains of the Sierra de las Nieves giving this region of Spain some of its highest rainfall. When I arrive back I am ushered through to join the table of the Maestro. It is only now that I realise that Cayetano has taken over the entire hotel and that its only guests are him and his girlfriend, his manager, the ex-matador Curro Vásquez and his wife and myself.

We embrace and talk about inconsequential things and I get the feeling that he, like me, is aware that we have fallen into a friendship that has aspects of convenience, my book research and his public profile, but also has something honest in it. The age we live in may be media-driven, but the bullfight remains a pillar of honesty within it – at least on this side of the horns. He tells me what Ronda means to him and his family. And I ask if his grandfather ever knew he was going to become a matador.

'No. Although I do remember one time when we were driving around my grandfather's farm, I was about eighteen, and I said to him that I wanted to fight a bull in a village festival.' Such things are done with smaller bulls by *aficionado-prácticos*, who still qualify as *toreros*, but not professionals like *novilleros* or full matadors. 'My grandfather gave me one piece of advice, "Train hard," and that was it. When my brother Fran started, my grandfather was his manager, and I think he worked him hard. *Very* hard.'

From there we talk about the ring and how half his grandfather's ashes are buried under it in front of the *toril* gate because he wished the bulls to run over him as they entered. It is there, because the ring has a different structure to more modern rings, that Cayetano must stand to salute the president of the ring. He is clearly moved by the thought of standing on the shoulders of such a giant of bullfighting.

(The other half of the ashes are interred in the Camargue region of France, where I had just visited the two great French bullrings of Arles and Nîmes, which are built in restored Roman gladiatorial arenas. Stunning as they are, I saw no fights worth describing, and felt uneasy in these places where men once fought beasts and each other to the death with no thought of art or mercy.)

Realising the conversation had become a little morbid, Cayetano suddenly switched into a lighter tone and began to talk about his time on the west coast of the US, where he studied media and film in Santa Monica. He tells a story about how in one class they were discussing Orson Welles's film *Citizen Kane*, and the professor said Welles was buried 'somewhere near Málaga in Spain'.

'And I thought to myself,' said Cayetano, 'do I tell him? No, it would be too much, but I was so tempted.'

'What?'

'Orson Welles is buried under a tree at my grandfather's house. They were great friends and Welles loved the bulls.'

I ask him about his brother Francisco, another famous matador of this age. This fight will be Cayetano's third – last year he couldn't, due to extensive internal bleeding and liver damage caused by a bull. Fran fought the other two years beside him, and is the manager of the bullring at Ronda, a job he must be doing well, as it is the third most visited tourist attraction in the country.

'I think this year he thinks it is good if I fight alone, so it belongs more to me this time. I will miss my brother in the ring, though. It will be sad not to have him there.'

There is a pause.

'So, what will you do tonight?'

I realise that despite the *feria*, at which he is the man of the moment, Cayetano is staying at his hillside retreat and readying himself for the 'big push' of the day to follow.

'I was thinking of heading into town to see the *feria*.'

'If you want you can drop by my *caseta*, my *peña* [a club of *aficionados*] has one there. Let me phone ahead for you.'

■ ■ ■ ■ ■

Which is how I end the night standing by a vast electric fan being plied with drinks by the eager childhood friends of Ronda's youngest son in a tent heaving to the ecstatic *sevillana* music of yet another *feria*. It is far and away the most popular tent there, and the women dancing are far and away the most beautiful.

I give up at three in the morning, when things are still hotting up, and walk down crowded streets looking for a taxi. I pass a group of teenage boys and girls in hooded tops sitting drinking on a patch of derelict ground under a graffiti-addled wall. There is no one else in the street, and as I pass them in a dark suit I evaluate them as a potential threat. Then I realise that they aren't even looking in my direction. They are sitting in a circle with a guitar playing flamenco and taking it in turns to sing while passing around a bottle, lost in their moment. It seems things are different here from in England.

Indeed, everywhere here there is music. Two girls pass in the street and flirt with their eyes, and when I don't respond as they pass, they sing a few bars of a *sevillana* to me. It is half past three by the time I find a taxi, but still there are prams in the street pushed by smiling families heading towards the fair. I take a last look at the moon from my terrace before going to bed and hope that Cayetano does not end the same way as his father, dying on the horns of a bull. As I fall asleep, I read a little from a novel I have borrowed from the hotel library, *The Fencing Master* by Arturo Pérez-Reverte. I underline a single phrase in pencil which gives me some consolation for the matador's sake: *Siempre había opinado que a todo hombre debía darsele la oportunidad de morir de pie.* 'I have always had the opinion that every man should be given the opportunity to die on his feet.'

The next morning I crawl out of bed and head to the main terrace for a coffee, where I join Cayetano and his girlfriend Eva González. I realise that I have not had a chance to speak to her properly. She is a tall, powerfully beautiful young woman who won Miss Spain a few years before and has found further fame as a television presenter. However, now is not the time: even more than the night before Cayetano is distant and isolated in his mind, and her focus is on him. So I leave them to it and set off running again, this time in the midday sun.

Along a flat and painfully hot stretch of road a four-wheel-drive pulls up next to me. I stop and watch the window wind down to reveal the president of Cayetano's fan club, Juan Antonio, and another heavily set young man from the night before nicknamed Rubio, 'Blondie', for his light hair.

'*¿Tu eres loco como un torero también?*' 'You are crazy like a bullfighter too?' They laugh, pointing at the burning sun. I am probably five miles from the hotel.

'If you drink, you must run,' I reply.

'*Si, tu eres loco.*'

They drive off laughing, with affection, but laughing nonetheless.

■ ■ ■ ■ ■

My photographer Nicolás arrives around lunchtime and we start to unwind by the pool. Eva is at another table with a girl-friend and the friend's young daughter. Cayetano appears in boxer shorts at the window and waves to us. Soon afterwards his team arrive with suit carriers and he appears again, shouting down to the little girl: 'Do you want to see me dress?'

She runs up eagerly.

Nicolás and I take *siestas* and arrive at the ring, cameras, notepads and a chilled bottle of sherry at the ready, to see the vast crowds outside. And these are the people who aren't even going into the ring. This is celebrity bullfighting, dwarfing what I have witnessed anywhere else. Although it is not just Cayetano who draws the crowd. The audience is packed with celebrities from the Spanish worlds of fashion, politics and the arts. French President Sarkozy cancelled at the last minute – he attended the year before – but the co-founder of Microsoft, Paul Allen, came in by helicopter.

Inside I see the understated beauty of the ring. It has something medieval about it. No whitewash, the stone pillars hinting at the mountainous rocks from which it was quarried. However, it is hard to see the detail for the packed ranks of the audience. There is not an empty seat in the house. Nicolás and I move down to the seats Cayetano has given us in the front row of the audience, so that our legs dangle down into the *callejón* behind where the bullfighters will stand. I begin to understand the favour Cayetano has done me.

At that moment, we see the matadors walking across the ring for the *paseíllo* and we also see the suit that his friend Giorgio Armani has designed and made for Cayetano, an impressive creation in a bluish grey laced with silver thread and Swarovski crystals, giving it the appearance of modern tailoring applied to something from the court of Louis XIV. As the most junior matador present – measured not by years since birth (Cayetano is a year younger than me at thirty-two), but years since becoming a full matador – he stands in the middle of the other two fighting that day – Miguel Ángel Perera and José María Manzanares.

Cayetano salutes the president standing on the ashes of his own grandfather and walks over to the *barrera*. He is as distracted as I have ever seen a man. The other two matadors are also wearing special outfits, but unfortunately the same one, scarlet trimmed with Goya's favourite black. Like two women arriving at a cocktail party in identical dresses, they avoid standing near one another. Their teams are also wearing different outfits as well, and one wonders about the expense to the matadors of having such things made which can only be used once. Even the ring assistants are dressed in costumes from Goya paintings, although these make them resemble deckhands on a Spanish galleon.

The first bull comes out of the gate at a slow walk, and I begin to think that it has no interest in fighting when he spies a flapping cape across the ring and accelerates from standing to gallop in a single bound. As he passes me, I notice that they do not place the *divisa* in this ring, the small pin carrying the colours of the breeder which agitates the bull before entry. This one is entirely untouched, and he charges hard. Manzanares meets him beautifully with the cape and I remember that although I do not like him as a matador, he has undeniable skill and flair. He looks like a young, lean Brando, with the heavy eyebrow ridges and overly strong facial bones overlaid by almost femininely smooth skin – a boxer's face unmarked by age or the glove.

The bull is then given only one lance by the mounted picador before Manzanares demands the horses leave and the first act is over. In the second, the *banderillas*, the barbed sticks, are placed fast and without drama. Everyone wants to cut to the chase, the matador's work with the *muleta*.

Twisting his form into the charging bull again and again as he wraps it round him with the cloth, Manzanares shows a beautiful line of the body, and yet there is an aggression and domination in his passes that is somehow ugly – my notes call the matador a 'beautiful brute' and 'a bull himself without art'. The bull itself is at this point an odd mixture of aggression and fatigue, rearing at the end of each pass, punch-drunk but far from spent. However, there is not much more to this fight than that, and when Manzanares goes in with the sword, I seem to see the bunched muscle of the shoulders actually preventing the blade from going in, catching the steel as though in a clenched fist. However, it does go in the second time and the death is quick.

The crowd seem an eager bunch, silent when necessary, but generous with applause for good work. They demand an ear for the performance, but the president is more sober than they and ignores the appeal.

The second bull comes out in the same way, with a noticeably massive *morillo*, the complex of shoulder and neck muscles that gives the fighting bull its trademark shape and unique ability to lift and throw anything from a man to a draft horse. This one looks as though it could make short work of an elephant. Perera, who some say is the most important up-and-coming matador and a real competitor to Cayetano, stalks out on his unnaturally long legs – the only matador I have met who is taller than me – and begins a sequence of perfect *verónicas* with his feet together which look as if they would not be out of place coming from José Tomás. In fact, I suspect he has been watching that matador whose effect on *aficionados* is so singular.

Again, the bull takes only one pic – the matadors seem to be competing to see who can inflict the least damage before the final caping with the *muleta*. With this small cape, Perera begins really to work, building up a *faena*, a 'display', of linked passes of interesting emotion and danger, again in the manner of Tomás, close to the body, not looking at the bull, feet together. However, unlike Tomás, Perera's judgement is minutely out; the bull hits him hard – I cannot tell whether with horns or shoulders – and he is sent flying to the ground. The bull comes after him on the ground, punching its horns into the dirt of the arena, before redjusting its aim and coming down towards the centre of his back. At exactly that moment the other matadors and Perera's team arrive, one flashing his cape before the bull's muzzle, cutting short the thrust so that it does not penetrate the jacket.

Perera gets to his feet, dusting himself off, and Cayetano asks if he is OK before they leave him to his bull again. The president signals for the music to start and he begins to cape again, but something is broken in his style. His rhythm is off, and the passes now just look dangerous without being moving or powerful. They have no link between them, and when he kills, it is clean but one is left with nothing of feeling.

Now Cayetano comes out in his almost foppishly elegant

suit, and the crowd sit up in expectation. He walks over to the planks and sits down on the ledge a foot up from the ground. The bull charges into the ring and is directed around it by his team, stationed at various points – this has been planned – until it reaches him. Against the wall, between an avalanche and a hard place, he passes the large cape over the bull's face in a beautiful *verónica*, and it turns and he does the same again and again. This is without doubt the best so far, even taking into account the inevitable prejudice I have developed.

The horses come in and the bull takes only one pic, but heavily so. Cayetano makes no pretence of wanting the bull pristine when it is returned to him. His *banderilleros* are the most efficient there, taking the least time, and he then dedicates the bull to the *plaza* with style, and to roaring applause.

It is when Cayetano first cites the bull, which is now stationary by the *barrera*, that I notice his brother Fran for the first time, himself wearing an immaculate suit of the business variety. He is banging the wooden wall to get the bull moving. It seems his brother is as much 'in the ring' as he could be without fighting himself.

Cayetano begins a lovely series of passes, furling his own body in the cape so the bull appears to be drawn in to wound him, while in reality it actually seeks out the fast-moving end of the cape, which it passes before it too is wrapped on to the matador's body.

For his next *tanda*, he begins on his knees with the *muleta*, passing the bull again and again, until the bull trips and stumbles and he stops, letting it get its breath back. Not that he stops performing, making his *muleta* perfect on the sword and appearing to slowly form his body into the correct shape for a pass, all the while allowing the animal to regain its wind.

He passes the bull again and this time it hits him, knocking him to the ground, although the bull does not turn from its charge, leaving him clear. Despite this, faster than any bullfighter watching, faster than one would have thought possible, a figure in a double-breasted suit is between Cayetano and the bull, caping with his bare hands. Cayetano's brother Fran has vaulted the high wooden wall and covered the fifteen-yard distance in less time than those who were standing one foot in the ring three yards from the fall. Of course, one only has to realise that they are all that remains of the family to see where the fraternal vigilance comes from. I remember a comment Cayetano made to me in passing: 'We don't like to fight together, my brother and I, we don't like to risk both of us in the ring on the same day.'

Cayetano sends his brother out of the ring and cites the bull for another charge; the bull calls to him, vocalising, and he answers, calling back in Spanish. They make another series of passes which are good, but not excellent, because the bull is now fatally tired. Cayetano collects the killing sword from his *mozo de espadas*, his 'sword-handler', and lines the bull up with the cape, before arcing the blade up backwards over his head in a semi-circle until it is aimed at the weak spot between the bull's shoulder blades, to one side of the spine. He calls, he charges, the bull rises to meet him and the sword goes in. Almost immediately the bull falls to the ground dead, and the crowd becomes a sea of waving white handkerchiefs. The president yields this time and Cayetano is awarded an ear of the bull. He takes his lap of honour.

There is now a pause, and Nicolás and I tuck into the bottle of sherry as a 1950s fire engine circles the ring, spraying water on to the fine sand so it is not blown up by the rising wind. The wind, which is the matador's worst enemy after the bull itself, stripping him of control of the life-saving capes. Cayetano stands in the *callejón* with his brother as various press photographers do their worst.

When bull four comes out, there seems neither drama to it nor to Manzanares, who is fighting. It would seem that everyone is bored; according to my notes that includes the bull, although I suspect that was not the case. My eyes wander to Cayetano spraying freeze-spray on an injured calf muscle. Towards the end, Manzanares tries to up the pace by working *en redondo*, wrapping the bull completely around him like a belt, his right hand leading it with the cape, his left apparently pushing its rump. However, as I have said before, the posture and facial contortions of this bullfighter seem to me annoying. He insists on himself and his greatness. A beautiful pass is a beautiful pass, I have no need for the matador to look me dead in the eye afterwards and say, '¡Olé!' I am annoyed when he is awarded two ears for his work.

Perera walks out into the ring and his bull comes into the ring like a demon, and Perera leans that long body into him and performs a series of excellent *verónicas*, most notable for the smooth turning of the body.

When the horses come out and the other matadors also enter the ring to help protect them, I notice that Cayetano's elegant suit has great patches of red under either arm as though he has been sweating thick blood. Then I remember how José Tomás had left the ring in Jerez with his crotch soaked in blood, but nowhere else. It is strange how a matador's style, and thus where he most frequently passes the bull, can mark him.

The bull takes one pic before the president changes the acts, and then the second act of the *banderillas* – because Perera also has an efficient team – is over in under three minutes. Perera has obviously told them to hurry to maximise his time with the *muleta* so he can truly show his stuff to the crowd.

He walks to the other side of the ring from the bull, places his feet together, the *muleta* held lightly by his side, and he calls the bull in this trademark José Tomás, 'you shall not pass' manner. It is beautifully done, but the bull hits the cape with such velocity that it is taken out of Perera's hands. Again, he puts in the best moves, but lacking rhythm, no feeling can be transmitted to the audience. Realising this, he tries to up the emotional ante by taking greater risks, but it is too late for me. I can see that the bull is tired and the danger is not real, he is resorting to trickery. As my notes say, 'Perera messes around with the bull too much.'

Now, when he has exchanged swords for the killing sword, the bull retreats back to the *toril* gate by which it entered. It has found a *querencia*, a 'lair', in which it feels safe and is thus at its most dangerous, acting on whim and refusing to charge. This is what happened when Perera got gored so badly in Madrid the year before. In losing his rhythm caping, he lost control of the bull and thus allowed it to dictate its place of death, endangering the man in the process.

Reluctant to go in over the horns in this place, he is given an *aviso*, a trumpet warning that he is in extra time, and so he steels himself and goes over the horns anyway, delivering a neat and brave kill. The crowd, who fell for his tricks (and are in full *feria* mood), demand ears for him, but the president rejects them. This time the crowd won't give in and Perera looks furious as the president becomes deliberately stubborn. Out of the corner of my eye I see Cayetano swearing under his breath, whether because the president is upsetting the crowd and he has to please them next, because the crowd is watching him as an Ordóñez in the family ring, or because he genuinely thinks Perera deserves it, I'll never know. Although I suspect all three.

It all becomes comic when the beleaguered president waves to signal that he wants the next bull out *pronto* and one of the ring lieutenants interprets this sign wrongly, fetching an ear from the body of the bull which has now left the ring. When he comes back with the bloodied lump, the crowd go quiet until the president, now furious, sends the ear back out of the ring again to rejoin the body. The crowd become angrier than the president and I am reminded of the early twentieth-century accounts of riots at bullrings over things like this, leading to the ring being burnt down. I take another swig of sherry and discuss this with Nicolás, deciding that it is unlikely in modern Spain, but at least this ring is built of stone rather than anything flammable.

Cayetano now has to walk into a hostile ring, and one can see his anger. The crowd are not against him, though. As one of them shouts, 'Matador, fight the president, not the bull.'

He sets his face into a hard mask of concentration and opens with some beautiful capework before rushing through the acts of the picadors and the *banderilleros*. He dedicates the bull to his girlfriend Eva and then he walks out on to the sand. He kicks off his shoes for the improved purchase and grounding of stockinged feet, and gives the best set of stationary, feet-together passes of the day. He then goes into an unusually good set of long, deep, strong right-handed passes, and the president tells the band to start.

Cayetano now starts a master class in how to combine dangerous and good capework with a sense of showmanship without sliding into the fraudulent or gaudy. The kicking off of the shoes may or may not have been necessary, but it is the closest a matador can get to rolling his sleeves up.

He is also the first matador I have seen who actually uses the music, taking long woodwind solos as pauses to give the bull time to regain its breath, while he angles his body slowly and places the sword in the right place in the *muleta*, so that when the brass and percussion strike up again, the bull is fresh and he is ready to begin the dance. However, this would not work unless he had the mastery of the *muleta* and the courage to bring the bull close to back it up. A beautiful frame still needs a beautiful painting within it. The most notable thing about his style is how much he brings the bull around his body, but without taking this dynamic too far. The beauty lies in the matador appearing to draw the animal around, not in pushing it yourself, as Manzanares does.

Nicolás and I become excited for our friend, who now

stands on the cusp of the great success he has been driving at for so long. The crowd are behind him, the president is behind him, and it is all in order for a great victory. All that remains is the kill. He is handed the steel sword and begins his trademark manoeuvre, squaring up to the bull then bringing the sword over in an arc above his head until he is staring down the blade at the bull. Then he calls, moves the cape in his left hand, and charges the bull with the sword, piercing deep and right so that the crowd are on their feet cheering before the animal has hit the ground, which happens moments later. The crowd take out their handkerchiefs and the president is quick to respond. Two ears are awarded and Cayetano begins his lap of honour.

As he does so, an enchantingly pretty girl in a dress, no more than eight years old, runs into the ring. Cayetano takes her hand and leads her round the bloodied sand to the roar of the crowd. This is his brother's daughter – and a granddaughter of the Duchess of Alba. A brother and daughter within the ring, a brother without, the grandfather beneath it – Ronda is certainly Ordóñez country.

The three matadors are hoisted on to the shoulders of the crowd and taken out through the main gate. I later discover that the crowd outside the ring reach such a frenzy that they begin to tear at Cayetano's clothing. Luckily, Armani's stitching is both crowd and bull proof.

I see something similar when leaving from another exit, where I witness Eva's fame as people mob her, although this I find genuinely disturbing, men's hands grabbing at a fragile woman as her companions try to hold them back. I am too far away in the throng to lend a hand and can only watch. Luckily she makes it into a waiting car, as do Nicolás and I.

■　■　■　■　■

We return to the hotel and change, and unlike other bullfights, there is not the descending sensation – sometimes happy, sometimes not – from an event into the night, but a feeling of escalating excitement. The garden is now changed, lit with candles from all the trees and on the half-dozen dinner tables carefully laid out for Cayetano and his friends.

Not knowing anyone, I talk first to Pom Piek, the Dutch husband of Tina and co-owner of the hotel. Tall, blond and tanned, with the easy laid-back charm of a lifelong traveller (he has just returned from a month of sailing between the islands of Indonesia), we fall into banter about the fight. It turns out that Cayetano stayed at the hotel before his very first fight in Ronda as a *novillero* and, since that was a success – and the hotel was so sympathetic to his pre-fight needs – he has taken the whole place over every subsequent year. So Pom has seen the evolution of the man and the fighter.

He remembers the first fight, when Cayetano paced the terraces through the night and finally asked for a chocolate drink to help him sleep at 6 a.m. Later in the morning the great figures of the bullfight arrived to support the scion of the house of Ordóñez, and Pom – who once lived with the Masai in Kenya – compared it to the senior elephants of a herd gathering around a youngster in time of trouble. He also spoke of the change: Cayetano is very much in control now, very much the maestro. We also discuss the change in his style, Pom thinking he has been learning from his brother how to reduce the risks, while I suspect he has simply got better at his own style and learnt how not to get hit while keeping to the same forms. The most striking thing about this brief taurine chat between two northern Europeans is the lack of fire and fervour that our Latin cousins would have put into it.

When the thirty or so dinner guests are all assembled, Cayetano and Eva descend from their suite – Cayetano's Armani *traje goyesco* exchanged for Giorgio's more normal look of black jacket, white shirt and jeans. I offer congratulations as

Cayetano leads me round the room performing introductions. A little later, when we descend on to the grass where the candlelit tables are, I ask him in a moment of quiet how he really feels.

'Have you ever done something with so much adrenaline that you are completely and utterly overwhelmed? More than a *tentadero* with the *vaquillas*? A bungee jump or a skydive?'

'Running the Miuras in Pamplona?'

'Yes,' he laughs, 'I forgot you were like that. Well, do you remember how numb you were after?'

'Yes. I seem to remember drinking through that part.'

'Food first, that later.'

I notice his smile is a little less forced now. I say, 'All the time I have spent with you up until now has been before a fight. This is the first time I'll get to see you after a fight. You know, relaxed.'

'Relaxed. Oh yes, my friend,' he said, 'tonight you'll see me really relaxed.'

I sit down on a table with Cayetano's manager Curro and half a dozen young women. I am next to Lucia Núñez, a family friend of the Ordóñez and cousin of my own friend Tilda. It is she who tells me how Cayetano's brother Fran is having his own party in town – the wild party as opposed to the quiet one out here in the hills. After the roar of the crowd, I know which one I would rather be at.

As the wine flows freely I start speaking to Curro – who does not speak English and whose rapid, economical Spanish I find so difficult to follow. We have all become a little bawdy by this time, and Curro mentions something about an incident he had with a nun when he was ten but will elaborate no further. Someone suggests that such a meeting was not spent on the knees, referring in Spanish to praying. I counter that unless it was a *portagayola*, a caping manoeuvre performed on the knees at the beginning of the fight at the 'cage-door'. I have no idea if my imagined sexual pun will translate, nor whether it is one step too far from a Protestant Englishman. There is a momentary pause as people take in what I have said, and what the pun is referring to, and then they almost fall off their chairs with the sort of explosive laughter that comes from utter surprise. After that we relax.

As dinner draws to a close, I notice that above on the main terrace large numbers of people are gathering. Lucia tells me her brother Xavier has gone to collect a group of gypsy flamenco singers and guitarists – the evening looks to be warming up.

From there on things blur into one. I remember meeting Cayetano's impossibly tall and elegant cousin Paola, the daughter of the great Luis Miguel Dominguín, and discussing something about bulls and something about theatre – her husband is an actor and director. I talked with him too, but in Spanish which I simply cannot remember. I remember the gypsies playing and singing, and Xavier introducing me to the leader of the group, in a beautifully cut suit over an elegantly thin figure, his grey-black hair slicked back from dark, clear-cut gypsy features. He took my arm and sang a flamenco song to me, for me, about *el escritor inglés*, the English writer. Cayetano strolled over to stand beside me, and the song changed to take in the matador of Ronda as well. It finished with a tragic flourish and a rush of applause from everyone else who had gathered around us.

Cayetano said, 'And now ... now you have lived.'

After that there was the usual, exhausting Spanish marathon of singing and dancing, from which I retired early, relatively speaking.

■ ■ ■ ■ ■

When I woke up, everyone had gone, and Pom and Tina suggested I stay on to recover and write for a few days at no cost. Cayetano was last seen sitting with the old gypsy at nine in the morning drinking rum, his friends passed out around him. Then he got up and paid his bill – and mine – and left. It was Sunday and he had a fight on Thursday and some recovering to do. But I had indeed seen him relax with singular style and resolution. If you can call it relaxing.

17

El estatuario

Side on to the bull, the matador holds the *muleta* perpendicular to his body, lengthened by the sword. He is a flagpole at half-mast. He does not move, does not look at the bull. He calls, moves the *muleta*, it charges. He is a statue.

In late September the madness of the media descended on Seville. Giles Coren, writer for *The Times* and best friend of my late brother Jules, came to town to do a piece about my research.

Giles's 9,000-word account does a justice to that long weekend I am not going to try to match, nor will I be graceless enough to point out the errors he both consciously and unconsciously included for dramatic effect. It is as much a moving paean to my late brother as a witty and sometimes thrilling account of a very hectic 100 hours in which I tried to combine the triple task of playing host, spin-doctor and bullfighter at a *tentadero* with Padilla and Adolfo Suárez Illana, and it was the last of these at which I was worst. The fact that I was still utterly untrained, had an audience of some of the better bullfighters of Spain, was being filmed and was even wired for sound at the time (which picked up mainly heavy breathing and swearing in English and Spanish) meant that the work I did in the ring with a frankly tiny animal was just embarrassing.

However, once Giles had left, I had another, far more important task. Although Giles thought that Adolfo was in the ring especially for him, it was actually part of his training for his first public bullfight in two years. Adolfo is not a professional bull-fighter, but for ten years he has almost annually stepped into the ring as that bravest of Spanish inventions: the *aficionado práctico*, the amateur bullfighter.

I had not seen Adolfo since our meetings in the early months of the year, although we had exchanged many messages in the interim. However, it was with Giles watching over the two of us like a journalistic hawk at the bar of Padilla's house that I felt we finally relaxed in each other's company, helped no doubt by hard liquor and the adrenaline of an afternoon spent in the ring with animals. There we discussed Adolfo's views of what a matador should be and who fulfils that ideal, weighing up the merits of the *figuras* of the day.

It turned out we had very different conceptions of what makes the bullfight beautiful. Tomás, whom I and many of the *aficionados* regard as some sort of genius standing above the standard ranking, Adolfo does not seem to feel is so special. He praises the elegance of his friend Enrique Poncé and, among the younger generation, Manzanares. In fact, elegance is Adolfo's dominant concept, which makes sense when I think of how he himself capes an animal, keeping his movements minimal. I ask why, given his tastes in bullfighting, he is so close to Padilla. For while I have seen Padilla exhibit unconscious elegance in training, in the arena he is a vigorous, grand gladiator of a bullfighter. Adolfo answers by talking of Padilla as something apart, fighting an older form of the bullfight, with the large and deadly bulls like the Miuras. Different rules apply there. We both agree that Perera, with whom we both spent a day the first time I got into the ring, is excellent but has some way to go. Morante, a good friend of his and Padilla's, has flashes of brilliance which, when allowed to emerge by his temperament and a well-publicised psychological instability, are so moving as to make him impossible to place. We also agree that Cayetano has something different too, especially at the kill, but he has been a matador for only a very few years.

It seems strange, and perhaps it is a function of spending so long in Spain, so long steeped in blood, that my doubts about the bullfight – about its ethical right to exist – appeared to have been placed firmly out of the range of conversation. Like a philosopher turned antique dealer, I no longer ask if the table exists, but spend my time discussing its polish, patina and the scrollwork in the carving. The doubts were still there: I was at the time rereading monographs like Mark Rowlands's *Animal Rights* and Roger Scruton's *Animal Rights and Animal Wrongs*. However, in the company of bullfighters those thoughts have, of necessity, gone underground. What is more, I've already heard all the arguments in favour of the bullfight and they're usually bad, so I'd rather not hear people I like come up with them.

At the end of our conversation, I confirmed that I would join Adolfo in the alley around the ring, the *callejón*, for his fight on Tuesday the 29th in Castellón. Padilla would be there as well, to give support, following his own fight in Granada on Sunday. Adolfo's fight is probably the finest *cartel* of the year, although it is a charity festival, rather than a *corrida*. So fighting six bulls of different breeders will be the great *rejoneador*, or horseback-bullfighter, Pablo Hermosa de Mendoza, followed by the footsoldiers, Fandi, Manzanares, Cayetano, Castella and finally Adolfo.

■ ■ ■ ■ ■

On Tuesday, I fly to Valencia and take the train up to Castellón, where, standing on the platform, I discover it is raining. Not the polite drizzle of England, but the great moving sheets of Spain that encase you in water in a matter of seconds. I arrive at the rather elegant late-nineteenth-century bullring to discover it under rising flood waters. Half an hour later Adolfo walks in to find me smoking, sheltered under an arch as various grizzled and thick-set men are unloading the bulls. He tells me a deal has been struck and the matadors have agreed that the fight will be delayed from the Tuesday until the Friday. We watch the bulls unloaded – damp furious beast after damp furious beast – until the last one comes out, the one that will face Adolfo. Chosen for him from the farm of his father-in-law, Samuel Flores, it is a particularly heavy animal: short of leg, shaggy of fur and massive – with horns to match. Adolfo laughs at his own fear and the laughter is real, but so is the fear. He tells me he is going to the ranch from whence it came, the *finca* of Samuel Flores, to relax on his own for the days leading up to the fight. Would I like to come? At first I say no, suspecting this may be politeness after I have made the effort to travel to his fight, but he assures me I am welcome.

I get in the four-wheel-drive Mercedes with Adolfo and a *banderillero* of some note who is called José Antón Galdón but is better known as 'El Niño de Belén', the name he had as a *novillero*, 'novice matador', before his hopes at fame and glory were removed – along with his right eye – by the horn of a bull. The loss of an eye has made him no less talkative, and my Spanish is run to the limit by his accent and the speed of his tumbling words. In the black Mercedes saloon following us is Adolfo's picador, the solid middle-aged figure of 'El Tuti', and Paúl Abadía, a polite and thin young matador who fights under the name Serranito.

I wake up as we turn off the road to a pair of gates inscribed with the legend 'El Palomar'. Adolfo buzzes the house and the electric gates open and we coast along the two miles of driveway to the house, the green grass all around spotted with trees and wooded islands. The ground is stony, the stones condensing into boulders as the land rises into great craggy hills all around us.

We pull up to the main house and Adolfo apologises for going in by the side door – 'My mother-in-law would never forgive me' – where we are greeted by a little dog called Toy with grey whiskers and bloodlines ranging from schnauzer to dachshund. There is an interesting change that comes over Adolfo with Toy, in which he reveals a most unexpected level of affection for the dog who is his constant companion and helper when he stays here.

We enter the house via the kitchen, so I am lulled into a false sense of normality, before being led out into the entrance hall and the first exhibits in this mausoleum of the wild and the taurine: bulls' heads, half a dozen of them. And antlers, a dozen of them. In fact, the entire house is laid out like this, the paragon of the Spanish country home, representing the embodied death on the inside of all the bustling life that teems outside. For El Palomar is as much a nature reserve as it is a functioning farm.

Adolfo installs me in the room next to his in the upstairs labyrinth and we freshen up before going down to the dining room. Adolfo and his father-in-law, Samuel, discuss the fight to come and the season's bullfights, which are now coming to an end. Talking about his own bulls, Samuel says that the modern bullfight with its obsession with elegant capework close to the body has made his animals almost out of date. He speaks of the 'Domecqisation' of the bullfight in the same way the sociologist George Ritzer spoke of the McDonaldisation of modern culture. However, this is not with disapproval for the actions of his friend Juan Pedro Domecq and his family, who produce the perfect bulls for the modern fight. What he bemoans is the lack of variety: 'Once upon a time you would see a poster for your local bullring with Saltillo bulls and you would know you were in for a certain sort of fight, or Murubes or Santa Colomas, now it is all trying to be the perfect Domecq fought by El Juli.' I wonder if this is because of television showing everyone how good that sort of fight can be, what the English theatre critic Kenneth Tynan called 'the slow, sad fury of the perfect bull-fight'. It seems strange to talk about modern media influencing the bullfight, but it is at heart a spectacle, so it is inevitable that this will be the case.

We retire for drinks into one of the living rooms, where Samuel shows me three vast sets of antlers, almost thirty points on each. Each was, in its time, the largest ever shot in Spain, all from this ranch: one by the King, one by Samuel's son (also called Samuel), one by Adolfo. Samuel bids us goodnight and Adolfo and I are left alone talking about his forthcoming bull-fight, or rather avoiding talking about it. It is obvious that it is beginning to weigh on him. We mix another drink and step outside into the cool dark.

'First thing you should know, Xander, there is a huge dog here, a real Hound of the Baskervilles. And when he comes at you, he comes fast ...'

On cue, one of the largest, strongest dogs I have ever seen comes bounding out of the darkness in a clumsily articulated silence, part Pyrenean mountain dog, part mastiff, part mastodon.

'... and he is absolutely harmless. Except the smell. His name is Super. He is the Hardy to Toy's Laurel.'

As he leaps up on me to say hello at the end of his gallop, I inhale the essence of pure outdoor dog. He is one of those great big gentle dogs you can't help but make a fuss of and then can't wait to wash your hands afterwards. We wander down the road for a while, listening to rutting stags calling to their mates from hilltop to hilltop before turning in for the night.

* * * * *

The next morning, I grabbed a bite of breakfast with Adolfo and then we left the house for a long walk across the property to loosen up his muscles before his team arrived to begin the day of training. We walked for a couple of miles until we reached the great lake, more than half a mile long and about a third of that in width. All around us were the bulls, held back from the road by fences, while at the far end the horse herds that are also bred here roamed free as well. We jogged back to the house to warm up properly.

Waiting at the house were Adolfo's team with capes and aluminium caping swords ready for some practice without bulls – *toreo de salón*, which translates terribly as 'drawing-room bullfighting'. Now, I have never done *toreo de salón*, despite having been in the ring three times, which may explain why I have been getting hit and suffering injury more and more frequently. As I said, the third time, which Giles came to witness, was in my eyes a shameful display. Bad because I lacked technique, but shameful because this had been catered for by the use of an even smaller cow than the time before, and the fact that I just went out there and took hit after hit from the infuriated animal in order to provide copy for a newspaper. All in all, it was a vainglorious failure in the name of PR.

So, with Serranito charging Adolfo with a pair of horns while Belén contributed comments on how Adolfo should refine his style, I stood to one side receiving the attention of these masters in the most rudimentary of passes, *el derechazo*, the right-handed pass with the *muleta*.

The *muleta* is the small red cape used at the end of the bullfight, when the bull has been worn down and damaged sufficiently (a cold phrase, I know) to be brought close to the body without intolerable risk (noting that what a matador will tolerate as risk far outstrips what you or I might, hence their scarring, disfiguring and death). However, at the beginning of this final act of the drama, the bull is still too fresh to be trusted. The *muleta* contains an eighteen inch wooden stick within it, the *palillo*. It runs along the edge of the fabric and it is by this that the *muleta* is held and manipulated with the right hand. Also intertwined between the same fingers are the hilt and guard of the sword, whose blade extends the *muleta* into a larger surface area to present to the bull.

The matador then advances towards the bull, slowing as he grows closer, until he reaches the edge of the bull's 'territory'. This edge is much like the 'biting point' of the clutch on manual transmission cars – the bull is trembling on the edge of committing to a charge. The stance of the matador, and where he places the *muleta*, at this point depends on his style. The older style is to stand face on to the bull; this then changed to sideways on, although most matadors nowadays, following the great Juan Belmonte, stand three-quarters on.

Arguments also exist about feet together or apart and whether or not the *muleta* should begin by the hip or go forward towards the bull. The fact is that the earlier style grew out of trial and error – and so worked – but was backed up by theories about the bull, especially about its visual field, which were simply wrong. This is why people thought that Belmonte's innovative style would lead to his rapid death in the ring, which it didn't.

Returning to the *muleta*, when it is at this 'biting point' it is then jerked while in place: a little at first, then, if nothing happens, with more force. This is accompanied by a call, usually '¡*Toro!*' or '¡*Je!*' This stimulates the bull into his destructive and headlong charge, and the matador then uses whatever shape he decides to draw with his arm to bring the bull close to his body for drama, and then away from his body for safety. Again, there are arguments whether the line of the cape should follow the natural line of the charge or materially change it, bending the bull around the body. Both have their aesthetic upsides and downsides, which may suit certain matadors better or worse, and also have their practical ones, which will suit, or not, different bulls.

However, my style is to start with the *muleta* clear out in front, feet apart, body in three-quarter profile, and begin to move it so that the horns catch up with it, but never actually catch it, following the line of the bull's charge which tangentially intersects the circle of safety around my body beyond which I do not want the bull to go. The *muleta* will start higher and end lower, bringing the horns and head down as he passes, which also slows him. My wrist will roll to facilitate this movement. At the end the *muleta* will turn like a revolving door so that the bull will spin to face it, ready for the next attack.

Using the language of the first matador, Pedro Romero, you need *parar*, *templar* and *mandar*. *Parar* means 'to stop' or 'to stake' – as in poker – and refers to the matador standing his ground. *Templar* means 'to temper' or 'to tune', adjusting the cape to the bull's charge and/or adjusting the bull's charge with the cape. *Mandar* means 'to send', with the sense of command, and refers to sending the bull safely away from the body to the place of your choosing. However, since you also need the bull to come back again, and by then he has lost sight of you, you must pass him so as to implant within him the desire to turn. This is the hardest of all, called *cargar la suerte*, which I translate as 'to load the dice'. This is to turn body, weight and cape during the pass so the bull's awareness is brought back to the cape even as he goes through it, so he will stop his charge beyond you, turn around, and be ready to be brought back.

However, why does the bull charge in the first place? Well, here it is necessary to say a little about the biology of the Spanish fighting bull, which I have avoided going into for long enough. For reasons both good and bad, the background of this symbol of Spain has made the messy slide from history to mythology. It is worth remembering what is at stake here. The killing of a savage beast invokes very different moral sentiments to the slaying of a confused but naturally placid mammal. The reality of this should be borne in mind when evaluating the writings of those who are either pro- or anti-bullfighting. Not least because it then becomes reported as fact by people who should know better. For example, in his book *Beef: The Untold Story of How Milk, Meat, and Muscle Shaped the World*, Evan Fraser, an environmental scientist, says:

> Spanish cows had a mixed bloodline. Much of it flowed from the light-coloured, utilitarian herds that had existed on the peninsula since Roman times ... In Andalusia, they mated with *Bos taurus ibericus*, the black-coated savage who had walked the hills since prehistory, and from whom the modern fighting bull is descended. The urbane Moors had hunted him and pushed him to the edges of their neat, furrowed earth, but in Las Marismas [the marshy floodplain of the Guadalquivir River south of Seville] he was free to do as he liked.

To Dr Fraser's credit, when challenged on this he said, 'As I look over recent literature ... maybe it's just a myth that these are the fighting bulls ... it's quite likely that I simply took the stories told to me in Spain at face value.'

On the other side of the debate, the anti-bullfighter Jordi Casamitjana says:

> Bulls, otherwise very peaceful animals that spend most of their lives eating grass, sleeping and playing with each other, are submitted to such an ordeal that not only inflicts serious physical and psychological suffering on them, but also forces them to behave in ways they would not normally behave, namely charging other creatures so they go away, giving them the false reputation of being 'brave', which any other herbivore would have in the same circumstances.

So, where does the truth lie? Well, when Adolfo and I walked near the herds, and when we drove in among them, there was simply no denying the fact that these react far more like the Cape buffalo herd I drove near in the Kruger Park – horns turned to face, constantly shifting, eyeing the threat, largest males coming to the front to protect the others – than the utterly docile herd of black and white milk cartons (Holstein-Friesians to be precise) that lived in the field next to where I grew up in East Anglia and among whom I used to wander freely. So, here is the biology of the situation.

In the kingdom Animalia, within the phylum Chordata (those with backbones), among the class Mammalia (those who suckle their young), a subset of the order of the Artiodactyla (the even-toed or 'cloven-hoofed'), are the Bovidae. Bovid is from the Latin *bos, bovis* for cow or ox. However, this family of animals (143 species) that ruminate or 'chew the cud', but neither have branched horns nor shed them (like deer), also comprises sheep, goats, antelope (including wildebeest), cattle and buffalo: African (Cape), Asian (water) or American (bison).

Now, the bovids are all herbivores, but not all herbivores are bovids. Alongside cattle and antelope we have elephant, hippo and boar; we also have the gorilla, the koala, the blue whale and the rabbit.

With specific reference to charging, this predator-inspired behaviour varies widely from species to species. For example, the kudu is both the second largest and second most common antelope in the Kruger Park, where I observed it. Despite its size and impressive horns, though, it is 'not a naturally aggressive species' (from *BMC Veterinary Research*). Indeed, it is so passive that in the Milwaukee County Zoo in 1988 two were bitten to death by a single zebra. At the other end of the spectrum within the same game park I saw the sable antelope, far rarer and one quarter lighter in weight. This antelope is treated with grave respect by all predators and is so violent within its own herd that, 'because of their aggressive nature, sable antelope present a challenge to captive management' (from *Zoo Biology*).

I use these examples to demonstrate the radical differences that exist between antelope species to show why stereotyping simply doesn't work. Cape buffalo are known by big game hunters as the 'Black Death', and are often quoted as the most prolific killer of lions (and sometimes humans) in all of Africa.

So, narrowing the focus, within the bovids, and their sub-family the bovines, we find the genus *Bos*. There are five living species of this genus. Ignoring the yak, the gaur, the kouprey and the banteng, we are interested in those currently classi-fied as *Bos primigenius*, which, according to the International Commission on Zoological Nomenclature, is divided into three subspecies. The humped zebu cattle of Africa, *Bos primigenius indicus*, all other breeds of domestic cattle, *Bos primigenius tau-rus*, and the ancestor of both, the vast, bestial aurochs, *Bos primigenius primigenius*. Of this animal we know:

> The last animal died in central Poland in the year 1627. Its former range was across much of the Old World, including Europe, north Africa, and large parts of Asia. [It is estimated] that the height of bulls at the withers [was] 170 to 190 cm [5' 7" to 6' 3"] during the Pleistocene period, with a curved, in-turning horn length of 60 to 110 cm [2–4 feet], and weighing between 450 and 900 kg [1,000 lb to 2,000 lb]. The species was a forest dweller and likely preferred marsh and wetter forests. [It is argued] that extinction was a consequence of the expansion of farms and pasture. (*Quarterly Review of Biology*)

We know that all the *Bos primigenius* subspecies – despite being wildly different in shape, temperament and circumstance – share their basic visual system. The bull does not have vision like a man, with eyes front: i.e. predator-vision. Instead, it has prey-vision, with increased awareness towards the vulnerable rear and excellent vision at the sides, while it has poor forward vision.

There are many bullfighters and *aficionados* – my past self included – who actually believe and propagate the myth that the bull has a large blind spot directly in front of it, the so-called 'anticone of immunity' that extends, point first, out from the animal far enough that a man directly in front of the horns is actually invisible to the bull. This is a nonsense. It would mean not only that it could not see what it was eating, but also that when two bulls fights, horns locked together, they would be unable to see each other's heads.

The eye placement and bone contours of the skull also cause the visual plane to be unusually low down, so they have to move their whole head up to look up. Because of the physiology of the eye itself, this idiosyncratic optical array is dichromatic – ranging from blue to green and unable to distinguish red as we do, having trichromatic vision. There are no red rags for bulls. In fact, what a bull is particularly sensitive to, what enrages it, is movement. The cape used at the end of the fight is red from tradition, not because of any natural antipathy in the bull to that colour.

The ancestral aurochs' natural opponent was a pack of wolves, which came at it from low down, camouflaged – so movement is a far better indicator than colour – and, when you are a six foot, one ton beast, it is not the 150lb predator snarling in front of your four-foot horns that you need to worry about but the one coming from the side or behind.

This visual set-up is a necessary, but not a sufficient, condition of the bullfight. It is the irritability, this overwhelming urge to charge the aggravating image that appears before it – rather than run away – that is the unique characteristic of the Spanish fighting bull over other breeds. Other cattle have been bred to be easy to manage – for milk or meat – and the fight has been taken out of them. Having said that, one must realise how dangerous a regular cow can be. A cursory glance at the archives for *The Times* for the past decade brings these headlines from Britain:

Cow kills man (29 August 2003)
Bull kills farmer (8 July 2005)
Bullock kills farmer (1 January 2007)

Dog-walker killed by cow (15 June 2005)

Bull on rampage (13 March 2007)

Man killed in bull attack on public footpath (13 November 2010)

Bull kills farmer (28 November 2010)

It is for this reason that the British Health & Safety Executive (HSE) passed the law that:

> Section 59 of the Wildlife and Countryside Act 1981 bans bulls of recognised dairy breeds (eg. Ayrshire, Friesian, Holstein, Dairy Shorthorn, Guernsey, Jersey and Kerry) in all circumstances from being at large in fields crossed by public rights of way. Bulls of all other breeds are also banned from such fields unless accompanied by cows or heifers, but there are no specific prohibitions on other cattle.

Notice how specific this decree is to the breed. And even despite this legislation, an HSE report titled 'Fatal injuries in farming, forestry, horticulture and associated industries' states:

> In 2006/07 injuries from animals caused more deaths than any other category. Eleven people were killed by animals, five more than in the previous year (2005/06). Three involved bulls, seven cows or other cattle and one a horse.

Given the machinery that is in use on farms, from combine-harvesters to chainsaws, this is a remarkably high fatality rate from animals, and over 90 per cent of it from cattle. In the US the picture is similar, with a report titled 'Occupational fatalities due to animal-related events' in the journal *Wilderness & Environmental Medicine* finding that from 1992 to 1997: 'Cattle were responsible for 142 deaths [more than any other animal] … Most deaths from cattle were from attacks or mauling from the animal, especially bulls.'

So we begin to see that even when the animal has been bred for docility, it is still dangerous.

Now, imagine if it was bred for aggression, or rather, if the aggression had not been bred out of it. The Spanish fighting bull is distinguished from the animals described above by a matter of degree so extreme that it becomes a difference of quality, not just quantity. It will relentlessly charge whether it is fresh or tired, strong or weak, hale or injured. This is what the Spanish mean by calling a bull *bravo*, which means brave when applied to humans in Spanish, but for animals means fierce. As it once did in English, the etymological ancestor of 'brave' and 'bravo' being the Latin word *rabidus*, which most famously applied to animals driven insane, and then later to the most common disease which causes that madness, rabies.

Despite these basic facts, the circumstances of the fight also contribute to the aggression of the animal. The ring is circular and has no exit, so the animal can neither run away nor find a corner to back into, therefore it must charge. However, this is only a partial cause. I have seen bulls in fights which have backed up against the fence and simply reared out at a matador standing inches away, but never charged. This is a situation of extreme danger to the bullfighter. At that distance the bullfighter is as likely to be identified as a target as the cape, and he has no chance to adjust the animal's focus. This category of animal – into which all other bovids including regular cattle fall – is simply not possible to fight in the style of the Spanish bullfight. It is the incessant urge to charge, and the total commitment to that charge without deviation, which is required by the bullfight. This is what the Spanish called *la nobleza*, 'the nobility' of the animal, in that it does not resort to 'ignoble' trickery, like stopping in mid-charge, or hooking with the horns, but is open, straight and honest.

So the question arises as to whether this aggression is a naturally occurring thing inherited from its ancestors or something man-made, bred into the animal for dark, cruel purposes. The evidence is hard to come by on a matter like this, but in a paper in 2009 in the journal *Animal Genetics*, a team from Madrid discovered that 'the high [genetic] diversity in the breed is evidence of a certain degree of primitivism'. They argue that the bloodlines that comprise the fighting bulls are some of the oldest in Europe. This would indicate that many of the genes that make the Spanish fighting bull are original, and although this does not prove that those which code for aggression are 'ancestral', it would be a little coincidental if it had been first bred out, and then bred back in.

Not that that hasn't happened elsewhere. It has been long known that the domestic dog descended from wolves somewhere between 16,000 and 36,000 years ago (the aurochs was domesticated only 13,000 years ago, hunting predating agriculture). Recently, like the cow, the dog has been reclassified as a subspecies of its ancestral form the wolf, *Canis lupis familiaris*. Just as there is between breeds of cattle, there is great temperamental diversity between breeds of dog. One might think of the docile Labrador as an analogue of a nice British cow, the Holstein-Friesian for example, whereas the boxer, bred at various times for both fighting and hunting large mammals like bear and wild boar, is more like the fighting bull. In fact, that analogy is obvious at first sight over all my examples: the sable antelope, the *toro de lidia*, the boxer dog all have heavy, broad, fighter's shoulders. The kudu, the milk cow, the Labrador do not.

This feeds directly into the argument about the conservation of Spanish fighting cattle breeds, which pro-taurinos say is a duty and requires the bullfight to continue to exist. In my eyes, the anti-taurinos quite rightly insist that is nonsense. Whatever the source of the bull's aggression, it is not itself an aurochs. It is one race among many within a subspecies that was the same species as the aurochs. Whether it is closer to ancestral type is in many ways incalculable (what do you mean by closer? What it looks like, behaves like, or number of DNA triplet codon matches?). The important argument really is that the vast landscapes within which this free-ranging animal roams remain entirely in their natural state. While it is difficult to believe that the fighting bull would ever be allowed to die out should the bullfight be banned, even if the vast herds were reduced to a few thousand individuals, wildlife conservation in a broader sense, as I have said earlier, is financially underwritten by the bullfights that pay for the landscape to remain *dehesa* (along with the preservation of a certain sense of Spanish national pride that has come to be symbolised by the fighting bull existing en masse in their countryside.)

So, the bull charges because that is its nature. There endeth the lesson.

■ ■ ■ ■ ■

After my lesson in the practice rather than the theory, we all walked into the nicest private bullring I have seen in Spain, nestled within the old, red-brick complex of the house, spanning the gap between the kitchen and one of the wings of bedrooms. With old, uneven walls forming an imperfect circle, ornamented with trees and hanging baskets, it seems far too sedate and informal for bullfighting – more the Senator's Estate than the Gladiator's Arena. Perhaps it is for that reason, perhaps the lack of journalists, perhaps the fact that I had been in a ring four days before, that I was infinitely calmer than when Giles came to visit. Lounging behind the *burladero* with Serranito and Adolfo, I watched them take turns to cape each beast as it entered, with El Tuti, who had now arrived, delivering his trademark of deft pic-ing with the miniature-tipped lance used on the *vaquillas*.

By the time we reached my *vaquilla* – number three – I was feeling much more comfortable than I had hoped and eager to try out the new technique I had picked up. I walked out to the *vaca* attempting a reverse cape as an easy opener, with the *muleta* in the right hand, but with the arm across the body so the fabric was on my left, wrist rotated so that the knuckles rather than the palm faced the animal. The body thus rotates to the left when the bull charges.

Sure enough the *vaquilla* swept past through the cape with a happy, but not ungainly, distance between its body and mine. I turn and face it for a *derechazo*, right hand open and outwards at the end of my arm at full extension, my body concealed behind the *muleta*, which I trill with one finger on the sword. It takes the lure and charges and I draw the *muleta* down by my side, wrist flexing down, then circling clockwise at the end to turn the animal as it follows the rotating doors of the red cloth. I turn, body once again concealed behind the cape, and perform the same action again. This time it comes closer to my body, but I am not panicked. And again.

This time something odd happens, and halfway through the pass it falls in the sand; as I reach forward in, what is for me, a bold effort to cape it to its feet, Adolfo tells me to stop. The *vaquilla* is lying trembling on the ground, not with fear, but something else. It turns out that its instinct to charge has exceeded its physical capacity to do so and now it runs the risk, I am told, of killing itself like a racehorse ridden so hard that its 'heart bursts' – a trait I was unaware that fighting cattle also share with thoroughbred horses.

Despite this odd event, my successful encounter with the cow invigorates and relaxes me, as it is so much better than my attempt in front of the audience I had a few days before. Samuel Flores sits watching the *tentadero* behind wrought-iron gates on a patio that leads to his kitchen. His *mayoral*, 'farm manager', Carmelo Clemente, sits with him as he makes his notes, and occasionally a member of staff will stop to watch, but that is it in its entirety: a family affair.

In this relaxed, odd state I start to watch Adolfo's caping.

He has become smoother and better, with more varied pass-sequences, since I saw him in spring. However, the one to watch is the young Serranito, whose smooth action is a joy. His style is still developing, but with easy limbs, effortless courage and constant practice there is no denying he will develop into something good given the right chances. He is also a quick learner, who has seen Daniel Luque's changing hands style in Nîmes and now tries it with perfect results on a *vaquilla*, though whether this would come as easily on a full grown bull is hard to discern.

However, the complex style seems to have consequences, as the *vaquilla* that he tries this on suffers a heart attack on its way out of the ring. A matador of consummate elegance has gone one step further and managed to kill without ever using a sword.

Or not quite kill. When I am called out to see, Adolfo, Serranito and one of the farmhands are standing over the animal on the sandy entrance area. Serranito, determined to put the animal out of its misery as soon as possible, calls for his sword, with which he tries to find a chink in the vertebral armour in order to sever the animal's spinal cord. Adolfo, a more practised killer outside the arena than anyone there, beats him to it. Taking a knife, he deftly cuts through the loose skin and fat layer on the throat, reaches into the incision with two fingers to find the carotid artery, pulls it out and cuts it as you would a length of rubber tubing. The failing heart beats a few times more, sending the bright red, oxygen-rich blood pooling on to the sand, and then it stops. The animal's white second eyelid closes, then its main one follows suit. I feel nothing. How far into this world have I come? How attuned was I to its ethics before I began? I don't know. Maybe it's just the adrenaline.

Soon I am out from behind the hide again, and this *vaquilla*, although smaller, is much fresher, catching me almost immediately in the hand and leg, snapping my – actually Adolfo's

– aluminium sword at the hilt because I refuse to let go. Adolfo berates me: 'When I tell you to get out, get out and don't try to be brave.' I don't think he understands that I simply didn't hear him. There is only one thing in the world for me in the ring, and that thing has horns and doesn't speak.

I replace the sword with an odd Mexican sword, a hybrid between a killing and a caping sword, and begin a series of passes, and although I avoid head-on collisions, the cow's horns scrape my thigh on each pass. Samuel calls out, 'Try *pase de pecho*,' and I begin the first real sequence of my life, done entirely in reverse to the normal order since it comprises three *pases de pecho* finishing with a *derechazo*. I don't think even the *vaquilla* knew what to make of it, but I knew what it felt like. It felt good, although not so good, as Belén would later put it with his one English word, as 'fucking'. Inevitably, though, I take an increasing number of hits. Interestingly, the brief success has so buoyed me that this does not throw me off, so I carry on, and Adolfo suggests that being unable to walk is not the way forward for a matador. Even a mere six hours later, when I am first writing this paragraph, I can feel my legs seizing up completely.

The *tentadero* ends with me happy for the first time on leaving a ring, with the words of Samuel Flores, '*bueno torero*', 'good bullfighter', ringing in my ears. That night I sleep the dreamless sleep of the content.

18

La manoletina

With *muleta* extended by the sword, the matador places it behind
his back, left hand keeping the corner by his hip, and cites.
The bull charges and the matador directs it to the lure with tiny
movements. It passes, the horns brushing his side.

Sitting down to a late breakfast before departing
for the fight, we find out that Padilla, whom we
had heard was injured in Granada, is in worse shape than we
thought. Samuel tells us he is supplying the bulls for a fight at
a festival in the local village and that Padilla was due to be one
of the matadors on a *cartel* topped by the Rolex of bullfighters,
Enrique Poncé. Samuel offers the job to Serranito, who has up
until then in his career had to attempt to fit his style to gladiatorial bulls like the Miuras and the Pahlas. Serranito nods with
a quiet smile, but you can feel the thrill of pride and excitement
rush through him.

A few miles along the drive to Castellón we pay an important visit to a large church in the hills above the little village
of Alcaraz. Here, Adolfo explains, seven centuries earlier, the
Virgin Mary appeared to a shepherd called Francisco Álvarez in
the hollow of an oak tree and as a result the oversized sanctuary
was built about a kilometre up the hill from the village. Every
year on 8 September, the statue of the Virgin is carried on the
shoulders of the faithful, up the hill, past tens of thousands of
pilgrims, into the chapel and down into its crypt.

'One year,' he says, 'I was one of the men carrying. It is

heavier than it looks. Now I must pray, my friend. I need all the help I can get.'

I leave the four of them on their knees and wander out into the colonnades, thinking about what he is going through, and about my own utter lack of faith. It must be a comforting thing, I think, but I do not regret having lost it early on in life.

I must admit that Adolfo mystifies me at this moment. He possesses great strength and power – physically and metaphorically – and yet his urge to kill is one of the strongest things in him, like a black fault in a crystal. And yet this is the same man who is on his knees now to the effigy of a man who said the greatest virtue of all is love. *Un espada*, 'a sword' – as the bull-fighters who kill are called – paying homage to he who said, 'All they that take the sword shall perish with the sword.'

Having dropped Adolfo's bags at the matadors' hotel – a five-star – Adolfo comes for dinner with his *cuadrilla* in our lesser accommodation, where the various teams were staying. We walk into the empty, soulless restaurant, where 1,000 corporate conventions must have dined, and take a table at random. There is something different about Adolfo at this moment, something I haven't seen before. He is not just distracted, but somehow lessened. For a man whose inner force is sometimes overwhelming, it is noticeable how much of it seems to be struggling with the idea of the next day. Or perhaps it is being held in reserve. It is Belén who insists on a bottle of red wine for the table, although Adolfo summons the presence to choose. We fall into uneasy discussion, largely driven by Belén, who is blunt to say the least.

'But why, *why* does an Englishman want to write about bull-fighting? This is not what the English are interested in? They are polite and weak and rich and mainly homosexuals. Obviously not you, Alejandro …'

I start laughing as I hear this and can't stop myself to respond. It is Adolfo who answers for me.

'The English were a hard race, Belén. They had the "empire on which the sun never sets", after we had lost ours.' *El imperio en el que nunca se pone el sol* is originally a Spanish phrase. 'They invented democracy.'

'In truth? I did not know this. But how does the Englishman get in the ring with our Spanish bulls?' asks Belén.

Adolfo warms to his theme. 'They had an industrial revolution which we did not equal for almost two hundred years, they all lived in cities, far away from animals, so they do not understand how they are treated in the real world. Alejandro grew up in the country, so he has courage.'

Adolfo winks at me – being on the side of Belén's glass eye he cannot be seen – indicating that he is aware this is a vast oversimplification.

'Is it not just because he is a little crazy, Adolfo?' Ever blunt, Belén continues, 'I think he has no idea of the danger of what he is doing?'

'Show him the photo of Pamplona,' Adolfo says to me. I take out my mobile phone and zoom into the image of me running beside the bulls, handing it to Belén.

'The Sunday of the Miuras, Belén,' he says.

Belén stares at it with his good eye.

'Fucking crazy!' He looks at me in genuine surprise. 'This, *this* Belén would never do. You and Adolfo' – Adolfo ran a few years before – 'you are both fucking crazy!'

The conversation returns to bullfighting in general, and Adolfo turns to me and begins to talk in English, in part because I find Belén so hard to understand, in part, as he points out, because he's heard it all before. I ask him why he fights bulls.

'You know there are twenty answers I could give to that and they would all be true.'

'Of course.'

'OK, I will tell you a story. My father killed bulls. This photo,' he brings up a black and white image on his mobile telephone, 'is of my father before killing a bull which he dedicated to my mother.'

Adolfo pauses for a moment; the death of his mother nine years before from cancer still hangs over him, I know. Only three years later his sister followed her, and a year after that Adolfo announced to the press that his father's Alzheimer's had taken away any memory of being prime minister.

'In 1981, my father's term as prime minister ended and his Socialist replacement was being confirmed in the Chamber of Deputies. To prevent this the Army attempted a coup d'état, and a colonel in the Guardia Civil entered the parliament building with 200 armed men. They walked into the chamber and fired into the air, shouting to everyone to get on the floor. And everyone leapt on to the floor, all except three men. The head of the Communist Party – and this was a right-wing military coup – took out a cigarette and lit it. He had fought in the Civil War, been trained by Stalin, executed his own men, he knew courage and he knew death. My father's deputy prime minister – who had also fought in the war on the other side, been imprisoned, had ended up a general and Chief of the Defence Staff – he leaped up and started to argue with the soldiers, calling them traitors, trying to wrestle with them even though he was nearly seventy. And my father, who sat there with his arms folded. How did he do that? He was never a soldier. How? Because when you have fought a bull, gunfire just becomes one more thing that can kill you. Just one more among many, and not the most terrifying at that.'

He pauses at this, remembering what he has to do the next day. Belén, who follows none of the words in this exchange, immediately notices Adolfo lapse into thinking about the bull; he decides it is time to put him to bed, pays the bill – as a *banderillero* always does, holding the money for his maestro – and we all get into Adolfo's car to accompany him back to his hotel. We are all a little 'merry' by this point, and Adolfo is going through his music collection, which up until then has seemed to be a mix of Beethoven and flamenco. However, he puts on something completely unexpected, which opens with the sort of sweeping chords that I associate with musical theatre (and dread as a result). As the voices come on, I react initially against the saccharine form of the song until I actually listen to the lyrics, and realise that verse after verse is about the singer's mother, who has died, and his sense of loss, and being lost.

As we get out of the car, in the dark of the car park, Adolfo quotes a line from the song, 'Mamma ... I hope you're happy with my life', and then says to me in English, in a voice thick with emotion, his face turned away from the streetlight, 'Tell me, Alexander, do you think she would be? I always wonder if she would be.'

Something glints on his face and I answer in the only way I can, hoping to the God in whom I have no faith that it is true: 'Yes, my friend. Yes.'

'Thank you.'

Adolfo shouts *adiós* across the top of the car to the other two, not turning his face towards them, and walks off into the darkness alone. We drive back in silence. They have not listened, they have not heard, but they have understood. Tomorrow he struggles with Death, so tonight he struggles with his life.

That night I am kept awake by the snoring of Belén. As is usual with matadors' teams, the three of us share a room which also has a fourth bed, not for the picador, who is sleeping at home, but for the photographer who is coming in Nicolás's stead, Carlos Cazalis.

■　■　■　■　■

Walking into the breakfast room the next morning I realise

how far I have come in this world of blood and sand because every single person in there, all twenty-something of them, is a bullfighter. Not matadors, but *toreros* nonetheless: *mozos de espadas*, 'sword-handlers', *banderilleros* and picadors. It turns out the matadors' *cuadrillas* are the only people staying in the hotel at that moment, and they all look up as I walk in. What is more, they all look familiar, as I have seen them around the rings of Spain (or, in the case of Castella, Nîmes in France). It is Cayetano's team who explain to the others who I am in a whisper, and I hear one of Castella's team saying that he has heard all about '*el inglés*'. I join Belén and Serranito at a table, and notice the respect with which Belén is treated, although you see this through the lens of rough humour.

'Belén, you still working, I thought you had died,' one of them says.

'Or lost his other eye,' says another.

'I did,' he replies, 'no one has noticed yet. And I can still give a *corrida* twice as well as you. Or at least that is what your wife said, José.' The room laughs, '*corrida*' also being slang for an orgasm.

As we eat, a familiar yet unknown face comes from the table of Fandi's *cuadrilla* and introduces himself.

'*Soy Óscar Padilla, hermano de Juan. Es un honor a encontrarte, Alejandro.*' 'I'm Oscar Padilla, brother of Juan. It's an honour to meet you, Alexander.'

And so I met the biological brother of my 'Spanish brother'. In all, for someone who less than a year before – exactly one day less, but still less – had been sitting in the stands looking down on the ring in Las Ventas and didn't know a soul, I had come a long way indeed. Whether I would ever find my way back was another question entirely.

■ ■ ■ ■ ■

We drove out to a rather desolate-looking patch of ground outside the town and found that they had erected a *plaza portátil de toros*, or portable bullring. It was an ugly-looking thing, constructed out of toughened plastic, wood and tubular steel, leaning on itself in the midday sun.

Normally this is the time of the *apartado*, 'separating', when the six bulls of a *corrida* are paired up – for example the largest with the smallest, the longest horn with the shortest – in a manner agreed by the ring officials and the matador's representative, which is usually his manager or *banderillero de confianza*, '*banderillero* of trust'. Having made three pairs, each of the three representatives draws lots, which means that the selection of the bulls, once evened up by the pairing, is left to chance.

I paid to attend one of these at Pamplona and found it a dull affair, although for certain fans of the fight – including those British I call the blood anoraks – it is an integral part of the day. My experience that day was that the *aficionados* were merely there to say they had been there, their judgement of the bulls bearing absolutely no relation to how they later behaved in the ring. However, today, each matador has his own bull.

The bulls arrive at the same time as Carlos, who recognises me from a photograph, comes over to shake my hand and starts taking pictures. His own grandfather had been a famous Mexican matador, which may or may not have left its mark on him, but there is certainly a dominating spirit in there.

The custom-built truck docks on the portable stalls and I join the people on top of a metal walkway, looking down on the animals being discharged below in the shade, like black sharks, into the pens below. One of the ring attendants balancing on a metal strut almost falls in and catches himself. The look on his face is pure terror.

Bulls observed, we all pile into the car to join Adolfo, who is breakfasting alone at his hotel, a newspaper propped up next to his plate of eggs, relaxed in suede shoes, slacks and an open necked-shirt. We exchange light banter and wait. About an hour before the fight we return to our hotel to change: Belén into his festival bullfighting uniform, the *traje corto*, cut along the same lines as the suit of lights but in dark colours without the gold braid, Serranito and I into regular suits.

In Adolfo's hotel room I join him in the strange silence of a man preparing for war. He has cleared the desk in the room and placed a wooden box on it, a portable altar of a type I have seen a few times before. He takes out of it keepsakes and icons: sketches from his infant children, a letter from his mother before she lost her life, his father before he lost his mind, small pictures and devices which represent Jesus and his Saints. Each is laid out in the same manner as he has done before, kissed and addressed in the same order, superstition dictating the ritual of faith. Then all too quickly we are ready.

Outside, Belén has pulled up in a rented white minivan, on the sides of which he has attached signs with Adolfo's full name. All around other minivans draw up, awaiting their masters. On the roads are signs with the full *cartel* for the fight, last of all being '*el aficionado práctico, Adolfo Suárez Illana*'.

As we drive to the ring, the atmosphere in the van is jocular, Adolfo joining in the banter, the only silent one El Tuti the picador, but that is just his manner. The undercurrent is as much one of excitement as of fear. As I take notes, Adolfo catches my eye and winks, as though to say yes, there is fear here, but we are at the centre of things, we are where we should be. Adolfo mentions that I already know Cayetano well and Belén, with unexpected enthusiasm, leaps on this connection to celebrity, begging me and Carlos to make sure we get a photo of him with the matador.

'For my wife, you understand. She says if she is going to have to have photos of someone as ugly as me all over the house, I can at least make sure I'm next to someone famous and handsome.'

When we arrive at the ring most of the crowd have already

entered, although some are still milling at the gates. As the least senior bullfighter present, Adolfo has arrived first, and we walk in and duck into the shade under the seating stands, watching out for the occasional trickle of spilled drinks the spectators have put between their feet. Adolfo leans against the outside wall, immaculate in his brown *traje*.

Next to arrive is Manzanares, whom Adolfo knows and for whom he does the introductions. Then Cayetano arrives, and I introduce him to Adolfo. People are milling around at this point: photographers, fans with backstage passes, and the bull-fighters are trying to find their inner equilibrium. Belén, Serranito, Carlos and I slip into the *callejón* just as the opening procession begins.

The first fighter up, following tradition, is the forty-three-year-old *rejoneador* Pablo Hermoso de Mendoza, who enters on a truly beautiful horse which shows astonishing bravery to the poor dumbfounded bull, leaving the man looking both far too much in control and far too divorced from the situation. I am more interested in taking in my surroundings. Adolfo is leaning on the railing next to me, Belén on the other side, and both are exuding fear and readiness in equal measure. Beyond Belén is Manzanares, whose sculpted facial bone structure gives away no feeling at all. Beyond him is the waif-like figure of Sebastián Castella, who was something of a highlight among the medio-cre fights I saw in France (unusually, he is French, of Polish immigrant parents). Today, he looks more as if he belongs in a café on Paris's Left Bank than in the bullring, with his tightly cut grey lounge suit and loafers.

After the *rejoneo* ends, El Fandi enters in black *traje corto* and begins the linked series of feats of athleticism that is his trademark style. Knowing his style, I find it hard to concentrate on Fandi at the best of times, but it is simply impossible in the tension of standing with the teams. People bustle back and forth carrying capes, water bottles, *banderillas* and swords and wherever you stand, at some point you are in the way. What is more, this is a particularly voluble crowd, placed very close to the fighters in the portable structure, and the matadors' teams – if not the maestros themselves – are feeling particularly talkative with the audience in the lighter atmosphere of a 'festival' rather than a formal *corrida*.

I try to offer whatever support and calming influence I can to Adolfo, but since the best I can manage in that atmosphere is standing still while being silent and staunch with a half-smile, I doubt it really helps. Not that Adolfo needs my attempts at emitting confidence; his excitability now seems to be just that, genuine excitement without a trace of fear.

As the next bull falls and Castella enters the ring, I join Cayetano, who looks infinitely worse than Adolfo.

'How's it going, Maestro?'

'Oh, hi, Alex.' He manages a half-smile.

'My God, you look worse than Adolfo and you do this for a living.'

'I know. Sorry, I'm exhausted.'

I look at him properly and realise that he has lost even more weight from his face, and that aside from the dark circles under his eyes, there are lines at their corners that from moment to moment deepen and soften. They are wince marks.

'*Cornadas*?' I ask, a word for 'wound' derived from *cuerno*, 'horn'.

'Yes.' With his right hand – which is covered in bandages – he gestures downwards. 'There is one down there that won't heal and is *very* uncomfortable. And I'm tired, a dozen fights a month for month after month. The season has been too long and I need to rest.'

I don't ask where he is gesturing to. The bull often aims between the legs, and, as a medical report I recently read put it, 'many *toreros* are missing a testicle or have serious problems with them'.

'Well, after this you can – ' I begin.

'Ha! Tomorrow I fight 500 kilometres away – we drive tonight – then the day after I fight 200 kilometres from there.'

He rests his chin on his hands, looking into the ring, brooding, and I fall silent.

Fandi changes to Castella, and I should mention how much the crowd are relishing what is going on. This is the highlight of this small town's little taurine *feria*, and to have such figures fight for them: they love it. The *rejoneo*, which was a little rich for their tastes, got an ear, but the ever popular Fandi is awarded both ears and the tail.

Sebastián Castella walks in and looks odd with the cape; it is almost larger than him, and although he is twenty-six, he looks like a boy of seventeen. His elegance with it, though, is phenomenal, his style almost feminine, and the young women in the audience respond to his prettiness vocally. It is not for me, that aesthetic – the pretty boy fighting the big bull – but it undeniably appeals to some.

The male–female dynamic in bullfighting is often discussed in literary circles in Spain. The bull is variously thought of as a mother figure and the matador as cutting the apron strings, a father figure and the matador is fulfilling his Oedipal imperative, a homosexual seducer figure from whom the matador must preserve his honour. Or the bull is simply a man and the matador a woman, using his skirts to taunt and entice before killing. John Hemingway sent me an interesting twist on this one: 'I once read that in the Carthaginian roots of bullfighting, the fight was seen as a wedding gift of the groom to his bride. The groom was the matador but symbolically he was the woman and the bull was the man, and only in the moment when the matador thrusts his sword into the bull and kills the bull was there union between the two and the differences in sex disappeared. Of course, it's just an interpretation but I know that my grandfather [Ernest Hemingway] and [Gertrude] Stein were aware of these "roots".'

The fact is that the critic who sees the bullfight in this manner is, in the language of that world, 'imposing a narrative' on the bullfight according to his own 'cultural norms', which are intrinsically sexual. Thinking about Padilla with a Miura, I personally am reminded of Cain and Abel; with Cayetano, David and Goliath; with José Tomás, Michelangelo with his block of marble. Castella's style is closest to Tomás's in his proximity to the horns, but it differs wildly in how it looks. And that strange, knowing smile he gives to the bull as it passes. It is a sort of vampiric malice. A beautiful, brave and fluent malice, but malice nonetheless.

Castella takes his two ears and his tail and then Manzanares enters to do what he does best. Carlos, who has been photographing from various vantage points in the ring, comes round and takes photographs of various combinations of Cayetano, Adolfo, Belén, Serranito and me – including the one for Belén's wife. Then, after Manzanares has taken his two ears, Cayetano goes in and Adolfo and I watch from the planks.

Cayetano's performance is muted and he is clearly in pain throughout. This is not helped by the poor quality of the animal he faces (from Victoriano del Río, whose bulls he often fights). The audience are firmly on his side, especially the female half of it, but even they can see neither party is up to the fight. When it comes to the kill, he has to go in three times with the sword before he gets it in – he is holding it in a right hand swathed in bandages – and then he has to finish off the bull with the *descabello*. He takes a perfunctory lap of the ring with his single ear and comes and leans back against the wall with us.

Now, finally, it is the turn of Adolfo. He enters into the *burladero* with Belén at his side and the *toril* gate is opened and out comes a great lumbering beast that cannot get up to a gallop. I remember Adolfo tipping the attendant at the ring where the bull was housed to make sure it was well looked after, and a later phone conversation where the attendant says the bull has been eating like a cow (equivalent in Spanish to the English 'like a horse'). It would seem that over-zealous feeding has delivered up a bull incapable of the fight.

Sure enough, Adolfo attempts some passes with the *capote*, but the bull is in no mood to charge at all. He does charge the horse; in fact, he does so with greater ferocity than any other bull there. Which gives one the impression that he does not view the humans as worth the effort.

He is equally tricky with the *banderillas*, placed not by the one-eyed Belén, but by the *banderilleros* of Fandi, with the exception of the last pair, which is placed by Bernardo del Valle, 'Vallito', a famous *banderillero* from twenty years before who was born in the town and now runs a restaurant. He places with great skill and bravery, his running speed that of a young Fandi, and the crowd rise to their feet to applaud him.

However, the bull now sinks back to the edge of the ring and point blank refuses to charge Adolfo, no matter how close he gets in with the *muleta*, flicking it across the animal's muzzle. For five whole minutes Adolfo tries to get the bull out and it refuses to make even a single pass. Needless to say, I and Serranito, who are standing together, feel absolutely awful for him. Cayetano, who is standing on my other side, says, 'And I thought I had a bad bull!'

Unfairly, members of the crowd start to mutter that this prime minister's son is no bullfighter at all. Adolfo feels the crowd losing interest and bites the proverbial bullet, coming to collect the killing sword from Belén and heading into the beast's own territory, its *querencia*, its 'lair', to kill. Manzanares says from beyond Cayetano, 'He's crazy.'

But what choice does he have? He lines up the bull as best he can – although its head is held very high, having suffered no fatigue from refusing to charge – and then Adolfo flies at the animal. The sword bounces off bone. He goes in again and the *pinchazo*, the 'prick', happens again. Finally, on the

15. Manuel Jesús Cid Salas, 'El Cid', performs a muletazo with a bull of San Mateo, in Valencia, 2011. He fights with the classical severity of a schoolmaster, sometimes finding great beauty within that.

16. Adolfo Suárez Illana, Spain's greatest amateur, passes a bull bred by his father-in-law, Samuel Flores in Castellon on the day I was part of his 'team'.

17. The Divine Cape, Morante de la Puebla, opens with a veronica of the large cape with a galloping bull of Juan Pedro Domecq in Osuna. Despite its vigour and wildness, his line of body and movement are absolutely flawless.

18. The Matador of Matadors, performing the pass invented and named after his precursor, the ill-fated Manolete in Córdoba. At no point during this pass did he even look at the bull, a Núñez del Cuvillo.

19. El Maestro, my teacher, Eduardo Dávila Miura, whilst he still wore the suit of lights in 2003 Feria de Abril in Seville. In the ten years he fought, no other matador took as many ears in that ring.

20. A close shave: I caught this calf's horns on its way into my chest cavity. Antonio, brother and banderillero the matador Ángel Luis Carmona, is just a little late with the cape.

21. The adrenaline-fueled movement between the last photo and this one both saved me, and cost me the use of my arm for a week.

22. The slow improvement after much blood, sweat from me, and patience from my Maestro, Eduardo.

23. Nearly there. Fighting the strong wind behind me for the cape, my posture here is finally right in this naturale.

24. Outside their dreaded square plaza, I am flanked by Eduardo and Antonio Miura, and their nephew, the matador, Eduardo Dávila Miura. Their bulls are the most famous and dangerous in the world.

25. José Pedro Prados Martín, 'El Fundi', tries to get one of the vast Miuras past him with a naturale, in Seville, 2009.

26. A wall of Eduardo and Antonio Miura's bulls carve through the streets of Pamplona. I am circled far right, keeping a wary eye on a bull coming up on the falling man behind me.

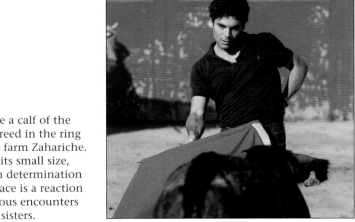

27. I face a calf of the Miura breed in the ring on their farm Zahariche. Despite its small size, the grim determination on my face is a reaction to previous encounters with its sisters.

28. Juan José Padilla places his own banderillas with his customary vigour, with a Miura in Seville, 2009.

third strike, the lunge goes in, an *estocada*, and the bull falls to the ground and dies. Adolfo stalks over to the *burladero* as the crowd politely but half-heartedly cheer, and demands his mobile phone, which I give to him. He is talking fast into it when the president awards him one ear from the bull, like the *rejoneador* and Cayetano. He hangs up, does his lap of honour, and then is back in the *callejón* talking fast to the other *toreros*. People in the audience realise something is up and stop leaving, returning to their seats. There is an announcement. Adolfo will fight another bull. As it is made, Adolfo smiles at me. 'I had to get the others to agree to stay until I am done. And I had to pay for the bull as well!'

To say that this is a proud man, I realise, is an understatement. He seems to think it is better to risk Death twice, the second time tired, than to suffer a bad fight.

A few minutes later, what everyone agrees is a real bull comes into the arena. (As I later discovered, the earlier bull was a three-year-old, a *novillo*, rather than a minimum four-year-old *toro bravo*. The substitute was a five-year-old *toro bravo* from the ranch of the Hermanos de García Jiménez.) Adolfo opens with some long sweeping *verónicas* with the cape. Now, I am not going to claim that Adolfo is the most beautiful bullfighter ever to grace the planet. He has killed one bull in public a year for ten years and has had a mere fortnight of training in the past twelve months. The total time in his life spent bullfighting and training is thus less than a professional does in a couple of seasons, and he is also forty-five years old. However, given those constraints it is quite astonishing how excellent he is. He has a natural relaxed rhythm, far less posed than the matadors, which neatly matches that of the animal. He has *templar*. After the picador and the *banderilleros*, he begins to cape with the *muleta* and truly comes into his own. In the words of the critic from *Opinión y Toros*, the bull was 'noble and continuous, serving the matador so he could cape with gentle slowness ... following excellently the *muleta* in a varied series of passes.'

Adolfo's delight was clear for all to see, and he ended with a series of *manoletinas*, the cape half behind his back, extended out to one side, the bull charging through and past, him turning and inciting it to charge again. And again. And again. He then lined up for the kill, bringing the now happy crowd to the edge of their seats in sympathy and support, and he killed on the second thrust, the crowd rising to their feet with handkerchiefs waving in the now floodlit night, as Adolfo kissed the tips of his fingers and touched them to the boss of the fallen animal's horns. The president awarded him two ears, and as Adolfo toured the ring to the applause and showers of gifts and flowers from the crowd he beamed with a smile that looked eerily saintly in the halogen light, a canonised killer.

We wait for Adolfo for about an hour as he meets members of the crowd who want autographs or to talk, all congratulations beginning with his fight and then moving on to thanks to his father for preventing another civil war. Then we return to his hotel for dinner, where he finally relaxes, delighted with his success, all of us swapping stories and laughing and drinking – Carlos, Belén, Serranito, El Tuti, Adolfo and me. Then we head into town, where we are met by a delegation from the town council, who lead us to the various drinking haunts of the *feria*. Adolfo decides to introduce me as his manager, which causes more confusion, as some have heard I am a new young bullfighter, others that I am writing a biography of Cayetano, or Adolfo, or both. I play along. At the end of the night, we stagger back to his hotel and say goodbye; he is driving back to his family the next morning. His wife is worried, he says, and not happy that he has been risking his life again, at his age. I can't imagine why.

It is for this reason that a little while later I asked Adolfo whether he would fight again. This is what he wrote in reply:

'Am I going to carry on? Yes, if you mean carry on being a bull-fighter until the end of my days and continue practising behind closed doors, joining forces with you. I will also carry on in my children. I have already planted the seed in them and they have already faced this summer their first "*calfing*". But everything has an end that must be accepted. As you know, I have a commitment to our mutual friend Padilla to kill a bull with him the day of his retirement as a matador, but beyond that, I already have withdrawn from the arena. My public career is over. In this world of bullfighting the finale can be chosen by the public, the bull or yourself, and I think it is highly recommended that it is you who chooses such an important date and that I finished – with a little luck and the magic finger of God that has always accompanied me – with a victory.'

19

El pinchazo

The matador draws the cape towards him in his left hand, inching it up his left leg to draw the focus of the bull; he then pushes it out in front so the bull lurches down, and then the matador leaps forward with the sword into where he thinks there is space between shoulder, clavicle and spine. And hits bone.

I arrived in England with winter to find my relationship broken by long distance and my mind uneasy.

I had enjoyed my year with the bulls too much. Before I began the project I had merely analysed half a dozen bullfights from the stands with a little biology, a little philosophy and a measure of intellectual honesty. The combination of these things put me out in front of the common run of pro- and anti-bullfighting commentators.

The idea behind the project was to go further, to give myself a clear lead over the pack. And, having watched fifty-something fights from every conceivable situation, immersed myself in the behaviour of the bulls on the ranch and in the ring, and been in the ring myself on two of the most historic ranches and one of the best modern ones, and even run through the streets of Pamplona, twice, I had given myself just that clear lead. However, I had been corrupted in my pursuit of that immersion. This wasn't Method acting, where the sole aim is to know the subject from the inside. I also needed objectivity, and this had been taken from me by a simple bribe. Or rather not a bribe, a blandishment. In fact the greatest blandishment of all, inclusion. As Aristotle said first, 'Man is a social animal.' The world of the bullfight had drawn me into its heart, which was what I had wanted, but in doing so it had won my affections, which was worrying.

I arrived at Oxford in a night-time snowstorm and set myself up in a room at my old college. I had decided to go back to the beginning. The next morning I tramped through the drifts to the Bodleian Library and ordered up to my desk copies of Peter Singer's *Animal Liberation* (1975) and Marc Bekoff's *Readings in Animal Cognition* (1995), both of which, especially the latter, by the saintly ethologist Bekoff, made me feel awful. That afternoon I ran ten miles, through the snow. Which succeeded in adding physical exhaustion to guilt.

However, I started to grow stronger. I won't list the slow construction of the philosophical edifice of how I made peace with the idea of becoming a killer. But I will say this about those philosophers like Singer, and after him the equally influential Tom Regan, who wrote *The Case for Animal Rights* in 1983: the end point of all their arguments is an unavoidable one. If man has a moral duty to minimise the suffering of non-human animals in so far as he is capable, then there is no way in this scheme, in theory, to distinguish between domestic animals and wild ones. So our duty would include, for example, stopping lions from killing antelope in so far as we are capable. And in a world with fewer and fewer wild spaces, we are becoming increasingly capable. The end picture, then, is one where 'the wolf also shall dwell with the lamb, and the leopard shall lie down with the kid; and the calf and the young lion and the fatling together'. For someone who admires the beauty of nature, that is, someone who loves animals living as animals, that is the worst sort of *reductio ad absurdum*. And it is that image that does it for me. The image of a predator forced to eat tofu because we can no longer deal with the reality of nature, of its nature; that finally made my mind up for me. I decided that I must represent the world of the bullfight as it is. And the only way to do that, I decided, was to go over the horns, sword in hand.

■ ■ ■ ■ ■

'Seville, she has not deserted me.' The city's motto rang true from the moment I arrived, when winter was just beginning to give way to spring in early March.

Within a couple of days, I heard from a friend that Eduardo Dávila Miura, the former matador I had met on my first night out with Adolfo and Padilla, was giving some lessons in bullfighting. I also knew that my friend Enrique Moreno de la Cova, the breeder of the Saltillos, knew Eduardo, because I had seen photos of a young-looking Eduardo at the inaugurating *tentadero* in the Saltillo testing ring in 2001, the same ring I had fought almost exactly a year ago. So I dropped Enrique a note and was told that Eduardo would love to meet me and would come to the *tertulia* at the Hotel Las Casas de la Judería that Thursday.

Meeting Eduardo, I quickly realised how wrong my first reading of him had been. His eyes, although blue, are not cold. Fair-haired and six foot, he is not the classic Mediterranean type. Anatomically he most resembles a thinned-down rugby player, with strong bones – clearly visible on the face – but the musculature is long and lean after years of training for bullfighting and his other love, playing football. He shook my hand and we got down to talking with Enrique.

After a few minutes we were agreed. He would teach me privately three or four days a week and he would take me out to *tentaderos* about once a week – he was managing a matador called Rafaelillo, so was kept informed about them even though he no longer fought – and we would see where we were after three months.

Eduardo's career as a matador had been impressive. His grandfather on his mother's side was the same Eduardo Miura who had bred the bull that killed Manolete, while the grandfather on his father's side was a breeder of bulls as well. So when he became a matador, he had all the advantages of the inside track. And as a result, the critics took every opportunity to savage him. Despite this, the crowd loved him, and in his native Seville, in the ten years that he was a matador, he took more ears in the Plaza de Toros de la Real Maestranza than any other. He retired in 2006 aged thirty-two (the age I was when I first entered the ring).

My one remaining worry was the cost of private lessons with a young, former top-level matador. I have mentioned in passing the ranking of matadors, the *escalafón taurino*, but not in any detail as, along with most serious *aficionados*, I regard it as meaningless. This is because it is based on the number of fights a matador appears in, opening it to manipulation by those willing to fight in a multitude of smaller rings and avoid injury. However, it is worth saying that Eduardo was usually found in the top ten. Personally, I was more impressed when I discovered that the great Abel Moreno had composed the *Paso doble Dávila Miura* in his honour, which was played by the bull-ring band when he fought. So I was more than a little surprised when he suggested €35 for an hour. I actually had to haggle him up to €50. And even then, he refused to take payment for the *tentaderos*, which last all day. The bull, which would normally cost over €1,000, was to be supplied free of charge by Enrique.

I had found an apartment adjacent to the bullring, with a terrace on which I could train with my newly purchased capes (Pedro Algaba, the tailor for *toreros* whose family have supplied every major bullfighter from Manolete on, and whose shop is part of the bullring itself, charged me €600 for a *capote*, *muleta* and *ayuda*, 'aid', the aluminium caping sword). Within a few days of arrival I had truly settled in for my task. Seville, it doesn't let you down.

■ ■ ■ ■ ■

For my first lesson, Eduardo collects me from beside the statue of the matador Curro Romero by the bullring, Romero being one of Seville's favourite matadors of the late 1960s and 1970s (he once took eight ears from six bulls in one afternoon there, the highest number ever).

We discuss the fact that our mutual friend Adolfo Suárez Illana has just published an article in the national newspaper *El Mundo* in defence of bullfighting. It seems that just as I have finally made up my mind in its favour, the autonomous province of Catalonia is having doubts. Eduardo and Adolfo both seem firmly of the mind that this is a political question. They see animal rights as a bandwagon the Catalan nationalists have hijacked and are trying to ride straight through the democratic constitution of Spain. However, I can't see it like that, despite friendship and my increasing approval of bullfighting. When I was in Barcelona, it did seem as though the locals I spoke to were against bullfighting, as they were against smoking in bars (strangely, I thought, for people smoking cannabis in the streets and playing bongos all night). Whatever the truth, there may be something in the claim that bullfighting was forced upon them by Franco as part of his campaign to culturally unify Spain. However, as a liberal, I just don't believe in banning things, especially when in terms of animal welfare it is better than many other human activities. Liberals don't ban things without good reason, and that even includes things once supported by the illiberal regimes that came before them.

We drive up into some hills just outside Seville to the house of a friend of Eduardo's, the Hacienda El Vizir, which happens to have a full-size bullring with seating for a couple of hundred people built on to it. Then Eduardo gets me to warm up with him, fast jogging, not just forwards but also backwards and sideways, both vital in the ring, he says. He tells me that is something I have to practise, I need to be able to sprint out of a situation facing whichever direction the bull is in. After twenty minutes we are both sweating but he notices that he is breathing more heavily than I am. The training in Oxford has paid off.

Then he takes the large cape, hands it to me, and picks up a pair of horns, telling me to call him to charge and then to pass him with the cape. After he sees the result, he readjusts his expectations. (He had seen the article in *The Times*, and not speaking English had merely looked at the opening photo – a double page spread by Nicolás of me caping a Saltillo *vaquilla* far too large for me – and assumed I had not the faintest idea of what I was doing.)

As a bullfighter, it is clear from the first that Eduardo is a consummate technician. The mechanics of the pass are perfectly clear to him. There is no equivocation for him between styles or manners, there is merely 'the way'. Similarly, the elegance which he has in his movements with the cape, which is immense, derives entirely from its economy and its confidence. However, most impressive of all is his patience with how slowly I pick it up. The nature of the movement is so alien, requiring so many muscles moving in coordination to achieve it, that I am utterly useless. Eduardo forgives me time and time again until I have it, pointing out that he has had a cape in his hand since he was five and been in front of animals since he was eleven.

The basis of the cape is the *verónica* (you can find it described at the head of the first chapter), and it contains within its long, slow sweep something of the courtier gesturing to his sovereign that he should go before him. Which is entirely suitable. At the end of a *tanda*, 'series', of three or four such *lances*, 'casts', of the cape, a normal animal will be tiring and its charges becoming unregulated, so the *torero* must bring the series to a *remate*, a 'conclusion'. This is done by bringing the bull up short, making it turn so hard that it loses all momentum and thus reassesses the situation to see whether it is worth charging all over again.

The most common method of concluding is the *media*, 'half', *verónica*, in which, midway through the pass, the outside hand becomes inverted, knuckles towards the animal, and the cape is drawn around the back of the waist. The bull follows this, trying to turn around the human body, which basically throws all its momentum away in too sharp a turn.

The stationary matador is then assessed by the animal again and found to be unthreatening (or not, as some matadors have discovered to their detriment). The appearance to the audience is the matador moving from guiding the bull with the *verónicas* to dominating it entirely by ending its charge at his command. Which is what he is doing, but by guile rather than the force it at first appears to be. Thus the good matador's deceit is twofold, first in tricking the bovine eye that the cape is the threat, and then in tricking the human eye that he is melding the bull to his direct will, rather than via the cape.

After only a few minutes of practising these, my shoulders are aching, despite the running and the hours of press-ups and chin-ups every week. It is the equivalent of taking a six-foot-long, ten-pound steel chain at either end, holding it a foot clear of your body, and then violently swinging it in twenty different directions. What is worse, while the tear in the meniscal carti-lage in my right knee has ceased to be a problem (for now), the calcification and cyst within my right shoulder are causing it to burn beyond bearing.

We move on to the *muleta*. The basic pass with this is the *derechazo* (from *derecho*, 'right'). In the act of the *muleta*, the sword must never leave the right hand, so when the *muleta* is in the same hand, the sword is used to widen it, intertwining your fingers through the sword and the *palillo*, 'stick', within the *muleta*. Which puts an interestingly distributed five-pound burden on your fingers, wrist and forearm. The *derechazo* has the genuine feel of a lure, like trailing string in front of a playful cat, never so far away the cat stops, never so close he catches it. However, it should look like you are drawing a half-ton bull around you by force of will and superhuman strength while maintaining both hauteur and composure.

The conclusion to a series of these is most often the *pase de pecho*, 'chest pass', failing to turn at the end of a *derechazo* and merely waiting, back facing the animal as it charges, and drawing it past in reverse, turning it hard around the body and lifting the cape at the end, causing it to rear and lose momentum that way. With the might of the bull rearing past the matador, who appears to ignore it and then calmly walks off, the matador shows his impunity.

The equivalent to the *derechazo* on the right is called a *natural* because the *muleta* is unextended as the sword remains in the right hand (both are sometimes called *muletazos*). This is more dangerous because the *muleta*, the alternative target to the human body, has less than two-thirds the surface area presented to the bull. Also, with no extension to the cloth, the bull is worked closer to the body. It is for this reason, and the fact that merely holding a stick rather than stick-plus-sword allows free wrist rotation, that it is much more elegant. For the left-handed *pase de pecho* it is the same.

After twenty minutes of this, I am useless below the elbow on both sides, and we end for the day. Eduardo seems happy with my progress, which makes me happy. I also know that I can work with him, which makes me even happier. I am making progress.

■　■　■　■　■

It took my muscles two days to recover from our training, and then I took up the capes and began training on my terrace, along with running around the beauties of the María Luisa Park, which is like a little Latin enclave with its palms and shrubs from around Spain and South America. Eduardo was busy after our first lesson, but had told me to keep the 16th free. The previous evening he had called me and said we were going to a *tentadero* and to bring my cape. I stayed in that night, cooking myself a quiet supper.

The next morning, I wake up at 7 a.m., shower and walk through what is, for Seville, the early morning streets until I reach the statue of Romero, where Eduardo is waiting. We drive and he talks, watching me to see how I am feeling. I fall asleep. After a couple of hours I wake up and the countryside is rich in the spring sunshine. I ask Eduardo how much further it is.

'A little way. Do you have your passport?'

I look worried.

'It's a joke. You don't need it any more,' and he points out of the window as we cross the border into Portugal.

I fall asleep again.

At eleven o'clock we arrive at a *finca*, 'Baraona', surrounded by the same sort of flat country I have seen all around southern Spain. The *finca* itself is pretty, but spare and modern. People are already in the ring and I can hear someone calling to an animal, '*Vaca, vaca.*' We enter through a side door into a viewing room where a handful of middle-aged men are drinking sherry in overcoats – it is cold here despite the sun – watching another middle-aged man working a medium-sized *vaquilla* with a *muleta*. One of the men I recognise, and he says in English, 'Alexander, the English writer! I didn't know you were coming.'

Eduardo asks him how he knows me and I am reminded that this is Tilda Núñez Benjumea's brother whom I met in Jerez, not the elder one, Álvaro, who runs their ranches in Spain, but the younger one, Juan Francisco, aka 'Curro', with his lazy, easy smile and blond curly hair. I ask who is caping.

'Fermín de Bohorquez.'

Fermín is not only one of the most famous horseback bull-fighters, but also a breeder of bulls down in Jerez. I am introduced to the others there: all breeders, one who has also been a matador in Ecuador called José Luis Cobo. All are more than capable in the ring.

Eduardo walks out into the ring and replaces Fermín, who

has been caping with the relaxed, understated style of the gentleman-bullfighter. Eduardo's posture is that of a pro, though, with the long sweeping arm I saw in our class, the legs locked straight, although now he is constantly adjusting his feet after the *vaquilla* has passed so that when it turns he is in exactly the right spot to cite it to another charge.

As he finishes off a series with a *pase de pecho*, he shouts to me, 'Get ready, this one is a good one for you to begin on.'

And the familiar dread takes over as I unpack my *muleta* and sword from their bag.

'You're caping?' Curro says, surprised, 'This should be interesting.'

Eduardo fixes the *vaquilla* after another series and then calls to me, gesturing me to come round the ring, keeping further away from the *vaquilla* than he is and then, when he is between it and me, to approach.

'OK. Remember when we did the walking passes? Try that.'

I remember vaguely something about beginning in reverse, with a *pase de pecho*, and then, when it has passed, walking away from it at four o'clock to its twelve o'clock charge until I am five yards away, and then offering it the front of the *muleta*, and again away, this time at eight o'clock, then *muleta* in reverse again and so on. In the end, we form a pair of zigzags, meeting at my destinations, making the animal work to my path. I manage four in a row and the animal stops and I turn to Eduardo.

'¡Joder, qué bueno, Alejandro!' 'Fuck, how good, Alexander!' He is surprised. 'Now, *derechazos*.'

I cite the bull properly, right hand palm forwards within the *muleta*, and the *vaquilla* charges straight into me with a ten-yard run up, sending me sprawling in the dirt. Eduardo runs in with the cape and takes the animal off me before its horns can find me on the ground.

'Stand up. All right?' I tell him I'm fine. 'Again.'

I try again and have no idea what I did differently, but the *vaquilla* sails through the *muleta*. However, it turns hard the moment it's through and now it is standing with one horn an inch from my crotch, the other an inch from the *muleta*. I try to move my more delicate parts to one side, and it bolts forward at the movement. I catch its horn in my left hand and divert it past with main strength. However, once you have a bull by the horns, like a tiger by the tail, it's very hard to let go. Eduardo comes in again to the rescue.

'This one's not for you. Take a break.'

I join Curro in the little room by a brazier in the corner as the mild-mannered Ecuadorian José Luis walks into the ring and begins some wonderfully smooth capework.

'I thought you were a writer,' Curro says.

'I am. I'm training with Eduardo now.'

'Impressive. How long have you been training for?'

'This is my second lesson.'

Curro laughs explosively. 'Oh, that's all right then. Because I thought you'd been with him since last year, in which case you would be shit. For one lesson, you are very good. Have some sherry.'

I'd never drunk in the ring before, but it seemed like a good idea.

There were four more *vaquillas* after that one, and I went up against two. On the first I was better, managing three passes together before having my legs swept out from under me by a well-placed horn. The one after I was worse, since my body was complaining from the hits I was taking. Eduardo, unlike Adolfo, did not believe in intervening before I got too damaged to walk.

At the end we retire to the farmhouse, where we are more properly introduced and those who got too sweaty, or bloody from the pic wounds on the cows, shower quickly. Then we sit down to beers and *caña de lomo*, a particularly smooth cut of cured pork from the acorn-fed Iberian pig. We move through to lunch and I notice that not only is there not a single woman at the table, but every person is either a breeder or fighter of bulls. So, as the Rioja flows, there is a bass rumble to the conversation, combined with a fraternal aggression which becomes more voluble as the bottles pass.

At some point, conversation turns to Eduardo's generation of bullfighters and he brings up a matador I shall call X who was famous for fighting huge numbers of bullfights per year. Fermín de Bohorquez points out that although X ended his career by fighting in a vulgar manner, he began as the purist's dream. He was obsessed with templar, which gives the bullfight much of its visual beauty. At this point, Curro Núñez del Cuvillo replies that Fermín can take X and shove him where the sun does not shine.

'Art, he didn't have Art, you son of a bitch, and if bullfighting is about anything, it is about Art. X! *X!* Don't talk to me about X! José Tomás! José Tomás, now he has Art and he is a genius. There is a great bullfighter. There is the greatest bullfighter!'

This leads, inevitably, to a deafening explosion of argument from all sides, not least because everyone knows that Curro's family supplies most of the bulls Tomás fights. I catch the eye of the mild-mannered Ecuadorian José Luis Cobo Terán, a matador turned breeder who is laughing as he watches me observing the discussion.

'Gentlemen, is this how you wish to be remembered by posterity?' he asks, nodding towards me. They find this hilarious, and the dispute becomes even more enthusiastic. Afterwards, when they retire back to the fire, I join Curro in his office, where he reminds me that we met in Jerez after the Tomás fight.

'That was his greatest, you know. I've never seen fighting like that,' he says.

'Neither have I. You are right. Then … that … that was art.'

On the drive back, I reassure Eduardo that on this part of my project, I am not there as observer but as trainee bullfighter. It is for that reason they spoke so freely in front of me. And it is for that reason that I have withheld the name of the matador.

■ ■ ■ ■ ■

Our lessons moved to Eduardo's Seville home for convenience. He lives in an apartment building in Triana – the *barrio* of Juan Belmonte – with his family, so I take a walk across the river with my capes in the bag with *Pedro Algaba, Sastrería de Toreros* emblazoned on the side and a sword hilt sticking out one end. As they pass, people greet me with a nod and a single word, '*¡Torero!*' And I feel embarrassed and fraudulent, but accept the compliment with the best grace I can manage. One day, I even walk past two policemen lounging by their car and suddenly realise that the handle of a caping sword is the same as that of a killing sword, and for all they know I am walking down the street with an unconcealed three-foot razor-sharp blade on me. Their reaction? A wave and '*¡Torero!*'

In the gardens of the building, which are shaded by tall pine trees, there is a circle of benches with sandy ground on which the grass doesn't grow. This becomes our *plaza de entrenar*, 'place of training', in which Eduardo teaches me the various manoeuvres of cape and *muleta* which head the chapters of this book. As we train in the early evening when the air is fresh and the shadows long, his young family comes to say hello: his wife Carmen – always engaging, always perceptive – who teaches at the school and comes home with their two daughters Carmen and Rocío, aged six and four, and as pretty as their mother with the blond colouring of both parents. And little Eduardito, their son, who joins us training on the sand with a miniature *muleta* which he waves like a flag as he is only two and a half, his father charging him with a pair of horns which he is half afraid of but also half willing to fight.

Following the family theme is my next *tentadero*, four days after the last one, with Enrique's Saltillos. Eduardo cannot come, the bullfighter for the day being a *sevillano*, Ángel Luis Carmona, a twenty-six-year-old who has been a matador for only two years, although he has been performing in public since he was fourteen. I notice my fear of the ring seems to be getting worse, even though everything is done to minimise it. I travel to the ring in Enrique's car, he and his wife Cristina chatting in the front, myself and their daughter Cristina relaxing in the back. When we get to the ring we are joined by her brothers, and by Enrique's brother, Félix, and his children.

Enrique's eldest, called Enrique, helps out in the ring (his physical strength is formidable), while Félix's eldest, called Félix, also ventures into the ring with a *muleta*, reminding me of myself the year before, all courage and no technique. He even turns down my offer of a sword, saying, 'No. I have no idea how to use it.'

However, when I try to hone my technique, I get into more than a few scrapes with the cattle, as the photos by Enrique's brother-in-law, my friend Tristán Ybarra, show. In one, I appear to have caught the horn just before it stabs me in the chest and then wrenched it away. Which would explain why I couldn't write for some time afterwards. However, there has been a definite improvement, with me even managing a series of left-handed passes before the cow stops too close to my body, finds me, and runs me over like a truck.

However, as the adrenaline fades, my muscles and scrapes begin to ache – including a quarter of the surface of my left forearm which was removed as I was dragged across the ring under the *vaquilla* – and I walk out to sit and relax in the courtyard, where I encounter the younger Cristina. I realise how long I have been in Spain as I talk to her. I remember having dinner with a witty girl at their house in Seville the year before, and here is a beautiful woman. The combination of fatigue and injury makes me feel I have grown old, and I am pleased to return to my apartment where I wash off the sand and blood and collapse into a deep sleep.

■ ■ ■ ■ ■

I carry on training and Eduardo takes me along to meet some of his other students at the Royal Club Pineda, outside Seville. It is a seventy-year-old horse-riding, golf and sporting club set amid woods on the outskirts of Seville, and when I arrive with Eduardo we are met by his teaching assistant Jesús, a *banderillero* as competent as he is small.

The first class is of children, all between nine and twelve, one or two of whose parents I know. Eduardo directs in the basics of a pass and then they take it in turns to face Jesús, who charges at them with the *carretón*, 'cart', made of a fake bull's head mounted on a bicycle wheel with wheelbarrow handles. I am reminded how much children misbehave at that age. However, when it is their turn to go before the horns, they suddenly become focused, and it is very strange to watch what could be a class from anywhere in the world play up, play around, and then stand still and cape a simulated creature of charging thunder. As someone says to me that day, 'If you scratch the surface of any part of society in southern Spain, they bleed bull.'

Their fathers are similar, as I discover in the next class. A little more dignified in repose, but not much, as their friends come from the bar, glass in hand, to mock them. Eduardo uses me as a demonstration for the left-handed *natural*, as apparently my action is unusually smooth. It is a good day.

■ ■ ■ ■ ■

After a couple of weeks' more training Eduardo asks me if I would like to come to Zahariche, and I notice him watching me closely when I answer. I answer yes and try not to bat an eyelid. Zahariche is the name of the farm of the Miura family, who have been breeding the infamous 'Bulls of Death' for 150 years (and ten months and six days). I know that the Miura reputation is in part a clever PR ploy by the family, although having seen them fought, and run with them in Pamplona and been bloodied as a result (although it was not my blood), I know there is some truth to it.

I research further, turning to the bible of the bullfight, *Los Toros. Tratado técnico e histórico*, 'Bulls. A Technical and Historical Treatise', by José María de Cossío (four volumes when first published in 1943, thirty in the revised edition of 2007, thirty years after Cossío's death), and then to other sources. The story of the Miuras is steeped in myth, but I found one tangible, formidable fact. The only bullfighters' strike in the history of the spectacle was caused by the Miuras.

At the end of the nineteenth century the magazine *El Toreo* took to publishing various statistics about bullfighting (this was in the days before fans of such things switched to football in Spain). One of these figures was about how many lance-strikes, on average, the bulls of the various ranches would take in the ring. I don't like bullfight statistics, as I have made clear, but this one was indeed a fairly accurate determinant, as such things go, of the bulls' aggression and toughness. The top five in the 1897 league table looked like this: Saltillo 7.25, Campos Varela (now defunct) 7.17, Ybarra (as in Cristina and Tristán, now defunct) 6.58, Miura 5.33 and Veragua 5.34.

Combining that toughness with the growing number of important matadors who had died in the ring on the horns of Miuras (e.g. Pepete in 1862, El Espartero in 1894, Domingo Del Campo in 1900), in 1908 a group of the fifteen top matadors, led by Bombita and Machaquito, withdrew their labour, demanding double pay to fight them. So the impresarios of the bullrings responded by bringing on a younger and hungrier generation of bullfighters like Rafael 'El Gallo' (elder brother of Joselito), who were delighted at the chance to fight for any money. The strike was thus broken by the power of big business and the fifteen matadors returned to work. Two of them went on to be killed by Miuras. It is for this reason some say that the only honest part of 'los toros' is on the sharp end of the horns.

Juan Belmonte said of them, 'No bull ever showed greater offensive and defensive capacity in the face of the bullfighter. All the other bulls I have ever fought could eventually be brought to a point of absolute submission; the Miuras never.' His friend Hemingway spoke similarly: 'There are certain strains even of bulls in which the ability to learn rapidly in the ring is highly developed. These bulls must be fought and killed as rapidly as possible with the minimum of exposure by the man, for they learn more rapidly than the fight ordinarily progresses and become exaggeratedly difficult to work with and kill. Bulls of this sort are the old caste of fighting bulls raised by the sons of Don Eduardo Miura of Sevilla.' In May 2009 an escaped Miura so terrorised a stretch of road outside the farm that rather than even try to recapture the bull, the local police shot him, despite his value. It took thirty 9mm bullets before he fell.

Needless to say, when Eduardo picked me up from the statue of Curro Romero I was even more nervous than for my last two *tentaderos*. So much for familiarity breeding contempt. In fact, it was about fear that Eduardo and I spoke as we drove.

'Eduardo, how did you deal with the adrenaline before you fought? Did you feel fear?'

'Every bullfighter feels fear, Alejandro. The trick is to fight as often as you can. When I manage a matador like Rafaelillo now, I know that if I give him several days off, when he comes back, he is ten times as afraid as if he is fighting every day. Even though, as long as the fear does not get to him, he is safer fighting less often. Fear eats matadors. The trick is not to let it get hungry.'

We get to Lora del Río and Eduardo turns into a roadside café, where we stop for a coffee and a cigarette before driving into the ranch. (Second to bullfighting, the great cultural difference between your southern Spaniard and your southern Englishman is that they will always stop for a coffee or a glass of something a mile before their destination, so they always arrive refreshed and uncrumpled.) People at one of the tables immediately recognise Eduardo and come over to salute him for his work in the ring. I have grown used to this in the preceding weeks – people even stop at traffic lights to address him – and his introduction of me.

'This is Alejandro, who is training to kill a bull. He is a writer from England, from *London!*'

That I should be doing this while being English is always a shock, and the fact that I am from London invariably causes a comic double-take, which speaks volumes about their views of foreign urban elites.

After I'd added the artificial stimulants of caffeine and nicotine to God's own adrenaline, we drove up to the gates of Zahariche. I had expected to find something dramatic – after all, it was clear the family were well aware of their reputation. Perhaps something in the Seville baroque vein, with the motto from Dante's infernal gates chiselled in, 'Abandon Hope All Ye Who Enter Here.' (Which, in a perverse joke, my mother wrote on the bathroom door when I was a child.) Instead, the portal was a spare, brutalist installation composed entirely of hacksawed scaffolding poles and cattle skulls which brought to mind the original film of *The Texas Chainsaw Massacre* crossed with Steven Spielberg's *Jurassic Park*.

The ring itself looks equally forbidding, being the only rectangular ring remaining in Spain. Once upon a time all *plazas de toros* were square – that is what '*plaza*' means – however, the bull often backs into a corner in such situations, making them either impossible, or at least downright dangerous to fight.

Apparently the two elder brothers of Eduardo's mother Reyes, who now run the ranch, Eduardo and Antonio Miura, have no problem with presenting such difficulties to the bullfighter. When Eduardo introduces me to his two weathered uncles I get the distinct impression that they expect the people in their ring to take whatever is thrown at them. Their respect for their former matador nephew is clear, though.

So, having shaken the hands of several young South American matadors who have obviously come to Spain to make their fortune and must begin by fighting the most dangerous bulls, along with the various farmhands who will be assisting in the ring, I take up my spot behind the most heavily armoured *burladeros* I have seen in a ring. From them, the viewer looks into the ring through a slit in a wall with some iron bars, as though he were a besieged garrison rather than a bullfighter. I think of Padilla's 1,428lb Miura in the Feria de Abril the year before and realise why.

As I lay out my equipment I am joined by one of the young matadors from Venezuela. Dealing with my own worries, I probably come across as rather self-possessed or haughty (to quote Giles Coren on my pre-*tentadero* demeanour), although actually I am just thinking about what I need to do. However, the young matador looks genuinely scared. Which I find odd, as he must have killed full-sized bulls to become a matador. Miura's PR must be even better in Latin America than it is in Spain. Even his manager, who I later find out is his father, is looking a little pale. I give them both cigarettes and listen to the father – whose eyes light up when he hears I am a writer – try to sell me the concept of his son for my book (he talks so fast, though, I never catch his son's name). I lean against the wall with the young bullfighter and listen to various metal gates sliding backwards and forwards as they move a *vaquilla* from the holding pen to the antechamber of the ring.

Looking at where the antechamber must be beyond the wall

of the ring, we observe something that momentarily stops our breath. Above the ten-foot wall we clearly see a pair of horns sweep up into view in an arc and then disappear again. Now, I know the Miuras are famous for holding their heads high, but twelve feet high? We look at each other and look back. His father notices we aren't listening and joins us at the viewing slit as the horns sweep back in the other direction. The older man mutters under his breath and I swear I hear him say, '¡Es un jodido Minotauro!' 'It's a fucking Minotaur!' Which does wonders for my inner calm.

Of course, I realise that the *vaquilla* must be running at the wall and then running up it with its forehooves so that its horns appear over the top, but knowing that doesn't seem to help. Four-foot-tall cattle so angry they are trying to climb the walls with their hooves are less scary than twelve-foot-tall cattle, but there's not a lot in it.

When they open the gate into the *plaza*, it is indeed a very pissed-off *vaquilla* considerably larger than any I have seen before. I nod to the matador and say, 'That one's for you, my friend,' and light another cigarette, which raises a smile. Gallows humour is apparently universal. After he has caped it, with considerable skill and courage, even if it does leaving him pouring with sweat on the chill spring day, Eduardo has a quick go. He shouts my least favourite Spanish phrase. '¿Alejandro, es para ti?' 'It's for you?'

And I give the answer which is already getting a laugh from Eduardo, who has heard it before, '¿Por qué no?' 'Why not?'

And, as always happens, the fear vanishes in the face of the reality of danger, and once again it becomes about adrenaline management, remembering various techniques which have yet to become second nature, and maintaining the clearest, hardest and most intense focus I will ever experience in my life. One slip, one error, and it is on you. And unlike any other opponent you may have in your life, this animal will stop at nothing to destroy you – it knows nothing of pity, nor mercy, nor fear of prison, nor, apparently, fear of death. Once you are on the ground, it will come after you again and again with its horns until you cease to move, until you are destroyed. Whether or not, like the proverbial shark, it 'wants' to kill you is quite beside the point. It will.

As it turns out, I can pass this one quite well with my right hand, but not my left – probably because of the smaller *muleta* – and when it hits me in my shin with the flat of its horn, I feel as though my tibia has been hit with a hammer. Which is also what it sounds like. Eduardo calls me out of the ring, saying, 'There you go, that is for the book. You can say you passed a Miura.'

What he doesn't say is how many more there would be. Luckily, that day there was only one more for me, which, given that it was considerably smaller, wasn't such a problem. I took some damage, learnt a few things, and got out of the ring alive.

At the end of the fight Eduardo's two uncles come over to congratulate me, and what makes me genuinely happy is that the rather arch look in their eyes I saw when I arrived has gone. I may be limping like a Long John Silver, but I am clearly better than they had expected. Photography is not allowed in the ring at Zahariche, but they allow me a photo with them and their nephew just outside, taken by the young Venezuelan matador.

■ ■ ■ ■ ■

It is only three days after this that the pre-Feria de Abril bull-fights begin, in a sequence that runs every day for two weeks and two days until the end of the *feria* itself. Eduardo's schedule suddenly becomes more hectic, as he has to commentate from the Maestranza on every fight for Radio Sevilla, and then he does a discussion afterwards called 'Tertulias Taurinas' on Giralda TV. It is for this reason that I find myself being interviewed on television in Spanish. Which is hilarious, as the interviewer is one of the Andalusian Spaniards whom I would have difficulty following at the best of times, but on live television I genuinely have no idea what he is on about. However, having predicted this outcome while watching the earlier segment of the programme going out live, I realised something: that compared to the fear of walking into the ring, this is nothing. I could have happily sat on live television blankly. Compared to the Miuras, it really doesn't matter.

Of course, being unwilling to do that, I think about how to get around my problem, and my mind immediately springs to British politicians in the post-Tony Blair era. They never, ever answer the question as posed, merely sticking close to the subject. When asked, for example, 'Is your party going to raise income tax on low earners after the next election?' they will reply, 'Our party is committed to proper funding of the welfare state.' Which is equivalent to answering, 'Are you in favour of crucifixion?' with, 'We have as a party always believed in good carpentry.' And they get away with it.

So when I was asked a question with the words 'bull' and 'English' in it, I would answer, 'Well, the most interesting thing is this: that in England the overall view of the *corrida* is …' Given the fact that he only raised his eyebrows at three of my responses to his dozen questions, I reckon that I probably managed to answer more of his actual enquiries than most MPs faced by Jeremy Paxman or John Humphrys.

■ ■ ■ ■ ■

On the morning of 25 April, I woke up and headed to the newsstands to find José Tomás on the front page of every single newspaper. The greatest living matador – perhaps the greatest matador ever – had been caught while caping a Santiago bull in Aguascalientes, Mexico, in the final stages of the fight. A six-inch hole in his inner right thigh had absolutely destroyed the integrity of the femoral, iliac and saphenous arteries. He was rushed to the infirmary, where it was impossible to stem the bleeding even as they were pouring blood into him. They ran out of Type A Rhesus negative blood, so a call went out on the loudspeakers and the crowd charged to the infirmary to donate. As one *aficionado* put it, 'To think that my blood may even now be pumping through the heart of such a man, such a *torero*: what an honour!'

Tomás lost seventeen pints of blood before they stopped the haemorrhaging, more than twice the amount in the body of a man of that weight. By the time I got to a television to switch on the news, he was on a respirator in intensive care, hanging between life and death. On the action replay I could see the bull turn too fast and find him under the *muleta*. Then it lifted him, horn at that junction between thigh and torso, the iliac crest, where it so often finds them. In the slow motion, you can actually see him slide down the six inches as the horn finally finds its way between the muscle strands.

The amazing thing was the emotion in the streets in the small Mexican city. It turns out that he became famous on the Mexican circuit before he did in Spain, receiving the first of his fifteen serious gorings in Aguascalientes, and since then has given huge sums to local charities, becoming a hero to the people. The abiding image is of the crowds standing vigil outside his hospital.

■ ■ ■ ■ ■

The temperature in Seville rose steadily and the days lengthened, climbing towards the sixteen-hour days of 110 degree temperature that summer peaks in. From training in a tracksuit I found myself running around the María Luisa in only shorts and shoes, having to map my route to fit in every available water source to pour over myself to prevent heatstroke.

Eduardo and I moved our sessions later and later into the evening, although that did not help much.

Alongside the heat – to which, despite my colouring, I am peculiarly sensitive – my internal state in front of the cattle seemed to be changing, and not for the better. Where I assumed that each time it would get a little easier, the fear becoming a little less, in fact it got much, much worse. The sheer quantity of adrenaline did indeed reduce as the novelty wore off, but its 'flavour' darkened and congealed into a nauseating doubt about my own abilities, and a tremor began to develop in my hands before I fought. It began with my next visit to the Saltillos (my then girlfriend, Marie Kristin Köberlein, a German student on a year in Seville, kindly took photographs).

Despite the clear improvement in style that can be seen in the photos – and it was a windy day – one of the cattle tossed me into the air, landing me on my back and knocking the wind completely from me. When I got up, I was so shaken that I seemed to lack the strength to cape, and it didn't return that day. A similar thing happened when I returned to Miura and went to the historic ranch of Guardiola with the members of the Club Pineda.

However, the wind finally turned, and for two reasons. One was that I finally felt the improvement, and that was most likely because I was in front of easier – or rather more normal – cattle. The other was fighting alongside a matador whose own courage is so ridiculously great that he ended up making me laugh even as we were both being chased around the ring. The cattle were the Jandillas of Borja Domecq, and the man who made me laugh was Rafael Rubio Luján, known as Rafaelillo, 'little Rafael', because he cannot be more than five foot four in height. However, anyone who saw him leap over the raised horns of a 1,366lb Miura to deliver the fatal sword thrust, as I had only a couple of months before in the Maestranza, would realise his height is the only small thing about him.

The fact that he was actually gored in the chest as he delivered the fatal thrust, but masked it so well that nobody noticed (even though I was watching the kill through a zoom lens), only reinforces this. (The reason I know he was gored was because Eduardo told me the next day, Eduardo being his *apoderado*, 'manager'.)

Rafaelillo has that hard-burning inner energy that one often encounters among matadors, exuding a defiant physicality that is unnerving to spend too much time with, but good to have beside you in a tight spot. That day, 16 June, I finally had something of a 'breakthrough' with my caping, managing to link some passes into a genuinely good series because the *vaquilla* charged straight and long, meaning that when I turned to set up for the next pass, it was still a little way off, giving me ample time to adjust.

Eduardo, seeing the sudden improvement, shouted for someone to start taking photos, but as we had no one with us that day, Rafaelillo himself took my Canon EOS out of the bag. As I was completing one pass, I saw him aim the camera from behind the hide and start to shoot and then I turned to face the *vaquilla* in the other direction. I cited, it charged, and just as my body was turning with the movement of the animal, I realised that standing behind my shoulder was Rafaelillo holding the camera, asking me where the 'on-switch' was. I was dumb with surprise, my arm carrying on the movement aiming the animal squarely at the matador, who simply sidestepped at the last minute – he had no cape himself – and asked again how to work it.

I quickly gestured as he ducked round the other side of me, and then I lined up the cow again. It charged, I caped, he sidestepped and kept taking photos as he did so. The fact that not one of the photos was in focus in no way saddens me, as I have a perfect recollection of the greatest piece of action photography I have ever seen, as he ducked and swerved, all the while looking through the lens, thoroughly enjoying every insane moment of it. I could barely cape for laughter at his antics.

On 3 July I entered the ring for the last time before the extreme heat – and wound-infecting flies – closed the *tentadero* season at Zahariche with the Miuras. I entered the ring in front of a special audience of breeders including Enrique Moreno de la Cova, where the animals were to be caped by myself, Eduardo Dávila Miura, and the famous matador – now aged fifty-three – Pepe Luis Vázquez, son of a great matador of the 1950s of the same name. The day was so prestigious that Antonio and Eduardo Miura – and his son Eduardo – broke their usual rule and allowed photography in the ring, which was later republished on the website of Spain's most popular piece of taurine press, *Toros para Todos*, 'Bulls for All', under the title of 'An Englishman in Zahariche'. Which seemed a good note on which to leave Spain to its hellish summer and return to Oxford again to train and write.

20

La estocada

The matador capes the animal back into place, so its hooves come together and its shoulders spread; he lunges with his *muleta*, he flies in with his sword, and the point strikes flesh, the sword vanishing with unnerving ease within the bull.

On 28 July, as the regional parliament in Barcelona votes to ban bullfighting in the province of Catalonia from 2012, I appear on CNN to give my perspective, although I equivocate on how much this has to do with Catalan separatism and how much with animal rights. I end the interview on a strong note, though: 'Having spent a year and a half wandering around Spain, going to all the ranches, I can say with absolutely clear conscience that if you were to ban the bullfight across Spain there would be a diminution in animal welfare in that country as a result, as they had to turn that land into intensive agriculture.'

Four days later, in Oxford, I have a dream in which I meet a giant yet doleful-looking Minotaur who asks me the question, 'Why are you doing this?' I ask him what he means, and he merely repeats, 'Why are you doing this?' I wake up. In the library I dig out an old volume of the psychologist Carl Jung's writings from 1940 to read about mythological archetypes in dreams, even though his theories are long since discredited. I am still struck by the passage which reads:

Everything that man should, and yet cannot, be or do, lives on as a mythological figure alongside his consciousness.

■ ■ ■ ■ ■

I arrived back in Seville in mid-September to find my plans were not going to work. My maestro Eduardo was busy and there were no *tentaderos*. None. I spoke to matadors like Padilla and Cayetano, breeders like Enrique Moreno de la Cova and Álvaro Núñez del Cuvillo: nothing. I had a lesson at Eduardo's house in the little circular garden at his apartment building and his conclusion was that I knew what I was doing, had trained well, had the strength in my fingers and wrists for the cape and the *muleta*, and could just keep training on my own, so I did.

My training regime began to alter. Long-distance running wouldn't alter my oxygen needs, and the combination of extreme adrenaline and high-level activity had left me out of breath in the summer. So I started to intersperse the long runs with shorter, faster ones. All the while doing press-ups and chin-ups to give my arms strength, sit-ups to build up the natural body-armour of my abdominal wall, and hours of caping to give my arms stamina and my style a fluid grace I knew would never occur in the ring, but at least the habits would be ingrained there, below the conscious level, within the memory of the muscles.

I also went out and saw my friends in the *tertulia* and elswhere, but loneliness began to set in. Marie had returned to Germany, ending our relationship, and I had the distinct feeling of going into battle alone. None of my close friends in England is an *aficionado* and so they simply didn't understand the danger. My family didn't want to discuss it, finding it too painful in the light of my brother's death. And none of my Spanish friends understood the moral and artistic quandaries, so they never questioned that the risk was worth it.

What was more, my Spanish friends had bought into an image of me which was not entirely true, one best described as 'Alexander the Viking'. In part, I had inculcated this myth myself because I quickly grew bored of answering the Spanish question, 'What is an Englishman doing bullfighting?' So when one day someone in the *tertulia* went as far as to claim that the name Fiske could be Spanish, I responded that it was a Viking name, Fiskr, dating in England from the tenth-century battle of Maldon, ten miles from where my family live, and the horned helmet image leapt into the minds of all present and stuck.

Far from berserker simplicity, my psychology was far more divided and present-day. When I was running or caping, I became involved in some training montage in my own inner movie and felt fearless. Then when I sat at my desk to write and remembered the depth and breadth of my feelings as I described the events that had gone before, I felt all the fear, pain and sadness of someone trying to elucidate the emotion of a scene of combat.

One day, Eduardo and I drove out to the house of a friend of his who had a 'killing carriage', and I spent a day leaping over a rising pair of horns and slamming a heavy, iron practice-killing sword into a bale of hay. It was not lost on me that the sword was held in my right hand, while I hold the pen with which I write in my left: one destroys, one creates.

Meanwhile, the date had been set. It was to be 5 November. Enrique also decided that the fight should occur at five o'clock in the afternoon. This being the time mentioned in the refrain of the García Lorca poem every schoolboy in Spain knows so well.

> *A las cinco de la tarde.*
> *Eran las cinco en punto de la tarde.*
> 'At five in the afternoon.
> It was at exactly five in the afternoon.'

Of course, there was something more than a little ominous about that choice of time for, as the first verse ends:

> *Lo demás era muerte y sólo muerte*

a las cinco de la tarde.
'The rest was death, and death alone
at five in the afternoon.'

It is not called 'The Lament for Ignacio Sánchez Mejías' for
nothing.

It was at this time that I started thinking seriously about
dying in the ring. Or in the back of someone's car on the way to
hospital, which was a much more realistic probability. Unlike a
plaza de toros in a town, a *plaza de tienta* on a farm has no infirmary, no doctor is present, and Enrique's ranch is just over the
border in Córdoba province, but still an hour from the main
city. Those lines of García Lorca's other poem 'The Song of the
Rider' kept returning to me: *'La muerte me está mirando desde
las torres de Córdoba.'* 'Death is watching me from the towers of
Córdoba.' Now he really was.

I also thought about injury; after the pounding I had taken
from the cows, I wondered what a bull would do. I don't fear
the painful damage that can be mended – pain is annoying, and
I complain about it as much as the next person, but it doesn't
keep me awake worrying. It is the damage that can't that worries me. From among those I know, Cayetano's liver damage,
the bizarre bone deformity within Padilla's hip, Belén's missing
eye. Then there is the horrifying image from television around
the world of the horn punching through the underside of Julio
Aparicio's jaw in Madrid, and hooking around to narrowly miss
the hard palate and brain beyond, instead punching out again
through his teeth. And of José Tomás lying in a Mexican infirmary, his body a conduit for the blood of others as he loses
twice as much as a sealed body can hold.

At first, I tried to think my way through this. (Surely that
was why I had studied philosophy at university?) Everyone
dies. It is something we all know, but seldom fully acknowl-
edge. I reasoned that this means that the death itself cannot

be that important, it is the timing of it that matters. So the question became whether it was worthwhile to trade the years I might have left for a book on bullfighting?

And the answer I kept coming back with was yes. Bullfighting just *is* important. It defines Spain and those other countries linked by history and culture where it also goes on. What's more it tells us all a little about who we are as humans, even if it is only a whisper in the modern age. And although the dance with Death that fills the main body of the fight is astonishingly important, it is the point when the matador maximises his risk of death in order to kill it that defines the art form.

Following that decision, I made two others. First, I realised that you can't think 'through' the fear of death. Death is the end of thought. So, on a practical level, you just have to stop thinking about it. When death finally comes for me, I want to be thinking about something else, before I think of nothing at all. It is the idea of witnessing the fading of the light that is terrifying, not the unperceivable void follows. Second, I had to stop writing too, stop analysing and trying to feel everything I was doing, because that was just making it worse.

An old name for matador that you often see in cartel posters is *espadas*, 'swords'. An *espada* is any bullfighter who kills, and thus the end of my training was to *convertirse en la espada*, 'to become the sword'. I had to become harder and colder than I had ever been before in my life. Not an easy thing, but not impossible for me either.

It was in this state of mind that I set off with Nicolás and Eduardo and Enrique on the last Friday of October to choose my bull, and it was for this reason, I believe, that I felt as I did: content and unthreatened. Once we got there, the *mayoral*, 'farm manager', Antonio, whom I had met a few times, greeted us, although I noticed that this time there was a difference in his greeting. He had always been polite and friendly before. However, he had never thought that the crazy Englishman was going to kill a bull. Now, when he shook my hand there was the very slight step back afterwards, and the checking of my face for any signs of offence or unhappiness when he spoke which I had seen around matadors.

We set off in Antonio's pickup truck, with my manager and breeder in the cab with him, Nicolas and I in the open air at the back. The bulls were a herd of two- and three-year-olds, along with the two seed-bulls, who were much, much older. My bull was pointed out to me. Conséjote, who would be three years old in a couple of weeks, making him a *novillo*, as fought by *novilleros* in the official rings, after they have fought and killed at least a few dozen cattle first.

Despite this fearsome statistical truth, it was watching him and his brothers from the flatbed of the truck that I had a minor revelation. Yes, if I was determined to fight my bull as I had fought all the cattle I had met before, I would come off infinitely the worse for wear, but as the bulls started to fight each other for supremacy, I saw their one weakness: they were much slower than the *vaquillas*. When they fought, it was deliberately, slamming the horns into the inevitable block from a countering horn, with the intent to damage, rather than the quicker, jabbing movements of their naïve younger sisters. If I made sure my focus was intense, and I got the hell out of the way after each pass rather than trying to set up a Tomás-like series, I reckoned I could just about do it. It was a gamble, but I liked my odds. After all, I had tens of millions of years of evolution in dexterity and intelligence to work with, and as a biped – as Enrique had so elegantly proven against his horse – I could out-accelerate any bull provided I was ready.

■ ■ ■ ■ ■

However, my trials of courage were far from over. Having decided to really push myself in terms of fitness in the last few days, I did the unthinkable. Running alongside the Guadalquivir at a brisk trot for five miles, I decided to turn the final half-mile into eight sequential 100-yard sprints. On the sixth segment, sprinting high on the points of my toes, the wind rushing past my ears, I felt and heard a distinct popping sound from my right knee. I braked as quickly as seemed sensible while trying to avoid any further injury, and preventatively limped to the nearest stone bench to inspect the damage.

There was no visible injury, and I could flex my knee, but something was clearly very wrong with it when I tried to walk. My brain was not trusting it for stability, as though my real lower leg had been replaced with an artificial one that I might fall off at any moment. I was well aware that the long run, and then the exhilaration of the wind-sprints, would have anaesthetised my brain, and for all I knew the knee was silently screaming at me to stop using it. My one abiding thought, which I said out loud, was 'You fucking imbecile.'

Because, no matter the damage at the time, I knew there was absolutely no way out of fighting that Friday. Rescheduling that many people – and by which I mean those intrinsic to the fight – simply could not be done in the near future, certainly not within the projected publication date of the book.

So I telephoned the amazing Dr Michael Criswell in London. We talked a little, wondering whether or not it was the meniscus again or a torn anterior cruciate ligament. He asked what I had done since the injury. I told him I had taken a Spanish dose of ibuprofen (600mg, rather than the English 400), and elevated my knee with ice for an hour to minimise the immediate swelling, and then was going to have a hot bath to ease up the muscles around. He agreed and asked what my week held.

'Tomorrow is my day off, Wednesday I need to run at least five miles and train with the capes on my terrace, which involves some rotation with a straight knee, Thursday a *tentadero* with live animals, Friday morning practising the kill, Friday afternoon, I will fight some more cattle and then fight and kill a bull.'

'Ah, I see. A full week. Can you postpone?'

'No.'

'Ah, I see. Well, carry on exactly as you planned then. Oh, but buy a knee support.'

This encouraged me massively. I could see the medical logic, of course. Aside from the psychological blow of having to spend planned-for training time twiddling my thumbs in bed, if my knee was likely to seize up or give out then it was most likely to go during that sort of training, thus neatly forcing me out of the danger of the fight. If it held up until Friday afternoon, then it most likely would hold up through Friday afternoon as well.

The day after the injury, I limped out to the shops and bought a compression bandage and a neoprene knee support but otherwise rested. Then, with two days until the fight to go, and having externally applied the knee support I now lacked internally, I set off running around the María Luisa Park. I say running, but it was more a combination of scuttling, scampering, hopping and a variety of other improvised gaits to get around the pain and the uneven surfaces I was running on. I covered almost four miles before I gave up, with the people of Seville staring at my antics, which must have resembled Quasimodo fleeing the scene of a crime. Then I did an hour of *toreo de salón* on my balcony, before another bout of ice, hot bath and a powerful mixture of codeine, paracetamol, aspirin and ibuprofen.

That night my parents arrived in Seville. I had asked them to come out for both selfish and unselfish reasons. If something went wrong, it was vital to me – logistically and emotionally – that they should be present. And if it went right, it was as well. Over dinner there was undeniably both a ghost at the feast – my brother – and an elephant in the room – my fight – which weren't ignored in the conversation, but neither were they dwelt on. In fact, the pair of them were surprisingly relaxed, as was I.

■　■　■　■　■

The next morning, Nicolas, Eduardo, Rafaelillo and I went for my ninth 'taught' *tentadero* (thirteenth in total) at a small ranch outside Seville, where I limped into the ring for the first time in almost six months and caped two *vaquillas*. Both Eduardo and Rafaelillo noted my greater confidence in the ring, as did I. Most interesting to me of all, though, was that the stress of the environment reduced the pain in my knee, allowing me to get out of the trouble I inevitably got into with each animal. I was as ready as I was going to be without the dozen more training fights I had originally hoped for.

That night my oldest schoolfriend, Andy Cooke, arrived, for much the same reasons as my parents. We went for a late bottle of red wine and talked until 1 a.m., 'draining the poison out of the night', as I put it, and helping me to fall into a deep sleep the moment my head touched the pillow.

■　■　■　■　■

On the day itself Eduardo collected me for the last time for a training session at the statue of Curro Romero. We drove out of the town to meet Rafaelillo and his *banderillero* Abraham Neiro, who were going to assist me in the ring later that day. Eduardo was disabled, ironically, by the same knee injury I had. When asked about it, I simply said it was a minor sprain and tried not to limp. There was no way I was going to allow anyone to cancel on me now. We did a little *salón*, but focused on the kill, something I had tried only twice before. I watched Rafaelillo fly through the air with the sword into the bale of hay behind the horns, crying out like a kamikaze as he did so, and tried to emulate it. However, as I landed and swerved past the rising horns manipulated by Eduardo, the effect on my 'slightly sprained' knee was making me sweat and turn pale. Eduardo looked at me and suggested we were done for the day.

Funnily enough, although I was anxious about my fight, there was no sense of genuine nerves. I had seen the bull, I had been in the ring the day before and come out with nothing worse than a couple of bruises, and my knee continued to hold up. Most of all, though, it was Eduardo's confidence in my abilities which boosted my own immensely.

After training, I met up with Andy for a bite of lunch and a glass of beer to keep my mind off what was approaching before my afternoon siesta. At half-past three I walked out of my house with a suit carrier containing a brand new, off-the-peg *traje corto* in funereal black, the trusty brown boots I have always worn in the ring (and outside it, for almost twenty years), and my bag of capes and swords. At the statue of Curro Romero beside the Maestranza was waiting a white minivan with my parents and Andy inside. When I got in I noticed a not unnaturally tense atmosphere, but for once in my life I felt I had every right to ignore it. I sat in the back, put the earphones of my iPod in, and disappeared into my own world, listening to the flamenco guitar of Paco de Lucía.

When we arrived at the ring, it became clear that I was going to have a larger audience than I had expected. There were almost 100 people present, which was impressive given that the ring has no seating. I cut my parents loose among them, handed Andy my camera, and walked into the changing room to prepare. There I found Rafaelillo and Abraham laughing that so many people should turn up to a first kill – theirs were both done in private, with no ceremony, and a much smaller animal. Then I walked to the ring, waving to friends who were standing around chatting, but carefully avoiding coming up and saying hello. The atmosphere was one of general anxiety, excitement and respectful distance. Although I had really wanted only to conclude my research with the experience of the matador going over the horns to kill, exposing his body to the animal as the sword went in, what I was being given was a miniature version of all the tensions of the fight itself.

The predominant feeling walking through friends, acquaintances and strangers on my way to the entrance to the ring was one of focus. All eyes are turned on you, but it's unlike walking on to a theatrical stage. There, you are present to entertain, so you hand out smiles and signals of affection to get your audience in the mood. The bullring's basis – at my level anyway – is not about getting people to like you. It is about being ready to use your skill to create the movements you wish for, while avoiding the injury you don't. The audience is there to watch, but they are not an integral part of the dance itself. The only person whose hand I shook was the breeder himself, Enrique, who accompanied me to the ring door.

Eduardo was waiting for me outside the ring, and helped me to warm up with the capes before we began. And then we entered, followed by Rafaelillo and Abraham, and took up our positions around the ring. I saw that Enrique joined his brother Félix, and also Antonio and Eduardo Miura, behind the breeder's *burladero* next to the *toril* gate, through which the animals enter.

Enrique shouted across the ring, as I had seen him do so many times before, asking the various bullfighters if they were ready. Each shouted back his assent. Then, he turned to me last, and said, '*Maestro, listo?*' And I replied, '*Si.*'

And the Gates of Fear were drawn back.

The first two animals into the ring, in succession, were *vaquillas* for me to warm up on. Classic Saltillos, they were tough, wily, fast and damaging. They clipped me time and time again, and I began to learn the advantages and disadvantages of using the large cape, the *capote*. For this was only the second time I had ever used it, and at this point in the fight, the animals were fresher than I had ever fought, not having yet strained against the picador's horse with his *tentadero* lance (whose head has a three-quarter-inch point, rather than the four-inch one used in a *corrida*). However, I caped both animals with *capote* and *muleta*, managed a series or two, and received the cheers of the crowd, encouraged by Eduardo, who played master of ceremonies. Rafaelillo would occasionally enter to cape for a series, and Abraham would enter to cape either of us out of the difficulties these particular animals presented with their short charges and almost telepathic ability to find the man underneath the cloth. As one most noticeably did, hitting me exactly where bulls so often do: straight between the legs.

Panting and sweating and nauseous with pain, I retreated back to my *burladero* for the entrance of the star of the day: Conséjote, the bull. I was tense, I was ready, I was afraid, and I was extremely and vibrantly alive. The challenge I had planned for since February, and in some grander sense for far, far longer, was snorting and stomping and crashing into the gates as he made his way towards the ring. The gate opened and the animal came out and my first thought was, 'Shit, that is a *bull*.'

Now, I am not claiming that Conséjote was a 1,400lb Miura, or even a 1,000lb Domecq. No, he was one year and three hundred pounds shy of that (about the same as a full-grown male African lion with me riding on its back, or a very large male Siberian tiger unjockeyed). Everything was different. The movement of the animal is heavier, each foot strike on the floor being felt, heard, and seen as the impact ripples up through the muscles of its body. It seems to have more gears as well. Where the *vaquilla* is largely a matter of walk or gallop, the bull enters at a trot, selects his target at a canter and maintains that pace until he is a few yards away before lowering the horns and entering the gallop. On first entry, he cantered two laps of the ring, attacking the *burladeros* at our direction, with each of us taking it in turns to flap our cape out of the space at the side to lure him round.

Then I ran into the ring with the *capote* and took him off the horse while running backwards. I stopped – feeling a spike of pain from my knee at the movement – and used the cape far out from my body to make him pass. I turned and invited him again, and he visibily gathered his strength and launched at me, his right forehoof stamping on the sweeping cape, pulling me in towards him so his horn slammed into the lower part of my injured leg. I turned and performed a mockery of a *media-verónica* to cut its charge short, and limped at speed out of the danger zone.

The bull was then called to charge the heavily armoured horse. I noticed that the picador had not changed his lance, so the tiny lance head skittered and slid over the muscled hump, the *morillo*, which was already forming across his shoulders. Notably, no blood ran down his sides after this encounter. He was taken off the horse by Rafaelillo with his cape, who found him equally impossible to raise a series of passes from. He was pic-ed once more and then Eduardo called for the change of acts. This would be a fight of two acts, since no one saw the need to place *banderillas* in a three-year-old animal (although he had also been lanced much less than he would in a formal fight in a *plaza*).

I took up my *muleta* and entered the ring when Eduardo signalled for Abraham to draw the bull over to a *burladero*. Then he called on me to give a dedication. I realise now that I should have prepared something, but at the time it was the very last thing on my mind. I walked over to my parents and said something along the lines of: 'I dedicate this bull to my family.' I noticed a few grumbles of dissent from the audience at the brevity of my address, which I must admit made me think, 'You try fighting an *effing* bull,' but I moved on from the ungracious thought. Then I walked back towards the bull and laid my *muleta* edge before him and wondered what the hell was going to happen. The answer can be seen in the photos.

I would love to describe my internal state at the time, but I had none. I was living entirely in the placement of the bull's horns, the direction of the blackness of his eyes, and where exactly my hand – which ended not at my fingertips but at the edge of the cape – was in space. Nothing else in the world existed for me, not pain, not fear, nothing.

The bull, I was told afterwards, had been involved in a quite serious hierarchy tussle in his herd the day before, and so it was surprisingly quickly that his head began to lower with fatigue. And when I tried to cape him low to further accelerate this, I noticed that he fell over more than once. We had both of us, it would seem, entered the ring not at the peak of form. However, as I brought him closer so his flanks buffeted me on the passes, I felt the terrible solidity of the animal. He wasn't just larger than the *vaquillas* – which are mainly composed of bone and vital organs – but he was greatly denser, the muscles that were already bulking him up towards full adulthood weighing so much more than other biological matter. In one pass his forehoof caught my boot and the blow of his mass came as an agonising shock through my foot, and I said out loud, '¡*Qué peso!*' 'What weight!' Which raised a snigger from Antonio and Eduardo Miura, breeders of giants.

From time to time I would take a break and Rafaelillo would step in for some passes, and during these respites I began to realise that the time to kill was approaching. As I watched Rafa pass the animal, I realised that I was going to run into a problem of engineering. The killing of a bull, which I had seen several hundred times, and practised on two occasions with a carriage with a bale of hay placed behind the horns (a ridiculously small number, but that was the order of the day), has its proper form. The key point, though, is that when you go over the horns, the sword point should enter between the third and fourth, or fourth and fifth rib, the spinal column on one side, the shoulder clavicle on the other. This space is about the size of a fist. However, on this younger animal, the spot was so small that it was all but invisible. And now, genuine fear kicked in. Because I had no idea how, with the animal in front of me, angry, waiting to strike, I was going to possibly manage to find it while my entire body flew through the air.

Eduardo called me across the ring and took out one of his killing swords, his 'most beautiful', as he called it, the blade a flat shining three-quarter yard ribbon of silvered steel so highly polished that when it caught the sun it was blinding. The weight, ten times that of the aluminium caping sword, was reassuring in my hand, and I approached the animal and gave him two more passes to check that he wasn't suddenly going to lash out at me in an unexpected manner.

And then I stopped him, and took a step back so I was three yards away. His head was held low, as he was tired, waiting to see what was going to happen, as was I. I stood with my feet together, at right angles to him, lowered the *muleta* on to the ground in my left hand, and raised my right hand up so I could sight down the curved blade of the sword as though it was a gun. Then I half turned, my feet rising on to their toes, my right arm straightening towards him as I now aimed for his sloping side, where I hoped the utterly invisible soft-spot was, and, wrapping the *muleta* around its internal stick, pushed it towards the bull so he lowered his head down towards the movement.

And I leapt, using my full 13 stone of weight, both feet clear of the ground, deliberately ignoring the horns – which took some mental effort – and the sword point struck what felt like a brick wall. His horns reared up, and I pivoted my body around them – I have absolutely no idea how – until I was clear, with the sword in my hand. He turned like lightning to face me, and I threw the *muleta* out towards him and drew it away from my body so he followed. I took a step out of the situation and regathered myself, noticing how Eduardo, Rafaelillo and Abraham had all entered the ring from behind their *burladeros* in case it went wrong.

The bull was facing me again in the right position, seemingly unfazed. He had not cried out, I noticed, merely rearing at the shadow of me as I loomed mid-charge. I lined up, profiled and went in again. Again I struck bone. And I began to despair. What if I couldn't do it? I was getting weaker, especially my wrist, which was giving out a dull throb from the repeated equivalent of a flying punch into a cement block. I lined up a third time, sweat running into my eyes and my breathing hoarse. And I began my leap over-hastily, not coordinating the *muleta* properly first to bring his head down, so the bull reared early. My response was instinctive, using my last purchase on the ground – my toes – to give me that little bit more height in the leap to stay clear. As a result, when my sword struck home, it was behind the proper killing spot, between the sixth and seventh ribs at least, as I pivoted on the sinking sword around the swinging horns.

And then I was past him on the other side, staring at what I had done.

My first feeling, and the strongest one of all, was the dread that I had failed, that I had injured the bull and injured him horribly, but not killed him. I looked to Eduardo, who was gesturing to Abraham to swing the cape at the bull so the sword would move within him, severing something major and killing him quickly. Then he called to me to do the same with my *muleta* on the other side. I did so mechanically, somewhat in shock, unsure about what was going on – within the bull, within me. The feeling that I might have done something wrong with regard to the kill was growing into the feeling that I might have done something wrong overall. The people in the crowd were calling to me – this was an expert audience – to gesture as the matadors gesture for victory. For the bull was dying. I could see his legs shaking now. However, the idea of bouncing on my toes, thus, and gesturing outwards with my hands, thus, to demand that the bull die on my command as real matadors do, I simply could not bring myself to enact. It seemed to me it would be crowing over a fallen enemy.

All I could do was watch his slow and inexorable descent into darkness. He fell, first to his fore-knees, then to the floor. He never let out a cry, nor any signal of despair, just the slow shutting down of control, of defiance of gravity and all the other laws of nature that see life as an aberration and want to see us dissolve again into the formless matter from which we came. The fight, quite literally, went out of him. In a gesture both sincere and overblown, I kissed my fingers and put them on his brow. And for the first time I felt him: the hard bone, the muscles that drove him, the simple, strong and honest mind that steered him. As Rafaelillo came over with the *descabello* sword to sever the nervous link between brain and spinal column – no more movement, no more pain – I was washed over with the feeling of what I had done. I have no idea how to describe it; it was a thousand things at once. Guilt, shame, happiness, elation, pride, vanity, and a profound grief and loneliness. I felt that I knew him, that I had got to know him in the moments before his death. And that I had ignored him, focused hard as I was on fighting him and surviving him. But now I could appreciate him as the great, beautiful incarnation of the natural world that he had been.

Eduardo came and embraced me as a brother-in-arms, as did Enrique, and anyone else who was in the ring. A hundred photographs were taken with those present, from local farmers and their sons to the 'great and the good' of Seville, including the entirety of the *tertulia*. And yet despite the adulation of the crowd and my victorious killing, I couldn't bring myself to revel in it (and please note that two misses, *pinchazos*, followed by a killing strike on your first animal is absolutely unheard of, even ignoring the other abnormalities such as the bull being three, not one and a half, and it being my tenth *tentadero* rather than my twentieth, and my being thirty-four, not seventeen). And sure enough, when I looked closely at the photos afterwards, there was nothing in my eyes at all, only emptiness.

■ ■ ■ ■ ■

A few days later, a female friend who had been present that day joined me for a drink with two mutual friends, both matadors, one a grandson of Lorca's unfortunate and lamented friend Sánchez-Mejías, whose surname he bears. She remarked on how everyone found my coldness and distance afterwards disconcerting. The two bullfighters looked at me and Marco Sánchez-Mejías asked, 'What did you feel?'

I tried to answer. '*Mi corazón esturo con el toro muerto en la plaza.* [My heart was with the dead bull in the ring.] I just wanted to go and sit with him in the ring with a bottle of whisky. Only he understood now.'

And Marco said to her, 'Now, and only now, is he a bullfighter.'

The other *torero*, El Tato, considered me longer and said, 'He will be back. He will fight again.'

But that day, all I knew was that I didn't want applause or congratulations. I was alive and he was not. Where was the goodness in that? We all went for dinner at Enrique's house and I was stunned by his and his wife Cristina's generosity, and everyone's shared pride in my achievement, from the historic great breeders of the Miuras down to the gypsy *banderillero* Abraham, but a part of me – ungracious to the point of narcissism perhaps – would have preferred to have taken that bottle of whiskey and sat with that dead bull rather than given and accepted speeches on the behalf of the *fiesta nacional*, the national spectacle of Spain.

There are few readers who have made it this far who will not have been responsible for 100 times this number of deaths through their diet, some better, some worse. And 100 lives lived far worse and shorter than this one. Conséjote lived three years among his brothers, and died within their call, in the country where he belongs. And in that ring are all the tragic and brutal truths of the world unadorned. It is for that reason above all that you cannot ban the bullfight, because it is already contained in the very facts of life itself. All you can do is turn away. And persuade others to do so as well.

La vuelta para el toro

The bull, found to be brave, fierce, noble and strong up until his death, at the demand of the crowd, and a signal from the president, is hitched to the mules and taken on a lap of the ring, while the audience solemnly applauds him.

I look back on my two years in the heartland of bull-fighting, and feel sad. It is gone now, all of those moments have passed, and I am not convinced I ever enjoyed them as I should. As spectator, I was always afraid I was missing something. As protagonist, I was always … well, just afraid. There is much I missed out; in Hemingway's memorable phrasing, 'If I could have made this enough of a book it would have had everything in it.'

The book is dominated by men. This is because it is representative, but there are women in the world of the bullfight. Like the Venezuelan *torera* Conchita Cintrón, 'The Golden Goddess', who died aged eighty-six in February 2009, warranting obituaries in every major British newspaper as one of the greats of the bullfighting world, although in the write-ups her abilities were overshadowed by her sex. Antonio Ordóñez and Luis Miguel Dominguín were not so well covered in death. Or Cristina Sánchez, who was by all accounts a great *matadora* (not just a *torera*, as, by the time of her 'moment in the sun', a woman could officially take that title) but whose career stalled because the great men of the day would not fight by her side. Or the *novillera* Conchi Ríos, whom I saw turn the men's sniggers into *olés* in Casa Matías as we watched her on the television while she fought around the corner in the Maestranza in May 2010. Or another trainee, who partnered me in training once, and became even closer than that for a while, but it was a brief while. And to whom I explained that the bullfighter could be Lady Macbeth too, although what she did with that advice I'll never know.

Had it been more of a book, I would have spoken more of the history, of the living and the dead, and those who came close to stepping from one to the other. Of El Pilarico, who killed 150 bulls in Colombia and Spain as a *novillero*, but the last one broke his spine. I would have described how the cruelty of those with whom he recovered in Miami turned him against himself, so that, in his own words, 'I said to myself, this is how people think in a society more civilised than ours. There are more of them, they must be right.' And he became an animal rights protester for the same reason he became a bullfighter, because other people told him to. And I would have talked about his brother in injury, the *novillero* El Cobijano, except that when the bull took Cobijano's leg in 1958, life was both kinder and harder. So, his livelihood lost, the great matadors of the day gathered in his most beloved ring in Valencia to fight in his honour: Domingo Ortega, Antonio Ordóñez, Julio Aparicio, Luis Miguel Domínguín, Pepe Cáceres and Jaime Ostos, the greatest line-up possible that decade. And my friend Sarah Gracey's mother was there with her friend Ostos, who dedicated the photo I have reproduced in the plate section to her.

She told me how Cobijano wept as he was carried from the ring on the shoulders of the crowd, along with his heroes, and how he purchased a small farm outside Valencia, and a kiosk selling tickets adjacent to his beloved bullring where he worked every day until his death in February 2009, a few days before The Golden Goddess, and the day before I attended my first *tentadero* with Padilla, so I never got to meet him.

I would have talked about South America, and France, where they fight in different styles, but the Spanish one as well, and Portugal, where everyone thinks they don't kill the bull, but they do, it's just someone other than the man who fought it, someone who doesn't care and risks nothing.

However, I have said enough. I have given you everything you need in order to decide whether or not you want to see a bullfight, and hopefully something to help you understand a little better the glittering confusion of emotion and danger and gold that will unfold before you if you do. And if you do, and your heart goes out to the bull, as it should, let it also go out to the matador. For it is he who is your brother, while the bull is not. Not unless you are in the ring itself.

References

I have tried to write the best book on bullfighting by talking to those who compose this world today, but there are many good books about how it was, which is what made it into what it is. Ernest Hemingway's *Death In The Afternoon* (1932) remains the best account in English of the early twentieth-century bullfight and what came before it – although it does focus rather on the first word of the title. His only other non-fiction book on the topic, *The Dangerous Summer* (1985), is a nice update of how it was three decades later. *Aficionados* often say Hemingway didn't know as much as he claimed about the bullfight; in my experience this claim is more true of them than of him. The theatre critic Kenneth Tynan writes well and clearly in *Bull Fever* (1956), with an interesting angle on the drama of it, although he justly claims no deep knowledge. The out-of-print autobiography *Juan Belmonte: Killer of Bulls* (translated by Leslie Charteris) is not only very good in my opinion, but also the text my own maestro Eduardo, the most literate of matadors, claims as his favourite. Adrian Shubert's study, *Death and Money In the Afternoon*, is the most honest text on the history and economics of the spectacle, while Barnaby Conrad's *Encyclopedia of Bullfighting* (1961) and John McCormick's

Bullfighting: Art, Technique, and Spanish Society (1998) are both good in-depth studies.

For those who read Spanish, there is no better work than José María de Cossío's encyclopedic multi-volume *Los Toros* (first published in six volumes in 1943, the 2007 edition having thirty). More recently, serious works include José Alameda's *El hilo del toreo* (1989) and Gregorio Corrochano's *¿Que es torear? Introducción a las tauromaquias de Joselito y de Domingo Ortega* (2009).

The most important book on animal rights to read is one that tells you what the non-bullfighting world does to cattle in the name of 'entertainment eating', Jonathan Safran Foer's *Eating Animals* (2009). In Chapter 8, where I quote him on this topic, I also reference the following more academic texts:

Bateson, P. (1991), 'Assessment of Pain in Animals', *Animal Behaviour*, 42, 827–39.

Grandin, T., Deesing, M. (2002), 'Distress in Animals: Is it Fear, Pain or Physical Stress?', delivered to the American Board of Veterinary Practitioners – Symposium on Pain, Stress, Distress and Fear: Emerging Concepts and Strategies in Veterinary Medicine.

Mazzoleni, S. *et al.*, eds.(2002), *Recent Dynamics of the Mediterranean Vegetation and Landscape*, John Wiley & Sons, London.

In terms of bull biology, a great introduction to what we did to these children of the aurochs is Evan Fraser's *Beef: The Untold Story of How Milk, Meat, and Muscle Shaped the World* (2009). In Chapter 17, where I quote him on this topic, I also reference the following more academic texts:

Mansfield, K. *et al.* (2006), 'A molecular epidemiological study of rabies epizootics in kudu (*Tragelaphus strepsiceros*) in Namibia', *BioMedCentral Veterinary Research*, 2:2.

Thompson, K. V. (2005), 'Aggressive behavior and dominance hierarchies in female sable antelope, *Hippotragus niger*: Implications for captive management', *Zoo Biology*, 12:2.

Price, T. D. (2006), 'Review: *Retracing the Aurochs: History, Morphology and Ecology of an Extinct Wild Ox* by Cis van Vuure', *Quarterly Review of Biology*, 81:3.

Langley, R. L., Hunter, J. L. (2001), 'Occupational fatalities due to animal-related events', *Wilderness & Environmental Medicine*, 12:3.

Cortés, O. *et al.* (2008), 'Ancestral matrilineages and mitochondrial DNA diversity of the Lidia cattle breed', *Animal Genetics*, 39:6.

List of Illustrations

19. My teacher Eduardo Dávila Miura
20. A close shave
21. The results of adrenaline.
22. Slow improvement
23. Nearly there
24. With the Miuras
25. José Pedro Prados Martín
26. Miura bulls, Pamplona
27. Facing a Miura calf
28. Juan José Padilla

Credits for the photographs
Author 15, 17, 18, 25, 28; Sergio Caro Cadenas 19; Carlos Cazalis 16; Loomis Dean, Time & Life Pictures/Getty Images 8; Angela Gracey 9; Allan Grant, Time & Life Pictures/Getty Images 10; Nicolás Haro 1, 2, 3, 4, 5, 6, 7, 11, 12, 13, 14, 26; Marie Kristin Köberlein 22, 23; Pepe Sánchez 27; Olivia Soto 24; Tristán Ybarra 20, 21

Acknowledgements

My greatest thanks are owed to my family for their never-ending patience and tolerance of the madness that I live. My father Clive, my mother Barbara, my brother Byron, and my niece Isabella. However, this book, like my life, is dedicated to the brother who didn't make it: Jules. As the family motto goes: ourselves and our works are a debt owed to death.

My second greatest are for another family I have known almost as long, the Bancroft Cookes, especially to Andy, the oldest of friends, but also to Nick and Sacha and Alberto who opened so many doors. And to my other old friends, Hugh Dancy and Claire Danes, who argued so hard that I should do it, Dominic Elliot who came and helped, and George Pendle who helped from afar, as did Christoph Hargreaves-Allen, Steven France, William Wynne and Dr Edward Clarke. I ushered most of your weddings while working on this book, so thank you for the glimpses of your happiness, trickling light into my darker world. And especially to Samantha Mullins, who was there for me from the beginning and for so long after. (And Marie Kristin Köberlein, who was there during much of my time of fear.)

My Spanish friends are in the book itself, and need no further mention.

Thanks to Dr John D. Kenyon and Dr Tim Mawson at St Peter's College, Oxford, who taught me the difference between good and evil, and Dr Malcolm Coe, who taught me that nature has neither. Also to Dr Carl Hoeffer and Dr Eleonora Montuschi at LSE, Professor Paul Snowden at UCL and Professor David Papineau at KCL, who combined my science and philosophy into one. Thanks to Exeter College, Oxford, who gave me the space to write when Spain was too hot.

I also want to thank my agent, Peter Robinson, my editor, Peter Carson, along with Rebecca Gray, Penny Daniel and Rukhsana Yasmin at Profile Books, and Annie Lee whose patient copy-editing proved so vital.